THE BAKKE CASE

JOEL DREYFUSS &
CHARLES LAWRENCE III

THE BAKKE CASE

THE POLITICS
OF INEQUALITY

Harcourt Brace Jovanovich

New York & London

HBJ

Requests for permission to make copies of any part
of the work should be mailed to:
Permissions, Harcourt Brace Jovanovich, Inc.
757 Third Avenue, New York, N.Y. 10017

Printed in the United States of America

Library of Congress Cataloging in Publication Data

Dreyfuss, Joel.
    The Bakke case.

    Bibliography: p.
    Includes index.
    1. Bakke, Allan Paul. 2. California. University.
3. Discrimination in medical education—Law and
legislation—California. 4. Medical colleges—
Admission. I. Lawrence, Charles, 1943–   joint author.
II. Title.
KF228.B34D74   344'.73'0798   78-22249
ISBN 0-15-110536-7
ISBN 0-15-616782-4 pbk.

First edition

A B C D E F G H I J

For the

HONORABLE THURGOOD MARSHALL

and for

CAROL, MAIA, AND VERONICA

ACKNOWLEDGMENTS

Our initial gratitude must go to our first teachers and supporters: our parents, Roger and Anne-Marie Dreyfuss and Charles and Margaret Lawrence; and our sisters, Jessica, Carole, Marie-Françoise, Sara, and Paula. The inspirations and ideas that shaped this book were first formed within our families.

Many friends and colleagues, particularly Derrick Bell, Ralph Smith, Eleanor Holmes Norton, Stephanie Wildman, and Stephen Arons, have been generous in sharing their ideas and reading various chapters of the book. The secretarial efforts of Jody Anderson, Angela Balestrieri, and Lani Mailes were greatly appreciated.

We are especially indebted to Dr. Daniel Collins, who encouraged us to embark on this venture, introduced us to our publisher, and provided encouragement throughout. Our editor, Peggy Brooks, played an essential role in helping us organize and clarify our final product.

Not enough has been said about the remarkable tenacity of U.S. Supreme Court justice Thurgood Marshall in retaining his vision of an integrated America long after others lost their idealism. For similar reasons, we want to acknowledge the courage of the editorial board of the *New York Times* for insisting that the public understand the complexity of the issues involved in the *Bakke* case. The editors of Pacific News Service and participants in their Cities Seminar helped place much of this material in the broader context of the nation and the world around us.

Finally, we can never adequately acknowledge the sacrifice, support, good humor, and perseverance of Veronica Pollard, Carol Munday Lawrence, and Maia Lawrence. It is their love that sustained us in this effort.

CONTENTS

THE
BAKKE
CASE

One

BITTER MEDICINE

At about four o'clock on the afternoon of Friday, August 3, 1973, Allan Paul Bakke, an engineer at NASA's Ames Research Center near Stanford University, started his car for the drive up to the University of California at Davis. The 100-mile trip would take Allan Bakke little more than two hours, but it would be a giant step toward a fate he could hardly have imagined on that sunny summer afternoon. He had applied to the medical school at Davis and had been rejected. He was applying again and would be interviewed a second time in a few weeks. But Bakke was nervous about his chances of becoming a doctor, and he was grateful that a sympathetic official at the school had agreed to meet with him informally.

One hundred miles is not a great distance at the Ames Center, where space vehicles that will travel millions of miles over several years are designed and tested. Sprawled alongside U.S. 101 on the southern peninsula of San Francisco Bay, the center is surrounded by an unsavory collection of industrial parks, drive-in movies, fast food restaurants, and flimsy residential developments that have converted the brown hilly country between the cities of San Francisco and San Jose into a classic nightmare of American urbanization. The drab green uniforms and white gloves of the U.S. Marines at the security gates help differentiate the complex from the warehouses and factories around it. The guards and the high fences hint at the difference and importance of the work inside.

A NASA spokesman calls the complex "a college campus of ideas," and there is a thin patina of the university in the formal walks, circles, and lawns that connect the jumble of brick and concrete buildings. The dominant architectural features are the giant steel and aluminum barrels suspended between the buildings. These are the wind tunnels and centrifuges where experimental aircraft and space vehicles are tested. The science fiction world is real enough with its banks of sterile control panels and flashing lights, but the more gritty side of space research is very much in evidence. There are more laborers in yellow hard hats in view than scientists in white smocks and calculators. The scale model of the space shuttle *Enterprise*, our first real spaceship, pushed over in a corner of a dimly lit hangar, wears a fine coat of grime. The coiled snake of disconnected cable, the greasy rags, and the irritating whine of high-speed drills are a reminder that the pursuit of Truth in science requires painstaking measurements, physical labor, and a tolerance of monotony rarely considered in the epics of speculative fiction.

It was in this place that Allan Bakke decided to be a physician. An engineer trained in the philosophy that all problems can be solved and all mysteries deciphered, he came into contact with the medical doctors who had to make sure the frail human cargo of the billion-dollar machines could endure the punishment of our most alien frontiers. While the practices of engineering and medicine have converged in the use of the electronics and computers that are the basic tools of our time, man—the ultimate challenge—would have been outside the conceptual universe of a mechanical engineer. One can easily understand the delight of Allan Bakke in discovering a new world to conquer. After six years at NASA, the daily routine of the engineer paled before this new mystery of flesh, blood, and emotions.

But as Bakke drove past the warehouses and drive-ins, through the eastern edge of San Francisco and its rows of pastel houses on picture-postcard hills, he knew that he was on a mission against time. He had applied to twelve medical schools over two years, and all had turned him down. Two had been honest enough to tell him why: age. He was thirty-three years old, and this single fact was a great obstacle over which he had no control. As he wound his way through the heavy Friday afternoon traffic, Allan Bakke was making a transition. Soon he would cease to be a man with a private fear of growing old and would become the symbol in a struggle that would make his name a household word and his ambition an issue that divided a nation. Despite his efforts to shun publicity, his personal goal would have repercussions he could not have foreseen as his automobile climbed through the dry brown coastal hills and plunged toward the stifling Sacramento Valley.

Four years later the issues raised at that August meeting would be the focus of an emotional debate that shattered old alliances, sparked political confrontation, and caused men of wisdom to utter the same words with totally different intent. The issue—race—was as old as the nation itself, but because of it, Allan Bakke's ambition to become a physician would concern some of the country's finest minds. Tickets for the session of the United States Supreme Court of October 12, 1977, would be as much in demand as passes to the World Series taking place between the Yankees and the Dodgers. And while six umpires would judge that confrontation of old enemies, nine men would arbitrate the dispute between Allan Bakke and the University of California.

There had been another autumn twenty-five years earlier,

when nine other important men listened to arguments about justice, law, and color, and at that time, too, the Yankees and Dodgers had met to determine the championship of the world. In 1952 the Supreme Court and the New York Yankees were all white men, and the Brooklyn Dodgers were on the leading edge of social change in America. In that year the plaintiffs argued that racial separation contradicted the ideals of democracy and should be abolished. Eventually the Court would agree and launch a profound transformation in the relationship of black and white Americans.

How far had the country come for Allan Bakke to argue that sixteen blacks, Chicanos, and Asians had violated his constitutional rights by attending the medical school at Davis? His case appeared simple enough: the medical school, in an attempt to correct the injustices of that segregated past, had set aside sixteen places in each entering class for members of minority groups. Because Allan Bakke was white, he was prevented from competing for those sixteen places. He argued that because his grades and test scores were higher than those of some of the minority students, he was better qualified to become a physician. Yet his aspirations had been dashed by his color. How ironic for the American Dilemma to come full circle in just a quarter-century. If Bakke's contention was correct, white men had lost the protection of the Constitution they had drafted in order to create a unique form of government, with all those checks and balances built in to protect them against absolute power and absolute corruption. Now Bakke took his case to the court of last appeal and pleaded for redress.

But was the issue as straightforward as many wanted to believe? Had this tall, blond, intense hero of this unusual racial epic lost his rights to a new injustice with the catchy title of "Reverse Discrimination"? What profound rearrangement of power had taken place in the space between two

6

World Series to provoke such a reversal of roles? To believe *Allan Bakke* v. *Regents of the University of California* that simple is to succumb to the melodrama that has been constructed of this affair, a play of shallow characters and shallow solutions. Could any fair-minded person oppose a man who wanted so much to be a physician that he volunteered to be the "pink lady" in the emergency room of a hospital after a full day at his regular job? Wasn't merit the fabric that had made America a great nation? Who would want to be treated by doctors whose abilities were so negligible that only their color made them eligible for medical school?

The issues in the *Bakke* case are hardly as straightforward as they have so often been presented, and they are hardly resolved by the decision of the Supreme Court. There are no simple solutions for complex problems, but a careful examination of the facts can reduce the melodramatic aspects of the case. There are dangers in oversimplification, and this common sin has done much to obscure the problems we have identified as racial. The instances in our history when problems of color were considered rationally have been few indeed.

At the root of this dispute is the equal protection clause of the Fourteenth Amendment, which says that no state shall "deny to any person within its jurisdiction the equal protection of the laws." The concept is engraved in the lintel over the entrance to the Supreme Court building in Washington: "Equal Justice Under Law," a simple credo that has not been enforced for most of the nation's history. The distance between laws and equality is a familiar gap in the American matrix, and much effort has been devoted to closing this gap. There was a concerted push for equality in the 1960s that evolved into the concept of real equality rather than just theoretical equality. When members of minority groups were given an advantage through preferential programs, they would be able to overcome the handicaps of history and racism.

But this generosity lasted only as long as a healthy economy promised a place at the table for everyone. The recession of the 1970s fueled intense competition for jobs, training, and education. The few who had criticized such efforts found a new and more receptive audience for their complaints. They warned of the dangers of group or "ethnic" rights in a democracy that recognized the rights of the individual and predicated advancement on merit and qualifications.

Allan Bakke's case represented a confrontation of two concepts: equality as a theoretical right and equality as a reality. The problem had appeared after Emancipation, when slaves found themselves free and penniless and, as a result, often bound to continued exploitation by their former masters. The radical demand for "forty acres and a mule" was ignored and contributed to the creation of the two racially divergent and unequal societies of the twentieth century. The parallels between Reconstruction and this era are striking. After the initial ground swell of support for black aspirations, there had been a retreat. In 1877 the Hayes-Tilden Compromise, a gesture of conciliation between North and South, removed federal troops frcm the South and allowed a return to white supremacy. In 1977 a southern president sat in the White House in another gesture of reunification, and once again the struggle for equality by minority groups was cast as an encroachment on the legal rights of white Americans.

Indeed, there are serious moral and philosophical issues raised by the granting of group rights. But the argument that equality cannot be legislated and will come about only in the natural course of democracy assumes that racially hostile attitudes are no longer an important element in the American equation of democracy. There is little evidence to support the contention that a profound change of attitude has taken place. A number of polls taken in 1976 showed the majority of whites to believe that blacks were at the bottom of the economic and social ladder because of a lack of effort—a variation of the "lazy and shiftless" concept. Whereas the majority of whites believed discrimination a minor issue, the perception of most blacks was the opposite. A 1978 report by the Department of Housing and Urban Development showed, in fact, that the majority of blacks continued to suffer discrimination in housing, the area whites believed to be most racially neutral.

But the inability of such reports to change white perceptions lay in the economics of the situation. As the end of the 1970s grew near, there was a painful awareness that social problems could not be solved without costs to one group or another. Already a million college graduates were unemployed or underemployed. Although the rate of joblessness among blacks was double the white rate, this provided little comfort to those whose security in society was not at all guaranteed.

Allan Bakke's case was on the cutting edge of a serious dilemma for the majority. To make a place for those underneath clamoring for a share of the rapidly dwindling privileges of affluence, some members of the majority would have to give way. To critics of affirmative action, this "reverse discrimination" was simply unjust. But to do nothing at all was to sentence entire generations of black, brown, and poor people to suffer the effects of this discrimination. The nation's highest court was expected to play Solomon in this intense melodrama. The dreams of one Allan Bakke were easier to understand than those of countless, faceless people who seemed to be asking for the unreasonable. But what the justices were being asked to do, as playwright and executioner, was to choose the victim.

There could be no resolution without injury to one side or the other. The imperative for action lay in the future shape of the nation, in the vision of a multiracial destiny that would eliminate color as a subject for debate. More than once in our history race has been a magnifying glass revealing the warts and imperfections of our most treasured myths. As one looks at Allan Bakke's case for becoming a doctor, one can also consider the irrationality of forcing 42,155 applicants to compete for 15,774 positions in medical schools. While officials admit that the majority of rejected applicants are qualified to study medicine, the United States continues to rank near the bottom among industrialized nations in the quality of health care.

It is easier for demagogues to raise cries of "merit" and "discrimination" than to consider the more serious obstacles to the education of an Allan Bakke. Few have been willing to discuss the abuse of power that had much to do with Bakke's exclusion from the medical school at Davis, California. It takes courage to admit that wealth and political power still bring advantages in our democracy. It is even more difficult to realize that we all cannot have what we want or deserve because that undermines the greatest American dream of all. Instead, we are left with the spectacle of Americans standing on both sides of the issue, crying racism while actually making a choice of victims.

The campus of the University of California at Davis would seem an unlikely setting for an important racial and legal confrontation. The university squats in the center of the valley, the broad, flat plain that slices like an incision down the middle of this rugged and mountainous state. The northern end of the valley peters out as the coastal range turns away from the Pacific and merges with the rugged Sierra Nevada, which form California's eastern Great Wall. The mountains on both sides keep out the chill coastal winds that give the coast its perpetual autumn. In winter the valley is cold, and in summer it becomes a dry, hot plain, forcibly transformed into one of the world's most productive agricultural domains by a crisscross pattern of waterways and canals.

San Francisco, that reasonable facsimile of a European city, with its cosmopolitan charm, polyglot culture, and tolerance of sexual and political aberration, is only seventy-two miles southwest of Davis, but the hills keep out more than weather. This is conservative farming country, replete with decalled pickup trucks, silos etched against an unlimited sky, and the inevitable California "Far out!" delivered to the cadence of country music. The growth of city living has encroached on the farmland around here, and the ubiquitous developments have sprouted wildly around towns like Davis. Among these boxes for living, we see the flimsiness of this new middle-class status. The builders throw up airy wooden cages, cover them with plywood and tar paper, add shingles and glass, and declare them to be homes. If this be the goal of upward mobility, then the location of this dispute is not at all difficult to understand.

On that August day in 1973, Peter Storandt, a thirty-year-old assistant to the dean of student affairs at Davis, waited inside one of the green metal prefabricated buildings that housed the medical school while permanent facilities were being completed. The medical school had begun only in 1968, and the impressive facilities on the western edge of the 4,000-acre campus were still under construction. The old green barracks at the center of the campus were relatively inconspicuous, their starkness only partially softened by the hedges around the exoskeletal structural beams.

It was six o'clock that Friday evening when Allan Bakke drove off the exit ramp from I-80 and made his way through the maze of roads and driveways that crosshatch the campus. In California the weekends begin early, and the building was deserted. The temperature had reached nearly 100 degrees, but it was dropping rapidly, and soon that part of the state would plunge into the typically cool nighttime weather that never fails to surprise tourists.

Storandt insists he never meant to provoke Bakke into suing the university. But his meeting with Bakke and their exchange of letters would make him a principal character in the melodrama. He provided a sympathetic ear, crucial information about the school's admissions procedures, and important advice on legal strategy that Bakke would follow. More than any other single event, this meeting at Davis would crystallize Bakke's resolve to sue.

Storandt, the son of an admissions officer at Cornell University, had himself toyed with the idea of becoming a physician. In one of those adolescent moments of truth that move us closer to adulthood, he decided he did not have the aggressive character and intense competitive spirit to pursue a premedical education, and he switched to English literature. He had nearly completed his course work for a doctorate at the University of Massachusetts when his wife became pregnant. Realizing that doctors of English had difficulty finding work in the late 1960s, almost by accident he found himself in admissions, first at the medical school at Wayne State University in Detroit, later at the Medical College of Pennsylvania, and then at Davis. A shy, intense man of medium height, Storandt has a clear complexion that makes him appear younger than he is and leaves his cheeks in a permanent flush. Until the *Bakke* case became a major issue, he had a reputation as a dissident in a tightly controlled administration who often took the side of students in controversial disputes. When he left Davis, students picketed in protest, not aware of the peculiar role he had played in the affair.

Storandt had always been ambiguous about the Task Force that selected minority students for the medical school. He was bothered by the fact that no whites had been selected by the Task Force, although it professed to consider all disadvantaged applicants. He felt compromised because he had to answer questions from white applicants in ways he felt were not totally honest in order to cover up the faculty's failure to develop a well-thought-out and carefully articulated rationale for the program. He saw deserving whites and blacks being excluded by both the Task Force and the regular admissions committee, and he raised the issue a number of times with administrators at the medical school.

In conversation Storandt exudes an honesty and earnestness that must have been appealing to applicants and students at the medical school. Some administrators complain that he had an inordinate desire to please and often exceeded his authority in the process. Those traits resulted in his involvement with Allan Bakke's problems. Bakke's first contact with the school was a letter he wrote in 1971 asking how his age would affect his application. Dr. Alexander Barry, an associate dean, wrote back that no fixed maximum age had been established for applicants. "However," Barry went on, "the Committee does feel that when an applicant is over thirty, his age is a serious factor which must be considered. One of the major reasons for this is that such an applicant can be expected on an actuarial basis to practice medicine for about ten years less than the applicant of average age. The Committee believes that an older applicant must be unusually highly qualified if he is to be seriously considered for one of the limited number of places in the entering class."

Despite the concern generated by this letter, Bakke applied late in 1972 and was not interviewed until the following March, after most of the places in the class had been filled. It had to be difficult for a man who had been at the top of his class at the University of Minnesota, served his country in Vietnam, and worked among the country's scientific elite to accept the form letter that rejected his application. Davis was the newest and least prestigious of the dozen medical schools Bakke had applied to. The turndown by Davis made his chances of becoming a doctor seem more remote than ever.

On May 14, 1973, Bakke wrote to Dr. George Lowrey, the
dean of student affairs and the official in charge of admissions
at the medical school: "Your letter denying me admission to
Davis was a tremendous disappointment but I'm not yet willing to give up my commitment to becoming a physician."
Bakke asked if he could be put on standby status or could
audit courses until a vacancy developed. His letter went unanswered, and he wrote again on July 1, 1973. Noting the
"inexorable passage of time, I feel compelled to pursue a
further course of action. My commitment to becoming a physician and serving in medicine requires it."

Until now Bakke's communications with the school had concerned his age, and their tone had been respectful, even pleading. Now his anger and frustration came through clearly. Trying a new tack, he raised the issue of race for the first time:
"Applicants chosen to be our doctors should be those present-
ing the best qualifications, both academic and personal. Most
are selected according to this standard, but I am convinced
that a significant fraction of every current medical class is
judged by a separate criterion. I am referring to quotas, open
or covert, for racial minorities. Medicine needs the ablest and
most dedicated men in order to meet future health care needs.
I realize that the rationale for these quotas is that they attempt
to atone for past racial discrimination. But instituting a new
racial bias, in favor of minorities, is not a just solution."

Bakke called quotas illegal and said he was asking friends
in federal and state government about possibly challenging
the school in court. "My main reason for undertaking such
action," he admitted, "would be to secure admission for myself. I consider the goal worth fighting for in every legal and
ethical way. Further, I believe selecting medical students on
any other basis than demonstrated aptitude, ability, and motivation is wrong and should be challenged." He added that
many physicians and laymen he knew opposed "reverse dis-

crimination" and that he planned to poll the faculty of a medical school in California on the issue. After his somewhat vehement assertions, Bakke ended his letter by thanking Lowrey and adding, "I do still hope to be accepted to medical school. I won't quit trying."

Answering mail from unhappy applicants was one of the tasks assigned to Peter Storandt. Lowrey passed the letter on to him, and it was now his job to deal with Bakke, whose complaints struck a sympathetic chord in the young admissions officer. He understood Bakke's burning desire to become a physician, and while the engineer could hardly be classified as disadvantaged, neither was he a child of the privileged class.

By reading Bakke's file, Storandt quickly constructed a sketch of this troublesome applicant. Allan Bakke was born on February 4, 1940, in Minneapolis. When he was very young, his family moved to Florida, where his father was a mailman and his mother a schoolteacher. He went through the segregated public school system and Coral Gables High School. "He was one of our bright young men," recalls Harry Rath, who was principal at the time. Bakke was a star at a school with a respected academic reputation. He was a member of the National Honor Society, treasurer of his high school band, chaplain of his homeroom, and vice-president of his senior class. When he was graduated in 1958, he was a National Merit Scholarship finalist. Bakke went back to his home state and was graduated from the University of Minnesota with a degree in mechanical engineering and a 3.51 grade point average.

To defray his college costs, Bakke joined the naval ROTC, and when he was graduated in 1962, he served his four-year obligation as an officer in the Marine Corps. His tour of duty included a seven-month stint as commander of an antiaircraft unit in Vietnam. He was honorably discharged as a captain in 1967 and went to work in the space program at NASA.

Bakke's concern about lost time comes through clearly in his two applications to Davis. He starts both by referring to his age and the fact that he lost four years in military service. "Four years was a high price to pay for my undergraduate education and I would hope the admissions committee will not hold those years of service to America against me," he said in his first application. He described his good health as an argument against actuarial considerations and said he had taken courses in biology and chemistry while working full-time.

Bakke also took the Medical College Admissions Test (MCAT), an examination required by virtually every medical school in the country. He did well, scoring in the 97th percentile (top 3 percent) in scientific knowledge, 96th percentile in verbal ability, 94th percentile in mathematics, and 72d percentile in general knowledge. His scores were higher than those of the average student admitted to Davis.

But his high grades and scores did not help when he began applying to medical schools. In 1972 he applied to the University of Southern California and Northwestern and was rejected by both. Northwestern said his age was "above their stated limit." In 1973, the first year he applied to Davis, he also applied to UCLA, UC–San Francisco, Stanford, the University of Minnesota, the Mayo Medical School, Wayne State University, Georgetown, the University of Cincinnati, Bowman Gray Medical School at Wake Forest, and the University of South Dakota. He was interviewed at Stanford, Minnesota, and Mayo, an indication he was being seriously considered, but all three turned him down. This time UCSF told him age was a "negative factor."

When Bakke's first application arrived at Davis, it was one of 2,464 competing for 100 places in the class that would begin in the fall of 1973. All applications were sorted into three groups by members of the admissions committee. Line 22 of the application read: "Applicants from economically and educationally disadvantaged backgrounds are evaluated by a special subcommittee of the admissions committee. If you wish your application to be considered by this group, check this space." Applicants who had checked off "Yes" were put into a separate stack for consideration by the Task Force. The grade point averages of applicants with "No" checked off for line 22 were examined. Those with an overall GPA below 2.5 were automatically turned down. Applicants with GPAs above 2.5 were forwarded to the regular admissions committee. Bakke's file met the requirements of the third group and was moved on to further consideration. The process of selection it had undergone would become the heart of the *Bakke* case.

Bakke's mother-in-law was seriously ill with lung cancer in 1972 and required considerable attention from Bakke and his wife. As a result, his application was not completed until January 9, 1973. But his high scores, grades, and experience took him over the next hurdle in the selection process. He was among the one out of six invited to Davis for an interview. But medical schools select their students over a period of time, and by the time Bakke was interviewed on March 21, 1973, 123 letters of acceptance had already been mailed. (Schools accept more students than they can accommodate because many choose to go elsewhere.) Only thirty-seven more letters of acceptance would go out for that fall's class. Bakke's chances for admission had already been considerably reduced by his tardiness.

However, the interview with Dr. Theodore West, a Davis faculty member, went very well. "He is a pleasant, mature person," West wrote in his interview report, "tall and strong and Teutonic in appearance (not surprising from his Minnesota background)." West called Bakke a "well-qualified candidate for admission whose main handicap is the unavoidable fact that he is now 33 years of age." West noted Bakke's service in the emergency room of a hospital near his home in Sunny-vale and his interest in applying his engineering knowledge to the problems of medicine.

"He seems completely unprepossessing," West continued. "He was not dynamic or aggressive and articulated well in all areas except his response to my request that he express for me some of his reasons for changing from engineering to medicine. During that phase his conversation was more halting, more introspective and I sensed an air of frustration and emotion which I attribute to his concern about the impact of age and the fact that this is probably about the last chance for him to apply."

The only negative comment by West was that Bakke had "apparently not looked to any extent into the problem of health care delivery." Officials at Davis were aware that problems of American medical care stemmed more from the mal-distribution of physicians than from the shortages that had received so much publicity a decade or two earlier. The concept of attracting minority and rural applicants to medical schools was aimed at correcting this problem. Later another official would also complain about Bakke's lack of awareness of the nature of the delivery problem. Despite this, he went on to say that he saw Bakke as "a very desirable applicant to this medical school and I shall so recommend him." As in the case of other regular applicants, Bakke's file was then cir-culated among five members of the admissions committee to be rated on the basis of the test scores, grades, recommenda-tions, and the interview with Dr. West.

At the same time the other group of applicants was going through a similar process. The Task Force, consisting pri-marily of minority faculty and student members, had been set up in 1969 to help bring greater diversity into the medical school.

When Allan Bakke was applying to medical school, the

atmosphere of tension and racial confrontation that marked the 1960s seemed remote. But when rioting swept through Watts, Detroit, and Newark and when the Reverend Martin Luther King, Jr., was killed in 1968, white America seemed at bay, and the need to correct the inequities of discrimination was a subject to be considered seriously. It was in this spirit that the Association of American Medical Colleges (AAMC) recommended that "medical schools must admit increased numbers of students from geographical areas, economic backgrounds and ethnic groups that are now inadequately represented." The following year an AAMC committee suggested that 12 percent of all first-year medical school classes be black by the 1975–76 academic year. This goal would not be met, but more than 100 schools responded by setting up programs similar to the one at Davis.

The Task Force at Davis was created by faculty resolution and operated in an informal manner until the dean of the school, Dr. C. John Tupper, appointed Dr. Lindy Kumagai, a Japanese-American faculty member, chairman in 1970. Kumagai had been instrumental in setting up a similar program at the University of Utah, so he seemed a logical choice. Davis was then accepting fifty medical students each year, and eight slots were allotted to the Task Force. When the class size was doubled, the number assigned to the Task Force went up to sixteen. Between 1970 and 1974 the Task Force admitted thirty-three Mexican-Americans, twenty-six blacks, and one Native American to the medical school. The fact that no whites were admitted through the program would lead to charges that it was racial and not for disadvantaged students.

But Dr. Kumagai insists he followed the recommendations of the AAMC and the faculty resolution in defining who was eligible. During the four years he was chairman, twelve Asian students were admitted through the Task Force, while forty-one other Asians came through the regular admissions process.

Kumagai says minority candidates who showed no evidence of disadvantage were referred to the regular committee but had difficulty being admitted despite excellent credentials. On the rare occasion that blacks or Chicanos were admitted by the regular committee, their records were so outstanding that it was predictable that they would not come to Davis. Task Force members say that at least three blacks were offered admission through the regular process, but only one accepted because of competition from more prestigious schools. Kumagai and others who served on the Task Force insist that they interviewed several whites during that time. Some were turned down because they made no commitment to serving in inner-city or rural areas or because their disadvantaged status was questionable. However, the statistics used in court would show only that no whites were admitted through the Task Force between 1970 and 1974.

While regular applicants with grade point averages below 2.5 were automatically turned down, this was not the case for Task Force students. Many had grades and MCAT scores somewhat lower than the regular group's. In 1973 the average GPA of Task Force students admitted was 2.88, against 3.49 for regular students. On the science section of the MCAT, Task Force students averaged a ranking in the 35th percentile, while regular students averaged in the 83d percentile. Clearly, the Task Force was giving less weight to academic credentials in selecting candidates, giving rise to charges that these students were "less qualified."

However, the *range* of scores tells more about the selection process than the *averages* used throughout the case. At least one Task Force student admitted in 1973 had a grade point average of 3.76—higher than Allan Bakke's. In addition, a considerable number of whites were admitted with grades and MCAT scores lower than Bakke's. In a number of instances white students had lower grades than did some of the students admitted through the Task Force. Because the university did not choose to make the individual scores of white students a part of the trial record but chose instead to submit only an average of their scores, these facts were never made clear.

Bakke's main problem was that he applied late in 1973, and the benchmark scores, the rating of applicants by the admissions committee, had moved upward as places became scarce to a minimum of 470 out of 500 for admission. After Bakke's application made the rounds of the committee, he had a score of 468. There were at least nineteen other applicants who scored 468 and fifteen with scores of 469. Bakke's last hope would have been the alternate or waiting list, but while some applicants with scores of 468 went on the list, Bakke was not among them. The reason he might have been excluded from the waiting list was not disclosed anywhere on the file Peter Storandt examined and would not be revealed until much later.

On July 18, 1973, Storandt sat down and carefully composed a letter to Bakke. He apologized for the delay in answering, explaining the turmoil of commencement, the start of the summer session, and changes that were taking place in the school's administration: "Your first letter involves us both in a situation as painful for us as for you. You did indeed fare well with our admissions committee and were rated in its deliberations among the top ten percent of our 2,500 applicants in the 1972–73 season.

"We can admit but one hundred students, however, and thus are faced with the distressing task of turning aside the applications of some remarkably able and well-qualified individuals, including this year, yourself," Storandt went on. "We do select a small group of alternative candidates and name individuals from that group to positions in the class made vacant by withdrawals, if any." Storandt explained that regulations did not allow part-time enrollment, as Bakke had suggested.

"Your dilemma—our dilemma, really—seems in your mind to center on your present age and the possible detrimental influence this factor may have in our consideration of your application. I can only say that older applicants have successfully entered and worked in our curriculum and that your very considerable talents can and will override any questions of age in our final determinations." Up to this point Storandt was playing the role of the concerned and sympathetic official. He encouraged Bakke to apply again through the Early Decision Plan, which would get him an interview and evaluation before October 1 and would give him time to apply elsewhere if turned down again.

Now Storandt addressed Bakke's threat to sue: "In the event that our decision is the latter [rejection] you might consider taking my other suggestion, which is then to pursue your research into admissions policies based on quota-oriented minority recruiting." Storandt said he was sending Bakke a page describing the minority admissions program at Davis. "I don't know whether you would consider our procedure to have the overtones of a quota or not, certainly its design has been to avoid such designation, but the fact remains that most applicants to such a program are members of ethnic minority groups." Storandt brought the *DeFunis* case, which challenged the use of race in admissions, to Bakke's attention and suggested two authorities on the legal aspects of minority admissions he might consult. The young admissions officer closed the letter by urging Bakke to "make a second shot at Davis."

Storandt would deny later that he was urging Bakke to sue the school, but it is difficult to interpret the letter differently. At that point Storandt felt that the Task Force was unfairly excluding whites, and in his zeal "I overstepped my bound of propriety and authority." Later he would wish he had limited his contacts with Bakke to off-the-record statements.

Finally, they were face-to-face, the man racing against time and the admissions officer who had given him new hope. They shook hands. Storandt offered Bakke a cup of coffee and tried to make small talk. Bakke brushed the chitchat aside and pressed Storandt for information about admissions procedures and the performance of minority students at the Davis Medical School. Storandt was reminded of a character out of a Bergman film, "somewhat humorless, perfectly straightforward, zealous in his approach; it was really striking; he was an extremely impressive man and I felt he deserved a straight answer." Bakke was no longer a faceless stack of forms and numbers. He was barely under six feet, taller in appearance, and his blond hair was thinning and combed across his forehead in that fruitless effort of men not yet resigned to baldness. The crew-cut youth in the picture that would be seen across America had been replaced by an older, heavier man with a determined jaw and a strong, set mouth.

Bakke did not believe the official description of the Task Force program sent to him by Storandt. As the engineer fired questions, Storandt gave him details: no whites had been accepted through the Task Force; the grades and test scores of minority applicants were lower than those of whites who applied; yes, Storandt understood the number of minority admissions was set at sixteen for each class. Bakke's resolute air and his own ambivalence made Storandt talkative. When the conversation ended, Bakke knew nearly as much as Storandt about the admissions procedures at Davis.

Yet there was one area that neither man touched. The case would go through the courts with no reference to a third method for admitting students to the medical school. Storandt had learned about it soon after he came to Davis in 1972.

From time to time the dean of the school, Dr. Tupper, would submit a name to the admissions committee for consideration. Sometimes the dean's candidate had already been rejected in the regular admissions process. But the intervention was common at many medical schools, a tradition for making sure that the children of the wealthy, the influential, and the politically powerful inherited the spoils of privilege. Although some Davis faculty members objected to the practice—especially in cases in which the candidate failed to meet the minimum standards—they thought it a privilege of the dean. The understanding was that the dean could select as many as five students in each year's class.

University officials have never satisfactorily explained their failure to mention the dean's involvement in the admissions process. They argue that it was not an issue at the time. In fact, it would not become a controversy until 1976, when a medical student wrote about the procedure and questioned the dean's right to exercise this power. A number of administrators, including Storandt, resented Tupper's interference and made strenuous objections on several occasions. But Tupper exercised much power over the waiting list, and without this quota of privilege, Allan Bakke might well have been admitted.

After his conversation with Peter Storandt, Bakke's spirits must have been lifted considerably. He had been urged to try again, and if he were turned down, he would attack what he saw to be the only obstacle between him and medical school: the special admissions program or Task Force. As he drove into the coastal fog that night, the radio droned about FBI director L. Patrick Gray's testimony before the Senate Watergate Committee and his admission that he had read Howard Hunt's files and destroyed them. President Nixon warned Congress that the impending cutoff of funds for bombing Cambodia would have "dangerous potential consequences" in Asia. The good news was that unemployment had hit a three-year low. Hardly anyone noticed that black unemployment was double the rate for whites and going up. For Allan Bakke, race was rapidly replacing age as a concern in his ambition to be a physician, and he felt a great deal less helpless than he had when he had started the drive to Davis a few hours earlier.

The following Tuesday, Bakke wrote a thank-you letter to Storandt. "Our discussion was very helpful to me in considering possible courses of action. I appreciate your professional interest in the question of moral and legal propriety of quotas and preferential admissions policies; even more impressive to me was your real concern about the effect of admissions policies on each individual applicant." Bakke reiterated that his first concern was "to be allowed to study medicine, and that challenging the concept of racial quotas is secondary. Although medical school admission is important to me personally, clarification and resolution of the quota issue is unquestionably a more significant goal because of its direct impact on all applicants." Although the personal objective remained paramount, Bakke moved for the first time into his new role as a symbol. He proposed two plans. Plan A was to apply under the Early Decision Plan at Davis and to sue Stanford and the University of California at San Francisco even if Davis admitted him. Bakke was especially interested in Stanford because it stated categorically that it had set aside twelve places in its entering class for racial minorities.

Plan B was to apply to Davis and at the same time to threaten to sue Stanford and try to force his admission "as an alternative to a legal challenge of their admitted racial quota." Bakke would sue Davis and UCSF if Stanford let him in. If also admitted to Davis, he would sue only UCSF. Bakke added that he didn't want to jeopardize his chances of being admitted at Davis under the Early Decision Plan. He wrote that he also wanted to avoid any actions Storandt might oppose "personally or professionally" because the admissions officer had been so helpful to him.

Bakke then made Storandt his mentor by asking him for suggestions or comments about the actions he proposed to take against Davis and the other schools. He also asked Storandt about the academic performance of the minority students at Davis and closed the letter by thanking Storandt again. At this point Storandt realized that Bakke was quite serious about suing. He says he went to see Dean Tupper and told him about his meeting with Bakke and the exchange of letters. Tupper took no action and told Storandt, in effect, not to worry about it.

A more prudent official might have terminated his contact with Bakke at this point. Storandt says that he was only mildly interested in Bakke and that he was just giving him the sympathy he shared with any applicant to medical school. But he sat down and wrote another letter to Bakke on August 15. "Thank you for your good letter," Storandt wrote. "It seems to me that you have carefully arranged your thinking about this matter and that the eventual result of your next actions will be of significance to many present and future medical school applicants."

Storandt went on to comment on Bakke's proposed plans to sue. He was doubtful about plan A. Could Bakke sue Stanford if he did not have a current application for admission there? Storandt preferred plan B, in which Bakke would apply at all three places and sue the schools that turned him down. He agreed with Bakke that the Stanford program seemed the most vulnerable and referred him to articles in the *Journal of Medical Education* on the performance of minority students.

"At Davis," Storandt wrote, "such students have not required 'official' tutoring, although they and many of their classmates have organized an impressive series of study sessions during the year. A few of them—perhaps ten percent—have taken longer than four years to complete the M.D. degree (but not more than one year longer)." Storandt said that about half the minority students in the third-year class had failed their National Board exams on the first try but that all had passed these tests before being graduated.

Bakke's second application was already being processed when Peter Storandt wrote his letter. It was no longer being treated as a routine application. Officials were aware of Bakke's threat to sue and had passed the word around to members of the admissions committee. There had been changes in procedure for the new application year. Davis had joined the centralized American Medical College Application System (AMCAS), which allowed applicants to fill out one form and have it distributed to all the schools where they wanted to be considered. As a result, there was a tremendous upsurge in applications to Davis, an increase of about 1,200 to 3,737 candidates for the 100 places in the class that would begin in the fall of 1974.

There was also a difference in the wording of one important question. Instead of asking about disadvantaged status, the AMCAS form made a direct reference to race. Did the applicant describe himself or herself as "White/Caucasian" or a member of some other identifiable racial group, and did he or she wish to be considered as an applicant from a minority group? Bakke checked off "White/Caucasian" and "No" once again. In his written statement he once more referred to his age and his concern about the obstacle it posed.

"The usual factors which detract from an older applicant do not apply in my case. First, my only dependent is my wife, who is well qualified to assist in earning if needed," Bakke said, stressing his recent studies as evidence of his ability to do the work in medical school. He said he was in good health and could be expected to practice as long as a younger applicant.

Bakke then decided to confront the question of why he had taken so long to decide on medicine as a career. "I was not among those blessed with a built-in motivation, such as a physician in the family, or a parent who encouraged me toward a medical career." He said that he had been considering medicine since 1963 and had made inquiries while in the Marines but that after his discharge he had gone on to finish the master's degree in engineering he had started at Minnesota. He said he thought the engineering background could be applied to medicine and emphasized that he was not changing careers for financial gain. "More than anything else in the world," Bakke stressed, "*I want to study medicine.*"

Under the new procedures at Davis, there would be two interviews instead of one, with a student and with a member of the faculty. On August 30, 1973, Bakke drove up to Davis again to see Frank Gioia, a second-year student, and Dr. Lowrey, who said later that his assignment to interview Bakke was simply the luck of the draw and not a result of his concern about the threat of legal challenge.

Gioia had heard about Bakke and was pleasantly surprised at the interview with the engineer. He found the applicant "friendly, well-tempered, conscientious and delightful to speak with." The conversation got around to minority admissions, and Gioia reported that Bakke took pains to make clear "that he was not out to sue anybody but that he simply wished to question the logic behind such policies. He simply felt that medical candidates should be selected on" the basis of qualifications. "I felt that he was at no time 'uppity' or threatening about the matter," Gioia concluded, giving Bakke a "sound recommendation" for acceptance.

Lowrey and Bakke disagreed on almost everything. "He was very unsympathetic to the concept of recruiting minority students so that they hopefully would go back to practice in the presently neglected areas of the country," Lowrey wrote in his report. "One of the main reasons for being against such programs was that this decreased his chances of getting into medical school." Lowrey found Bakke "a rather rigidly oriented young man who has the tendency to arrive at conclusions based more upon his personal impressions than upon thoughtful processes using available sources of information." He rated Bakke "acceptable but certainly not an outstanding candidate for our school."

Considering all the attention that was to focus on this case, the final process for selecting students at the Davis Medical School would never be made completely clear. None of the testimony and no interviews ever established the relationship between grades, test scores, and interviews with the benchmark ratings that actually determined acceptance or rejection. Apparently, the rating was quite arbitrary, unlike the situation in some schools, which scored each segment of the application process and produced a rating through a complicated formula. At Davis the number of people voting on applicants had been raised to six for 1974. Each scored the applicant without seeing the vote of other members of the committee.

On Bakke's second application, Storandt gave him 92 points. Gioia, who had interviewed Bakke, scored him at 94. Bakke also got a 96, a 94, and an 87. Dr. Lowrey gave him his lowest rating, 86 points. His total benchmark score was 549. He was rejected under the Early Decision Plan, and when he was reviewed the following spring, he was turned down again.

Twelve applicants with higher scores than Bakke's failed to make the alternates list for 1974, and thirty-two applicants with higher scores than 549 were not admitted at all. In the class for 1974, the overall grade point averages of whites ranged from 2.79 to a perfect 4.0. The overall GPAs of Task Force students ranged from 2.21 to 3.45. The grade point average in sciences of the top regular student was 4.0, and the science GPA of the top Task Force student was 3.89. The most profound differences between the two groups would be found in the MCAT scores and would help build the argument that the Task Force students admitted to Davis were "less qualified" than Allan Bakke.

Two

BROTHER FOX
FOR THE DEFENSE

One day Brother Fox caught Brother Goose and tied him to a tree.

"I'm going to eat you, Bro' Goose," he said, "you've been stealing my meat."

"But I don't even eat meat," Bro' Goose protested.

"Tell that to the judge and jury," said Bro' Fox.

"Who's gonna be the judge?" asked Bro' Goose.

"A fox," answered Bro' Fox.

"And who's gonna be the jury?" Bro' Goose inquired.

"They all gonna be foxes," said Bro' Fox, grinning so all his teeth showed.

"Guess my goose is cooked," said Brother Goose.

—An Afro-American folktale

The natural dramatics of a courtroom trial would have been the preferable way of resolving the issues in the *Bakke* case. The gradual exposition of fact through examination and cross-examination is a device that has attracted writers ever since the invention of the written word. For that reason plays have been written as trials and trials have served the purpose of theater. In a case that has played the national stage to such acclaim, a courtroom confrontation would have been a fitting vehicle for sorting out the complexities of law and the motivations and passions of the principal characters and for resolving it all in a firm and definitive final scene with the passage of judgment.

But this case fails to offer a neat resolution. We see no penetrating examination of nervous witnesses, no dramatic appeals to judge and jury. At least three times judgment has been rendered. But this was a battle fought with paper, delivered with little discernible drama by messengers who insisted on signatures and receipts that ended up in the record. The combatants have been not the complainants and defendants most affected by this case, but attorneys and judges.

The mass of paperwork in the *Bakke* case tends to reduce the issues to abstractions because there is little sense of the flesh and blood in legal maneuvers. But even in cases where prosecutor and defendant stand eye-to-eye in moments of high drama, these theatrically satisfying confrontations often tell us less than the processes that take place outside the public view. Decisions to include or omit, to challenge or let pass, to protest or acquiesce, are important in the overall strategy of a case.

The lack of a trial in *Bakke* remains a major criticism of the handling of the case by attorneys for the University of California. In addition, a number of important omissions and concessions by the university have muddied the defense all the way to the highest court in the land. These unspectacular events have brought into question the university's commitment to the defense of the case and cast doubt on the competence of the attorneys involved. The facts indicate that the university lawyers were hampered not so much by a lack of lawyering skills as by the competing concerns of their client and an ambivalence about the issues central to the case.

When reporters for national news organizations began calling the West Coast to find out about the attorney who would represent Allan Bakke before the United States Supreme Court, Reynold H. Colvin couldn't resist slipping into what he called his "Sam Ervin shuffle." He would tell the press he was "just an ol' country lawyer from San Francisco" and ask about the distance from the Greyhound station in the District of Columbia to the Supreme Court building. Although his law practice may not have impressed Supreme Court pundits, Colvin already had to his credit an important federal court victory in a case alleging reverse discrimination.

A jowly, jovial man of average height and stocky build who appears a decade younger than his threescore years, "Rennie" Colvin has the carefully modulated tones of the practiced public speaker. A native of San Francisco, Colvin was graduated from Lowell High School, a selective public school in the city, and got his bachelor's degree from the University of California at Berkeley in 1938. He was graduated from the university's Boalt Hall Law School before being swept into military service by World War II. After his discharge he worked as an assistant U.S. attorney until 1951, when he ventured into private practice.

An active member of San Francisco's Jewish community, Colvin served several terms as president of Temple Emanu-el, the most influential and politically powerful synagogue in the city, and he has also been president of the San Francisco chapter of the American Jewish Committee. Colvin's interest in city politics brought him indirectly to the most important case of his career. In 1964 Mayor John Shelley appointed him to the traditional "Jewish seat" on the San Francisco Board of Education, a high-visibility position that has been a traditional first step to higher political office. Despite a term as president of the school board, the gregarious attorney was unable to capitalize on his exposure because Shelley's successor, the flamboyant Joseph Alioto, declined to reappoint Colvin in 1970.

But Colvin's tenure made him a lot of friends among school officials and administrators. In 1971 Superintendent Thomas

Shaheen, facing budget cuts and declining enrollment, proposed to demote and transfer more than 200 administrators in an economy move. In order to keep the handful of minority officials who had recently joined the school system, Shaheen decided to exempt them from the effects of the reorganization. Because a strong affirmative action plan set goals for hiring and promoting minorities, the new arrangement would have virtually eliminated future advancement for white officials in the school system.

The administrators asked their friend Reynold Colvin to represent them. The "Zero Quota" case made a public figure of their attorney. After a series of confrontations with the school board, the case ended up in the federal district court. The decision in *Anderson* v. *S.F. Unified School District* did not receive a great deal of national attention. The ruling by federal judge Joseph Conti, a conservative whom San Francisco civil rights lawyers avoided when they could, concerned a specific employment situation and did not seem to have broad implications. But it was one of the few cases that had considered the issue, and it would provide important theoretical elements for subsequent attacks on preferential treatment of minorities at Davis and elsewhere.

"Preferential treatment under the guise of 'affirmative action' is the imposition of one form of racial discrimination in place of another," Conti ruled. "Any classification based on race is suspect: no authority exists which discriminates on racial or ethnic lines which is not being implemented to correct a prior discriminatory situation.

"No one race or ethnic group should ever be accorded preferential treatment over another. No one race or ethnic group should ever be granted privileges or prerogatives not given to every other race. There is no place for racial groupings in America. Only in individual accomplishment can equality be achieved," Conti concluded in reversing the school district's action.

Judge Conti's ruling turned up in the case Storandt had suggested to Allan Bakke, *DeFunis* v. *Odegaard.* Marco DeFunis, Jr., was a Phi Beta Kappa graduate of the University of Washington who sued his alma mater after he was rejected by its law school in 1971. DeFunis charged that the law school's minority admissions program had allowed less qualified applicants in ahead of him because of their race. A lower court supported DeFunis and ordered him admitted, but the Washington Supreme Court reversed the lower court and declared the university's program constitutional.

In his first letter to Bakke, Peter Storandt pointed out that DeFunis had been able to attend the University of Washington Law School while his case was in the courts. This sparked Bakke's interest, and with the thoroughness of the research scientist, he wrote to DeFunis in Seattle. By return mail he received copies of briefs and documents filed in the case. Among them was a brief by the Anti-Defamation League of B'nai B'rith on behalf of DeFunis referring to Colvin's case against the San Francisco Board of Education.

Reynold Colvin met with Allan Bakke in January of 1974 to discuss the merits of his case against the University of California. "I told Mr. Bakke he appeared to be a very sane, very intelligent, confident person and that the road of litigation was long and hard and rough." Colvin pointed out the parallels in the *DeFunis* case, which was going to the U.S. Supreme Court, and suggested that they wait to see the result.

On February 26, 1974, the High Court heard oral arguments in *DeFunis.* But the plaintiff was already completing his third year of law school. On April 23, to the bitter disappointment of both sides, the Court declared the case moot by a 5 to 4 vote. Within a couple of days, Bakke was back on the telephone with

Colvin. "Well," he said to the attorney, "what are you going to do for me now?"

There were fundamental differences between Bakke's case and that of the school administrators. The changes proposed by the superintendent had been made public; Bakke had obtained his information from conversations with Peter Storandt. While it was clear which administrators would be affected by the San Francisco plan, Bakke, as an outsider looking in, had to establish the important legal condition of standing. He had to show that he was genuinely affected by the procedures at Davis. As Colvin saw it, Bakke had to prove not only that there was a quota for minority students but that he had been injured by this quota. The crucial issue would be how close he had come to being admitted. Storandt's assurances that he had been very near admission were not enough. Bakke had to show that the Task Force students had specifically kept him out of the medical school.

While the thrust of legal action would aim at getting the special admissions program declared illegal, the real objective was to get Bakke admitted in time to join the fall class. The time element would dictate Colvin's tactics and would pay off in unexpected ways. When DeFunis sued the University of Washington, a local judge ordered him admitted, and he was able to stay in school even when the U.S. Supreme Court sidestepped the case. Colvin decided his best bet was to take the case to the superior court in Yolo County, where the medical school was located. He hoped that a state court judge at the local level, familiar with the Davis campus, would view the case in terms of real benefits and damages to Bakke. If they went to federal court in San Francisco, the judge might view the case as an abstract exercise in law and keep Bakke out until a decision was issued.

Colvin's decision to pursue Bakke's admission as a primary objective also dictated another tactic. The case would not be pursued as a class action. "While he had no constitutional right to be in medical school," said Colvin, "he did have the constitutional right not to be discriminated against. From our point of view, he was there as an individual." The emphasis on the individual, Colvin hoped, made it more likely that a judge would order Bakke admitted than if several plaintiffs were involved. This pragmatic decision would also reap benefits for Bakke. Whenever the case threatened to become too abstract, Colvin would focus attention on his client. The case would no longer involve an amorphous white person deprived for the public good. It would become a case about Allan Bakke, Vietnam veteran, aerospace engineer, and a man with a strong commitment to medicine.

On June 20, 1974, Reynold Colvin filed a complaint on behalf of Allan Bakke at the Yolo County seat in Woodland. This important first step was strangely lacking in drama. The complaint covered a modest four pages and had a fifth page asserting that Allan Bakke was telling the truth. The complaint charged that Bakke was "and is in all respects duly qualified for admission to [the Davis] Medical School and the sole reason his application was rejected was on account of his race, to-wit, Caucasian and white, and not for reasons applicable to persons of every race."

Colvin charged that "a special admissions committee composed of racial minority members evaluated applications of a special group of persons purportedly from economic and educationally disadvantaged backgrounds; that from this group, a quota of 16 percent, or 16 out of 100 first-year class members, was selected; that, in fact, all applicants admitted to said medical school as members of this group were members of racial minorities, that under this admission program racial minority and majority applicants went through separate segregated admission procedures with separate standards for admissions; that the use of such separate standards resulted in the admission of minority applicants less qualified than plaintiff and other non-minority applicants who were therefore rejected." The complaint concluded that Bakke's rights had been violated under the Fourteenth Amendment of the U.S. Constitution, the California Constitution, and the U.S. Civil Rights Act of 1964. Colvin asked that Bakke be admitted to the school while the case was being considered.

The University of California is an independent entity created by the Constitution of California. While the university depends on the state legislature for much of its funding, policy decisions are in the hands of the University Board of Regents, a body consisting of the state's top elected officials and private individuals named by the governor of California. The university is the top tier of an educational system that includes the state colleges and the community colleges, each having its own ruling body. But the university system is the most prestigious, a sprawling complex of nine campuses stretching from San Diego to Davis, an enrollment of nearly 122,000, a teaching staff of 9,400, and an annual operating budget of $1.8 billion.

On the day that Bakke's complaint was filed in Woodland, a copy was delivered to the fifth-floor offices of the university's general counsel in University Hall, Berkeley, a dull, colorless blockhouse of concrete, glass, and brick that serves as the administrative center for the entire system. All legal matters for the nine campuses are handled by the staff of eighteen attorneys under the supervision of Donald H. Reidhaar.

In many ways, Reidhaar presents a sharp contrast with his opponent in the *Bakke* case. Where Colvin is extroverted and garrulous, Reidhaar is self-effacing and closemouthed. Where Colvin is expansive and dramatic in making a point, Reidhaar has the lawyer's talent for cloaking an important point in boredom. A native of Idaho, Reidhaar is a slim, pale man, distinguished by healthy sideburns that seem out of place in his otherwise conservative demeanor. After being graduated with a degree in business from the University of Washington in 1957, Reidhaar earned his law degree at Boalt Hall and clerked for a justice on the Oregon Supreme Court. In 1961 he returned to the Bay Area and joined the prominent San Francisco law firm of Pillsbury, Madison, and Sutro. After just eleven months as an associate, Reidhaar crossed the bay to join the university counsel's office. He spent nine years as an assistant counsel, was promoted to associate, and in 1973 was rewarded with the job of general counsel. He had been in office less than a year when Bakke's complaint reached his desk.

Although the debate sparked by *DeFunis* had been raging for some time, the university had been amazingly complacent about the possible repercussions of that case. Large corporate institutions like the university retain full-time attorneys as a preventive measure against legal problems. Yet no guidelines had been issued on affirmative action, and no efforts had been made to formulate admissions guidelines for the university system. Instead, each campus and each professional school were allowed to set their own standards for admission and to draw up their own affirmative action plans. The result was a hodgepodge of approaches, some clearly more defensible than others. Reidhaar would explain that this diversity was a result of the university's policy of encouraging autonomy on the individual campuses.

The university had received complaints about affirmative action and special admissions programs from individuals and organizations such as B'nai B'rith, but Bakke's was the first definite legal action against these programs. The regents had expected that a U.S. Supreme Court decision on *DeFunis* would provide some guidance on special admissions; but less than two months had passed between the Court's rejection of *DeFunis* and the filing of Bakke's complaint, and they were no more ready in June than they had been in April.

Initial reaction to the complaint was low-keyed. Reidhaar assigned three lawyers from his staff to determine the facts of the case. They went to Davis and interviewed medical school officials involved with admissions: Dr. George Lowrey, the dean of admissions; Peter Storandt, who had corresponded with Bakke; Dr. Lindy Kumagai, who had been chairman of the Task Force; and Dr. C. John Tupper, the dean of the medical school.

Storandt remembers his own response to Bakke's complaint as a combination of concern and relief. Maybe now, he thought, his reservations about the Task Force would be resolved in court. "We believed it was going to be a strictly social issue," he recalled. "It was going to be one of those precedent-setting decisions that would help the medical school devise a better program and maintain its commitment to minority education. Maybe we were optimistic and idealistic and maybe all of these things."

But some of the people interviewed by university attorneys were not so confident about preparations to defend the program. At least one Task Force member thought the lawyers somewhat casual in their approach. "I think they tried to win the case with one hand tied behind their backs," said a faculty member. "They didn't realize they couldn't win it off the cuff." Dr. Kumagai, who had set up the guidelines for the Task Force, thought at least one of the lawyers was "overtly against affirmative action. I said to one of them, 'With friends like that, who needs enemies?'"

The facts assembled by the university attorneys would become the foundation of the case for both sides. Unfortunately, mistakes or omissions in the university's preparations would prove most harmful to the defense. There was no dispute over the fact that applications were sorted into two groups—regular and Task Force—and that members of separate subcommittees interviewed and rated applicants, then presented them to the full admissions committee for consideration.

For some reason the lawyers decided to build their defense around the testimony of Dr. Lowrey, who had never worked directly with the Task Force and was therefore not completely familiar with its operation. Two key arguments in Bakke's complaint, which would remain undisputed throughout the legal battles, might have been challenged or undermined if Task Force members had been brought into the defense of the special admissions program. Early in the case the university virtually conceded that a quota was in operation by submitting statistics showing that in each year Bakke applied, sixteen students were admitted through the Task Force. Not until later would Dr. Sarah Gray, a black faculty member, go through the records of the admissions office and find that in 1974 only fifteen students came through the Task Force. One slot was given back to the regular committee, apparently because Task Force members felt they didn't have a qualified candidate. This information would have been helpful in refuting charges that unqualified applicants were being admitted to Davis because of a rigid quota.

The most damaging evidence against the Task Force was the total absence of whites admitted as disadvantaged, although more than 200 applied. Nowhere would the university show that a number of white applicants were interviewed by the Task Force. Dr. Kumagai and Dr. Gray say none of the whites were admitted because they failed to meet the economic and social qualifications applied to minority applicants or because they indicated no plans to practice in underserved or ghetto areas. In their defense, they point out that minority candidates from middle-class backgrounds were referred to the regular committee for evaluation. Dr. Kumagai complains that the regular committee often turned down well-qualified minority applicants. "They would say he or she only has a 3.4 [GPA] instead of a 3.6," he recalled. "I would point out that they were accepting whites with 3.4 and much less." Dr. George Sutherland, who as a student at Davis studied admissions practices at the medical school, concluded that both committees failed to practice what they preached. Dr. Lowrey would admit later that good middle-class minority candidates and whites from disadvantaged backgrounds often fell in the cracks between the two committees and were turned down.

The most crucial defense omission, of course, was the dean's intervention on behalf of well-connected applicants. Long after the California Supreme Court ruling in the case, Tupper would admit to a Davis paper that he had "intervened hundreds of times" in the admissions process "on the side of fairness." One prominent instance involved Ramona Mrak, daughter-in-law of a former chancellor of the Davis campus. Another Tupper admittee was the son of B. Kent Wilson, a former president of the Yolo County Medical Society. Others included the sons of the state senator and assemblyman who headed finance committees responsible for the medical school budget. In one case, Storandt recalled, a student was not interviewed at all but simply placed on the waiting list and admitted after the admissions committee had disbanded for the summer.

At the time that university attorneys were preparing their case, most faculty members, even those opposed to the practice, believed Tupper to be within his rights. After all, most professional schools made some exceptions for wealthy and influential friends. "I don't think those places were on anybody's mind as they worked on the court case," recalled Storandt. "It never came up when we were working with the university attorneys." Considering reports that Tupper was admitting as many as five applicants each year, this was a considerable oversight. A similar practice at the university's San

Francisco medical school had been debated some years earlier and abandoned when slots traditionally controlled by the dean were used for a new affirmative action program.

Bakke's entire case rested on the premise that the "quota" of sixteen places in the first-year class at Davis left just eighty-four slots open to competition. What if he had known that he was really competing for seventy-nine places because he lacked political connections? More important, Tupper often exercised his authority by placing students on the waiting list and selecting them from that list when vacancies occurred. In each year he applied, Bakke never made the waiting list. But because the details of the admissions process remained curiously fuzzy, he would never know that social status had at least as much to do with his exclusion as race.

Thirty-three days after Bakke filed his complaint, the university made its first official response. The lawyers admitted the existence of a special program that let "officials of the Davis Medical School consider minority group status of qualified applicants as a factor in filling a limited number of spaces in each first-year class for the purpose of promoting diversity in the student body and the medical profession and expanding medical educational opportunities for persons from economically and educationally disadvantaged backgrounds."

The university argued that Allan Bakke had no standing to sue because he had fallen far short of admission and because there was nothing illegal about the special admissions program. So far the university's response followed standard procedure. But at this point the attorneys made a move that would come back to haunt them. In filing an answer to Bakke's complaint, Reidhaar filed a cross complaint explaining the stiff competition for places in the medical school and the rationale for using race as a factor.

"An actual controversy has arisen and now exists," the university lawyers said, "relating to whether the special admissions program" violated the law. They asked the superior court to determine the validity of the program "so that it may ascertain its rights and duties with respect to the evaluation of [Bakke's] application and others." With this simple statement in the cross complaint, the university had opened itself up to a new line of attack. Up to this point the legal debate centered on Allan Bakke's right to be admitted to medical school. Colvin had suggested in his complaint that the method of selecting minority students was illegal but that all he wanted the court to do was admit his client. Quite possibly, the court would touch on the legality of the program in deciding whether to admit Bakke, but state trial court judges tend to shy away from sweeping decisions. This was the reason Colvin had gone to the Yolo County court. Now the university, of its own free will, was broadening the target for Bakke.

Litigation is the sweat and blood of law, essentially an unglamorous business of nuts and bolts, technique and technicalities. One axiom of litigation is that the defense tries to narrow the grounds of a case while the plaintiff makes every effort to widen it. The university lawyers had violated this rule, and they would pay for it. Another common tactic of corporate defendants is to slow the proceedings and increase the costs to the plaintiff. Again, the university gave no sign of resorting to such practices.

Bakke was fortunate that Reidhaar and his staff were after bigger game. The general counsel would refuse to discuss his strategy on the grounds of the lawyer-client right of confidentiality, but he conceded "the great uncertainty about the validity of such programs in the wake of *DeFunis*. There certainly was an institutional interest in having their validity clarified and sustained." Like Peter Storandt, the university lawyers had decided to turn their troubled consciences over to the courts.

The next step for Bakke was to find out as much as possible about the facts of the case. Under the rules of discovery adopted by most states in recent years, one party can interview the other in a legal action to determine these facts. On July 12 Colvin filed a formal notice of his intention to take a "deposition" from Dr. Lowrey. He asked the school official to bring all records of Bakke's applications, including documents having to do with his evaluation and rejection. Colvin also wanted information about the special admissions program and any documents defining the terms *educationally disadvantaged* and *economically disadvantaged.* Understandably, most of Colvin's requests for information were vague, but there was one specific item he wanted: "documents setting forth summaries and tabulations of information relating to said special program including, without limitation, the documents prepared by the University of California, Davis School of Medicine, Office of Student Affairs, Admissions Office, entitled: 'Statistics, Admissions Office, May 20, 1974.'" This document had been prepared by the medical school at the request of the Department of Health, Education and Welfare's Office of Civil Rights in San Francisco. The reason: a complaint of reverse discrimination by Allan Bakke. Colvin knew that those statistics, marked "Confidential," would provide information essential to Bakke's case.

Dr. Lowrey was interviewed by Colvin in the presence of Reidhaar at University Hall on Tuesday, July 23. For the first time Bakke and his attorney had full access to the files and letters in Bakke's application folder and a statistical comparison of Task Force and regular students at the medical school. Colvin took Dr. Lowrey through a step-by-step explanation of the selection process at Davis: the separation of files into "disadvantaged" and regular groups; elimination of regular applicants below the 2.5 GPA limit; the interview process; and the method of grading according to benchmark scores.

Lowrey emphasized that the score was a "benchmark for selection but is not rigidly followed throughout the admission period." He explained that students were admitted in batches and that their scores were sometimes changed because of additional recommendations or material added later. He said students selected from the alternate or waiting lists were not picked strictly by scores but for "balance" or "special skills" they brought to the class.

Colvin concentrated on the statistical differences between Task Force and regular students. He pointed out that some Task Force students admitted had grades well below the 2.5 set for regular students. In one class the average science GPA of regular applicants was 3.36, but that of Task Force students was 2.42. Lowrey conceded the difference. Colvin wondered if the purpose of looking at the relative scores was to determine whether applicants could compete successfully in medical school. Lowrey said no; the process tried to judge more than just academic qualities—for example, character and motivation.

Lowrey rephrased the comment he had made in his unfavorable evaluation of Bakke: "I think we are concerned about such things as imaginativeness. We also consider the possibility of what kind of practice and where they are, at that point in their lives, thinking of practicing, recognizing these things can change." Colvin asked if benchmark scores for Task Force applicants were equivalent to those of regular applicants. Lowrey was unsure, but he conceded they might be lower than those of regular applicants, possibly as much as 30 points lower.

"Below the 468?" Colvin asked, citing Bakke's score when he was turned down the first time.

"Below the 468, right," Lowrey answered.

Colvin wanted to know if any exceptions were made to the admissions procedure described by Dr. Lowrey. Lowrey conceded there were some exceptions.

"Those exceptions were made by the committee as a whole?" Colvin asked.

"Some, yes, because of further information. A letter from a dean of the applicant's undergraduate school would come through and be very strong and this would make that original rating somewhat higher than it had been." Lowrey gave another example: when a married couple applied and one spouse had grades somewhat lower than the other's.

"Were the exceptions made by determination by yourself, Dr. Lowrey?"

"In some cases, yes."

"Some cases, I see. Was this understood by the Admissions Committee that this was the rating process: that exceptions would be made to the numerical order which was proven out by the rating?"

"Yes," said Dr. Lowrey, remembering instructions from the university's lawyers not to volunteer additional information.

This was as close as the record would get to the dean's discretionary admissions prerogative. The exceptions made by Dr. Lowrey were often made at the instructions of Dean Tupper. But Colvin dropped what might have been a revealing line of questions. The university had been very cooperative, and he had no reason to suspect that anything was being hidden. In addition, Lowrey's comments on the exceptions were not especially useful to his case. Colvin was going to argue that Bakke was better qualified than others on the basis of his benchmark scores. The concession that some students were selected without regard to their ranking on the waiting lists undermined that argument. Lowrey was painting a picture of an admissions process than was extremely subjective and arbitrary, while Colvin preferred to exploit the statistical differences between the two groups. For this reason he would never examine the grades at the upper and lower end of each group admitted, preferring instead to emphasize the averages. His interview of Lowrey would turn out to be the most critical confrontation in the case.

In every case there is a point where each side assesses its position and considers the possibility of settlement. After taking Dr. Lowrey's deposition, Colvin had to feel fairly confident. In his eyes the administrator had virtually admitted that a quota existed and that the admissions process was segregated. During the interview Reidhaar had made little effort to direct the flow of Dr. Lowrey's statements, an indication that he considered little of the information damaging to the university's case.

But time was running out for Bakke, with classes just a few weeks away, and Colvin's priority was to get his client into medical school. He met with Reidhaar to discuss the possibility of a faster and less costly resolution. "Look," he said to Reidhaar, "Allan Bakke belongs in medical school. He should have been admitted in the first place. There's a law of the universe that there is always room for one more, so why don't you find another cadaver for Mr. Bakke up there at Davis? He will go to medical school. There will be no more lawsuit, and since there are no other plaintiffs in this case, it will be over."

The proposition would have tempted the ordinary trial attorney. If the university agreed to admit Bakke, there would be a respite until another case was filed. The next plaintiff would have to go through the laborious process of preparing a case without all the information that Bakke had collected. The university would gain valuable time to prepare a defense and correct weaknesses in the Davis admissions procedure. There might even be time to issue guidelines for the entire university.

But Reidhaar rejected the offer. The "institutional interest" in a definitive resolution took precedent. In pursuing a constitutional decision, the university had discarded caution and forgotten to protect the special admissions program. In light of the growing pressures against special admissions, this concern was understandable, but what if the university lost? Little attention had been paid to the possible impact of a decision against the university. If anything, there were no indications the university attorneys ever considered that they might lose.

But where had this directive come from, to get a definitive ruling on special admissions? Reidhaar informed the regents about the case at their July meeting, but several who attended the closed-door meeting do not recall any specific instructions to the general counsel. At that point the *Bakke* case was just another lawsuit before a lower court, and few could have guessed the impact it would have in just a few months.

Reidhaar's determination to pursue a legal judgment would add to the controversy over the handling of the case. The opportunity to set legal precedents must have seduced the university's chief lawyer, but his failure to bring out the complete story of the admissions process at Davis greatly jeopardized his chances of getting a favorable ruling.

The great frustration that *Bakke* presented to minority groups was their exclusion from the preparation and defense of the case. *Brown* v. *Board of Education* and other important civil rights cases were the result of a well-prepared legal assault on segregation drawn up by black attorneys under the direction of black legal expert Charles H. Houston in the 1930s. The unraveling of the separate-but-equal doctrine had not happened suddenly with *Brown* in 1954 but had begun with a long line of victories in the courts dating back to the 1940s and all based on the master plan dictated by Houston and others. But *Bakke* was a defensive action, and minorities found themselves on the sidelines, reminded that despite the rhetoric of progress so popular in the 1970s, most American institutions remained solely in the hands of white men who made decisions that would profoundly affect their welfare.

Colvin went back to court on August 6, and armed with the new information from his interview of Lowrey, he asked the court again to admit Bakke while the issues were considered. In addition to his request for action, he filed his first detailed legal argument on behalf of Bakke. His "Memo of Points and Authorities" listed laws and court precedents in support of his arguments. Bakke had been turned down twice, Colvin argued, although his grade point average and his MCAT scores were "both high and in fact higher than those of some who were admitted." He charged that the Task Force was exclusively for the admission of "racial minority persons" despite the assertion about "disadvantage."

"The selection process for the Task Force students paralleled but never intersected that used in the selection of nonminority students so that at no time were Task Force and nonminority applicants compared." Pursuing the thrust of his complaint and his interrogation of Dr. Lowrey, Colvin argued that the two groups of students were selected by "different standards." As evidence, he listed the differences in the grades and test scores of the two groups.

Colvin then launched into a legal argument that had definite echoes of the decision in the *Anderson* case he had won in federal court. Any classification on racial grounds by a state is suspect under the equal protection clause of the Fourteenth Amendment, he said. These racial classifications had prevented Bakke from competing for all the places in the entering class of the medical school. Bakke was excluded solely because of his race from a significant number of places that were set aside and reserved for other races. Had Bakke been a member of a racial minority, Colvin contended, such exclusion would have been unconstitutional. "The intent for adopting the quota is irrelevant. Validity of state racial discrimination is measured by effect, not motive."

Following the lead of the *DeFunis* case, Colvin quoted UCLA economics professor Thomas Sowell, a black critic of affirmative action and quotas. Paraphrasing Sowell, Colvin said Task Force students were being labeled as incapable of meeting the higher standards of admission applied to non-minority candidates. Colvin concluded by noting that there was no demonstrated history of race discrimination at the University of California to justify the use of such quotas—an exception often made by the courts.

The university filed its response on September 3. Again, Reidhaar and his staff insisted that Bakke had not been rejected because of the special admissions program. Even if there had been no such program, they said, he ranked so low he would have been excluded. They also repeated their belief that the program was legal under the law. The university argued that the courts had clearly given educational institutions the right to set admission standards. "The special admissions program is designed to serve the legitimate needs of the Davis Medical School, the medical profession and society. This delicate and complex process of deciding which of the many qualified applicants best serve those needs must be left to the informed judgment of those administrative officers."

As an example, the university cited the need for family physicians over highly trained specialists. "The issue is not whether preference should be allowed; they are basic to the admissions process. The question is whether the Constitution is to deny members of minority groups from disadvantaged backgrounds the kind of preference which is routinely granted to a myriad other individuals and groups." The test of "rationality" for racial classifications, the university argued, was intended to protect minority groups from capricious acts of racial discrimination. "There is every indication that this extraordinary exception to the rational basis test is a shield protecting minorities against discrimination and not a sword preventing society from redressing the effects of historical discrimination against minorities."

Colvin was not impressed with the eloquence of the university's arguments. On September 24 he filed a response suggesting the university had admitted the existence of a racial quota. If this were true, Colvin argued, the burden of proof in the case should be shifted from his client to the university, a practice frequently used by the courts in cases involving discrimination. For the first time Colvin used the term *reverse discrimination* and argued that "qualified applicants such as plaintiff are passed over because of their race in favor of minority applicants with less potential ability."

Colvin proceeded to bolster this argument by reducing the issue to numbers. "Defense must show, statistically speaking, plaintiff would not have been admitted even if there had been no special admission program. Only in this way can defendant prove that race was not a factor in the evaluation of plaintiff's application."

Of course, the university had already admitted that race was a factor in the selection process. Colvin was making the key argument of opponents of race-conscious admissions: that race had no positive value in a selection process, that being black, Asian, or Chicano and presumably from a poor background gave an applicant no advantage over one from a middle-class background. This argument prevented race from being an experience that might make a better physician or lawyer but reduced it to the level of a somewhat superfluous characteristic such as hair or eye color.

In a deposition taken by university lawyers after his interview with Colvin, Dr. Lowrey attempted to show the positive value of the presence of minorities in the medical school class. Lowrey said that these students brought a perspective and a concern about minority communities beneficial to both students and faculty members at the medical school, that minorities were most likely to return to their communities and provide medical services as well as role models for young blacks, Asians, and Chicanos.

Nowhere would the university argue that these minority students were actually "better qualified" than Bakke and other white applicants in fulfilling these objectives. After all, the admissions committee had never made a comparison of the two groups or, as some schools had done, combined the two groups of applicants before selecting students. Bakke's attorney would emphasize the difference in tests and scores and put the university on the defensive. Much time would be devoted to explaining the history of poorer educational opportunities and financial need that forced minority applicants to work while in college—all valid enough reasons for placing less emphasis on grades.

But there was the underlying assumption that Allan Bakke had to be an unfortunate victim of temporary measures that were probably less than just. Few of the foxes in the defense could make the leap of faith to a concept that minority students with lower grades and test scores could possess human qualities growing out of their individual racial experiences that made them better qualified than some whites who wanted to be physicians.

Reidhaar defended the motives and actions of his staff and the university. He said the issues needed to be presented as "sharply and cleanly" as possible. His involvement with the case, he admitted, was a great educational experience. "A person cannot be involved with a case like this without being deeply impressed with the consequences of the legacy of discrimination against persons of color that we have in this country." The man from Grangeville, Idaho, spoke eloquently of the high qualifications and credentials of minority students admitted to the University of California through race-attentive programs. But in the end he conceded that there were no blacks or Asians and only one Chicano on his staff of eighteen attorneys. "It wouldn't be fair," he said, "to bring in someone who couldn't cut it. But we are always on the lookout for qualified applicants."

Three

MASSACRE IN
YOLO COUNTY

In late summer the coastal hills shut out the Northern Pacific breezes and turn the Sacramento Valley into a cooking pot. Along the ocean the temperatures rarely rise above the 80-degree mark, but a mass of superheated air settles over the valley, undisturbed by the moderating influence of the sea, and temperatures above the 100-degree mark are common. State Route 113 connects Woodland, the county seat of Yolo, to I-80 and Davis, eleven miles to the south. The terrain along this road gives a strong impression of the Midwest. The heat and scenery are right, the fertile fields stretching to a barely visible wall of purple and dark blue mountains in the west and as far as the eye can see at the other cardinal points. The grain elevators and the mechanized farm machines shimmer in the hot sun, vague and intriguing structures that seem concerned with far more than the production of tomatoes, sugar beets, maize, and soybeans.

The monotone of the fields is broken occasionally by the old wooden farmhouses, generous in dimensions, trimmed with Victoriana, and framed by the old shade trees planted when these houses still smelled of the sea from the long trip around the Horn. The illusion of middle America is broken by the palm trees in the yards or in gauntlets along the road, possible only in a land that doesn't know snow or ice in winter. Woodland is a modest, quiet city of 25,000, complete with its Main Street and a handful of stores touting everything from farm equipment to consumer goods. There is little of the psychedelia and poster trade that differentiates Davis from any other valley town. Agriculture dominates here, as it has for more than 100 years.

Yolo County has not always been in the mainstream of California history. The first settlers were stragglers from the mass migration across the Bering Strait, mysterious and complex people who 2,000 or 3,000 years before Columbus buried their dead stretched out in their tombs, facedown, with their heads toward the west. One of Spain's ubiquitous missionary explorers sailed up the Sacramento River in 1817 and found the Patwin Indians living modestly in a land abounding in waterfowl, salmon, deer, the now extinct tule elk and acorn.

One of the first ranchers was Francisco Guerrero y Palo-Mares, a leading citizen of San Francisco, but like most of the Spanish grantees, he was an absentee landlord. Yolo was still a backwater when the gold rush drew thousands to the Sierra Nevada, but once again the stragglers and disappointed prospectors saw the value of this flat, fertile land. "In the conflict of the races," says the official history of Yolo County, "only the fittest survive. Civilization and epidemics destroyed the California and Yolo Indians." Civilization came in the form of rough-and-ready white settlers, who made slaves of the Indians and robbed and killed each other with alarming frequency. In 1850 a sheriff in Yolo quit, complaining that "there were more cattle thieves than gold dust to pay for hunting them."

When a man known as Uncle Johnny Morris built the first log cabin in Woodland, it was a wilderness of oak trees inhabited by grizzly bears. In the 1880s Indians were still a common sight on the streets of Woodland, their women clad in many skirts, colorful bandannas, and brightly colored plaid shawls. By the end of the last century Woodland had settled into a placid agricultural life, and farmers brought their families into town in the evenings to watch the seven o'clock train come in.

A fire in 1892 destroyed most of the evidence of Woodland's colorful past, leaving only the Spanish and Indian names and a relatively poor community, where change has been slow and relatively peaceful. A new breed of educated Chicanos has refused to accept the traditional arrangements of class and color and begun a push for political power. But their efforts are hampered because the best and the brightest prefer the more exciting life of Sacramento, San Francisco, or San Jose. The older Chicanos can remember when the Chinese were not allowed to live in Yolo and when Mexican farm workers had to hitch rides to Sacramento to get their hair cut.

The county building provides a measure of how much the recent past has been rejected. Its imposing Greek columns and the sweeping staircase would fit better in a European city than in a county whose name means "the place abounding in rushes." The main courtroom on the third floor of the building is a medium-sized room, lit unsparingly by a battery of fluorescent lights that succeeds in blurring the last remaining Greek revival details of the original architect.

Court clerks and officials were excited about the case when it first appeared on the docket in 1974. They didn't think of it as an important legal landmark, just a welcome break from the normal routine of minor civil suits and domestic disputes. Still, the two sitting judges of the court were already swamped by the backlog of cases when Colvin filed his complaint on behalf of Allan Bakke. A third judge, F. Leslie Manker, sixty-seven years old and retired at the time, was called in to handle the *Bakke* case. Manker had been a prosecutor and municipal court judge in Sonoma County before being appointed to the superior court bench in 1964 by Governor Edmund ("Pat") Brown. A native of California and a Boalt Hall graduate,

Manker stepped down in 1969 but came back occasionally to help handle the overflow. Until his trip to Woodland, little of his judicial work had gained the attention of the press or the public.

With the preliminary skirmishes completed and the positions of the parties committed to paper, September 27 was set for the hearing on Colvin's motion to have Bakke admitted immediately to the Davis Medical School. With just a few days left before the start of classes, Bakke's chances of getting admitted in time seemed very slim. When time is an important factor for one party in a suit, an argument can be made for immediate relief on the grounds that irreparable injury will take place unless the court takes immediate steps.

Colvin had observed the performance of the lawyers for the university, and he understood that their primary objective was a ruling on the constitutionality of the special admissions program. "They were not taking the view of hard-nosed litigators," he said. "What it gets to is neither apathy, incompetence, nor malicious motive. They were as anxious to get the case to issue as I was, but for a different reason. I thought the best thing I could do for my client was to get to the issue as soon as possible. They saw it as a great constitutional issue."

On the day of the hearing the courtroom was nearly deserted. Bakke and Colvin sat at one table in the carpeted inner area of the courtroom, Reidhaar and members of his staff at the other. The only spectators were Bakke's wife and three-month-old daughter and Dr. Lowrey. Bakke's key pieces of evidence were Lowrey's deposition and the statistics obtained from the medical school. In its defense the university had sent a list of twenty-four questions to Bakke, asking about his background, his qualifications, and his efforts to get admitted to Davis and other medical schools. In his arguments Colvin had continued to exploit the differences between Bakke's scores and those of the Task Force students. In the deposition taken by Reidhaar, Lowrey had reemphasized the preference for attributes not measured by grades and test scores and the need for minority physicians. Lowrey continued to stick to his assertion that the Task Force was intended for disadvantaged students of all races. ". . . the special admissions committee considers the applicant's status as a member of a minority group as an element which bears on economic or educational disadvantage and indeed, almost all of those admitted through the special admissions process have been blacks, Chicanos and Asians."

This was really the essence of the case, whether race or ethnicity could be taken into consideration in selecting applicants for the medical school. In the hearing before Judge Manker the university argued that it could use race as a factor. Colvin replied that race was the main determinant of who was eligible for the Task Force and was therefore illegal. All the statements, depositions, and briefs were meant to support one side or the other of the issue. As the hearing neared an end, Colvin knew that the pressure of time was against him. Feeling he had no other choice, he told Reidhaar he was willing to let the hearing serve as the trial in the case. This meant there would be no more discussion, no further testimony, and no further discovery or gathering of evidence.

"I was somewhat surprised when Colvin made that offer," Reidhaar conceded, "because it seemed to me he had not gone as far as he might have gone in the attempt to develop evidence supportive of his claim. It seemed to me at the time the documentary record contained essentially all the evidence we had detailing and supporting the program." But considering the glaring omissions in the record, the offer was even more attractive. There would be no further investigation of admissions practices at the medical school and no contradiction or challenge of the record as it stood. Colvin had gambled on the general counsel's anxiety to get a constitutional ruling, but he had also lost any opportunity to find out about the dean's discretionary admissions. Reidhaar was so eager to agree that he forgot to make an oral argument in support of the cross complaint he had filed asking the judge to declare the program at Davis legal.

Later he would defend his decision to accept Colvin's offer as a "trial tactic," but it would add to the concern about the university's commitment to defend the program. But the second-guessing would be based on the importance the case was yet to acquire. Although the issues involved were complex, it would have taken the gift of prophecy to guess that affirmative action was about to be ambushed in the nearly empty courtroom of a small town in a relatively minor county of Northern California.

In cases involving racial preference, Judge Manker had two main categories of decisions to draw from in reaching a decision. He would be guided by the Anglo-American system of precedents, rulings by other judges and other courts that are the building blocks of important legal principles. Most of the decisions in favor of preferential treatment involved institutions in which there was clear evidence of previous discrimination: school systems that had been intentionally segregated, all-white unions and municipal departments, segregated job categories. With some reluctance the courts had ordered some form of corrective action: recruiting, hiring goals, and, in some cases, hiring quotas. The pattern was less clear in cases in which there was no documentation of earlier discrimination. Here the judges preferred to tread lightly. Without clear evidence of wrongdoing, the courts shied away from quotas and the dangers of "group rights."

There was another important legal element for Judge Manker to consider. In cases involving school desegregation, busing did not involve the exclusion of whites from schools.

Despite the protests of some white parents that their children were excluded from better schools, the judges saw no victims. At least in theory, all children were getting an integrated education. But *Bakke* picked up where *DeFunis* left off: a redistribution of opportunity. A decision to admit minorities meant the exclusion of some whites, and this posed a much more serious problem for the judges.

The Supreme Court of the State of Washington had concluded in the *DeFunis* case that there was a "compelling state interest" in making a choice by race. Lowrey's deposition had pursued this argument, saying that more minorities meant better services for the poor and benefits to both students and faculty through the presence of a minority perspective. But the university had not fleshed out these arguments with any evidence or expert testimony that might persuade a judge whose understanding of minorities was largely unknown.

The most concrete evidence available to Judge Manker was the compilation of grades and test scores. Colvin had pounded away at the differences between the average grades and the average scores of regular and Task Force students. The university had failed to point out that at least on the basis of grades, a number of the regular students ranked lower than some of the Task Force students. In the areas where the differences were most glaring, the MCAT scores, the university provided no detailed breakdown of the scores and no evidence to support the argument that these scores told little about a student's eventual ability to become a physician.

In *DeFunis*, law school applicants were given a benchmark score determined by a precise mathematical formula. The process of scoring applicants at Davis was left unclear. If the ratings were as arbitrary as the testimony implied, with little weight given to test scores and grades, there seemed little reason to segregate minority applicants. If the scoring was not so subjective, much had been omitted from the record that

Reidhaar considered complete enough for his purposes. Maybe the lawyers had planned to introduce additional evidence at a full-scale trial, but they had bargained away that opportunity by agreeing to Colvin's offer.

Bakke's hopes of quick admission faded as summer melted into fall. Classes were well under way when Manker took his first tentative steps toward a decision. On November 25 he filed a Notice of Intended Decision, a preliminary announcement that gave attorneys for both sides a chance to respond before his decision became final. In the notice Manker rejected the university's argument that Bakke had no standing to sue. Although Bakke had not proved his right to be in the medical school, the judge said, the university had admitted he was a qualified applicant, and he therefore had a definite interest in the resolution of the issues. The first round had gone to Bakke.

On the basis of figures submitted by the university, Manker said, it seemed obvious that whites were being excluded from the special admissions program. In 1973, of the 297 applicants to the Task Force, 73 were white. In 1974, of the 628 applying for minority or "disadvantaged" status, 172 were white. Since none had been accepted, the superior court judge had to conclude that the special admissions program was "in fact open to and available only to members of racial minority groups and that it excludes consideration of applicants who are members of the white race."

Manker expressed some reservation about Bakke's qualifications as a plaintiff, saying he would have preferred someone who had applied to the Task Force and been turned down. "Nevertheless," he went on, "the use of this special program did substantially reduce plaintiff's chances of successful admission to medical school for the reason that since 16 places in the class were set aside for this special program, the plaintiff was in fact competing for one place, not in a class of 100, but in a class of 84, which reduced his chances for admission by

16 per cent." Manker had decided that the sixteen places were in fact a quota.

The judge reviewed the precedents that favored the use of race, including the decision by the Washington state court in *DeFunis*. But he chose to rely on the dissenting opinions in that case in formulating his position. "Racial bigotry, prejudice and intolerance will never be ended by exalting the political rights of one group or class over that of another," Manker quoted from the dissent of Chief Justice Frank Hale on the Washington Supreme Court. "The circle of inequality cannot be broken by shifting the inequities from one man to his neighbor."

Manker now shifted to William O. Douglas's powerful dissent to the U.S. Supreme Court decision that the *DeFunis* case was moot. "What places this case in a special category is the fact that the school did not choose one set of criteria but two, and then determined which to apply to a given applicant on the basis of race." To rally additional support for his decision, Manker quoted from *Anderson* v. *S.F. Unified School District,* the case Colvin had won for the white school administrators.

"This court cannot conclude," said Manker, "that there is any compelling or even legitimate public purpose to be served by granting preference to minority students in admission to the medical school when to do so denies white persons an equal opportunity for admission." As a result, Manker concluded, the program at Davis violated the equal protection clause of the U.S. Constitution. Round two had also gone to Allan Bakke, but he had fallen short of victory.

Manker said there was not enough proof that Bakke would have been admitted if the special admissions program did not exist. In addition, "the admission of students to the medical school is so peculiarly a discretionary function of the school that the court feels it should not be interfered with absent a showing of fraud, unfairness, bad faith, arbitrariness or capriciousness, none of which has been shown." The net result was a standoff. The university's program was declared illegal, but Bakke would not be admitted. "What happened at Woodland," Colvin would say later, "was that both sides lost."

Manker's decision was still in the formative stages. He had invited the attorneys for both sides to respond, and they did, each trying to claim victory and offering to write the decision for the court. Colvin proposed a declaration that the special admissions program at the medical school was illegal and an order that Bakke's application be considered without regard to race. Reidhaar objected, noting that Colvin was now asking that the special admissions program be halted, something he had not done earlier. The university lawyer failed to mention that his cross complaint had opened up the issue. "Plaintiff's complaint sought only to compel [Bakke's] admission to Davis Medical School," Reidhaar argued. "Defendant's cross complaint sought only a declaration as to the constitutionality of its special admissions program." Now Reidhaar was arguing a technical nicety—saying that the university had asked the judge to determine if what it was doing was legal but that it never intended to stop.

Colvin was still trying to push Manker into a more active role. He pointed out that the university's cross complaint had brought up the issue of legality and that Bakke was entitled to a ruling about the special admissions program. He also told Manker that Bakke had no other recourse for getting his application considered. "Indeed, what can be more unfair than to discriminate against an applicant on the basis of race? The violation of one's constitutional right is the classic form of unfair treatment and once a constitutional violation is established, the court not only has the authority, but also the duty to intervene and grant relief."

When Manker issued his final judgment on March 7, 1975, it was apparent that Colvin's arguments had been persuasive, but the judge was still reluctant to involve himself in the admissions process at the medical school. He repeated his earlier ruling that the special admissions program was illegal, but he did not order the program halted. He did tell the university that Bakke was entitled to have his application considered without regard to race.

Now that the university had been rebuffed, it started to play the kind of game that might have been expected earlier. A few weeks afterward Reidhaar made a cavalier offer to have Bakke's application considered on the same terms as "any other application coming in at this late date." This, of course, meant that Bakke would not be admitted. This gesture could have no other effect than to make sure that Colvin joined Reidhaar in taking the case to a higher court.

Once the case left Yolo County, it would move into the special environment of appeals courts, where the legal issues would be debated in a highly abstract and unemotional atmosphere. But the facts had been established in Judge Manker's court, and his findings would have a profound impact on subsequent decisions about the right of Allan Bakke to attend medical school.

Critics would question the paucity of the record and the lack of a vigorous defense by attorneys for the university. Indeed, the defense seemed to be a litany of missed opportunities. The university's main argument against Bakke was that he was not a particularly extraordinary candidate. Yet it never made much of a case against him. On the basis of grades alone he seemed much more qualified than most applicants—black or white. But because of the peculiar blur that occurs at the most critical point in the selection process—the benchmark scores—the reasons for his low rating and his failure to make the alternate lists are never explained. Bakke's own admission that he had been turned down by twelve other medical schools was never used by the university, nor was the most obvious obstacle of all, his age.

Bakke had begun his quest for a seat at Davis with a fear that he was applying too late. But because there was so little information about the way applicants were rated, the impact of age on at least his initial rejection is not clear. At least two other schools had turned him down flatly on the basis of age. Apparently they felt secure from a suit on the basis of age discrimination.

The suspicions of minority groups would inevitably center on the racial makeup of the people defending the university. It was not difficult to conclude that a group of white male attorneys would see the *Bakke* case as a simple matter of law and an opportunity to settle once and for all a practice that was generating considerable public resistance as the mood of the nation changed and the number of opportunities declined.

The battleground had also been an important factor. Had Bakke filed a complaint in Los Angeles or San Francisco or a major eastern city, the response from minority groups might have occurred sooner and affected the process of litigation at any of its crucial points. But neither Davis nor Woodland was a flash point of racial confrontation. Both were small, basically rural communities, like much of California north of San Francisco, and racial issues there had never reached the critical status of those in large cities in the 1960s.

This, perhaps, was why Judge Manker could see no compelling state interest in having minority doctors. He had weighed the most tangible evidence before him, grades and test scores, and found the minority students less qualified than did the university. He had stayed away from the issue that subsequent decisions would also do their best to avoid: the new awareness that opportunities, like natural resources, were limited in America. To have made such an admission would run counter to the entire mythology of advancement in America and the belief in places like Yolo County that survival was the prerogative of the fittest. As for the arguments that preference was not unusual, they would fall by the wayside. After all, the university had failed to point out that the most ancient and honored form of preference—wealth, power, and privilege—could still be an obstacle when the son of a mailman and a schoolteacher tried to become a doctor.

Four

"A VERY SAD IRONY"

Once Judge Manker's decision was made final, it was clear that the case would have to be appealed. If Bakke surrendered his struggle to get into medical school at this point, he was really giving up his dream. The university was in a worse predicament. Manker's ruling had made the program at Davis, and by implication all similar affirmative action programs in the university, illegal. Reidhaar and Colvin filed with the state's court of appeals, the next rung on the judicial ladder. But they soon decided they might as well go directly to the state's highest court for a definitive ruling on the issues.

The university's motion to the California Supreme Court made it clear that the *Bakke* case was no longer a local matter before a local judge. Reidhaar billed it as "a case of great and pressing statewide importance" and said that "a decision by this court will avoid a multiplicity of litigation." Without the court's intervention, he warned, all special admissions programs would be of "questionable legality."

The petition for transfer went to a court with an enviable reputation as one of the most active and progressive in the country. The California Supreme Court had anticipated many of the most liberal rulings of the U.S. Supreme Court in protecting the poor and extending constitutional rights. It had preceded the U.S. Supreme Court in ruling against the death penalty. When the Nixonian majority emerged on the nation's highest court and began cutting back on the rights of criminal suspects, the California court was extending those rights.

The California Supreme Court had also broken new ground by ruling that discrimination based on sex was suspect and that school financing systems that resulted in discrimination based on wealth were unconstitutional. On racial matters, it had rejected the U.S. High Court's attempt to differentiate between de jure and de facto segregation, holding that all segregation violated the rights of black children. This was a court that was viewed as a champion of the underdog and that gloried in its activist reputation.

It was not surprising that the court quickly agreed to accept the *Bakke* case. "All of the justices were concerned that this was not the ideal case upon which to decide such an important issue," recalled a court staff member, "but they also agreed that it was an issue which needed to be faced head-on." On June 26, 1975, the California Supreme Court agreed to hear the *Bakke* case, and this automatically raised it to the level of importance Reidhaar had sought. Immediately several organizations asked to file friend of the court briefs in support of one side or the other. As in the *DeFunis* case, the battle lines were quickly defined. Jewish organizations such as the Anti-Defamation League and conservative unions such as the American Federation of Teachers attacked the use of race and "quotas" on behalf of Allan Bakke. Civil rights groups such as the NAACP and associations of medical and law schools joined the university's side of the fray.

The arguments in the briefs filed by the two parties and in the oral argument of March 18, 1976, were not much different from those made in the Yolo County court. Bakke contended that the equal protection clause of the Fourteenth Amendment applied to all races and that "only in remedial situations have the courts tolerated racial discrimination." He also attacked the still-vague description of the admissions practices at the medical school in pursuit of his argument that it was up to the university to prove that he should be excluded. Because there were no clear standards by which the university judged medical school applicants, he argued, it could not objectively demonstrate that he was rejected for a reason other than race.

The university countered that there was a difference between programs instituted to assist minorities and those which discriminated against them. Reidhaar also urged the court to differentiate between programs that completely excluded whites and programs, like the university's, that attempted to include a limited number of minority students. As for Bakke's eligibility, the university renewed its arguments that Bakke was so far from acceptance that even without the special admissions program he would have been rejected.

Immediately after oral arguments, the seven members of the California Supreme Court met to discuss the merits of the *Bakke* case. It was soon clear that two members of the court would play pivotal roles in the forging of opinions on the case. Mathew Tobriner and Stanley Mosk had both been appointed to the court by Governor Edmund ("Pat") Brown, Tobriner in 1962 and Mosk in 1964. In their years on the state's highest court the two men had become close friends. They were both Jewish and longtime Californians who had acquired reputations as legal scholars and liberals, but their responses to the issues in *Bakke* could not have been more different.

Mosk remembers his family's struggle during his childhood: his father's fight for survival as a "small businessman" during the Depression, his job on Chicago's South Side for $7.50 a week during his days as a student, and his migration to Southern California in search of opportunity as a young attorney. He recalls with pride his courageous stand on civil rights as a judge in Southern California, where he outlawed restrictive racial covenants; as the state's attorney general, in which capacity he banned the segregated Professional Golfers Association from using state golf courses; and on the supreme court, where he authored many of its most liberal decisions.

But Mosk, a settled and comfortable man, is not so much at ease in discussing the *Bakke* decision, for his majority opinion has provoked strong reactions. Seated at the head of the T-shaped desk in his office, he has surrounded himself with documentation to defend his position on the case. He refers to William J. Wilson's book asserting the decline of the importance of race, and under the gold *M* on his desk he has secured a copy of Theodore Gross's *Saturday Review* article attacking open admissions at the City College of New York. He talks about quitting the Elks and the Eagles because those fraternal organizations had racially restrictive policies and adds that he also left the San Francisco Bar Association because it filed a brief supporting affirmative action in the *Bakke* case. "They're not discriminatory in their membership, but they are advocating a discriminatory position which I think is equally bad."

Mosk has been vehemently attacked by minority groups who felt forsaken by their formerly liberal ally. A conservative judge might have been viewed as the enemy, but Mosk is now seen as a traitor. Hundreds of chanting students have massed below his office window on San Francisco's Civic Center Plaza to denounce his decision, and his appearances at local campuses have been met with pickets and demonstrators. When, through bureaucratic insensitivity, Mosk was invited to give the commencement address at the Davis Law School, minority students wrote him to express their displeasure and to ask him to decline. With the same aggressive defensiveness, Mosk responded that he would not be intimidated, and he chastised the students for "their defective knowledge of the First Amendment." Yet he sees no contradiction between his insistence that they should hear his views and his own resignation from the Bar Association because he disagreed with the organization's position.

Mosk has been made tense and besieged by the outspoken opposition to his views. "I have been harassed a good deal by the Third World Coalition," he says of the protesters. "I see no difference between their position and that of George Wallace. They both want race to be a factor, and I don't."

On the other side was Mathew Tobriner, who would stand alone on the side of the university. It is clear that he has enjoyed the role of the intellectual maverick. "I was always considered the radical," he says.

Tobriner grew up in a magnificent Victorian house built by his father right after the 1906 earthquake, and he lives in that house today. "I'm not very adventurous when it comes to my own living," he explains, "but I'm more adventuresome in my theories of the law." After leaving Stanford, he went to the Harvard Law School, but he found the atmosphere isolated and repressive. "We had some wonderful teachers like Powell in constitutional law and Frankfurter, but most of the teachers were pretty orthodox."

After Harvard, Tobriner returned to San Francisco to practice labor law, and from 1928 to 1959 he represented many agricultural cooperatives and labor unions. It was during his early days as a lawyer that he met the man who would eventually appoint him to the California Supreme Court. Both he and Edmund Brown were registered Republicans, but the two young men were impressed with Franklin D. Roosevelt's New Deal. After a discussion of the merits of FDR, Tobriner talked his friend into switching to the Democratic party.

Twenty-five years later, when Brown was governor of California, he offered a vacancy on the California Court of Appeals to his old friend. Two years after his appointment to the court of appeals, Brown elevated Tobriner to the California Supreme Court.

The fact that Mosk was unhesitating and definitive in support of Bakke's position had a clear effect on the other justices. Judges are as sensitive of their image as politicians, and considering the fragile power of courts, they must often weigh public reaction to their opinions. This was, after all, a court that had great pride in its liberal reputation, and it surely was easier to believe the justices had not abandoned that image if Stanley Mosk was speaking for all of them.

While six of the justices debated the issues, one would play a minimal role. Justice Marshall McComb, eighty years old at the time, had ceased to be an active member of the court. A year after the decision in *Bakke*, the state Commission on Judicial Performance would recommend his removal for senility and incompetence. However, McComb would cast his vote with the majority that was forming around Stanley Mosk.

Although Mosk and Tobriner respected each other's independence, they both tried diligently to persuade each other. There was a steady flow of newspaper and magazine articles from the offices of one justice to the other. "I argued very loudly and long and strenuously," said Tobriner, "but as you know, I received no other vote." In a stunning 6 to 1 decision, the California Supreme Court upheld Judge Manker's ruling that the special admissions program at Davis was illegal and ordered the university to go back to the Yolo County Superior Court to determine if Bakke would have been admitted in the absence of the special admissions program.

To the educated eye, the opening sentence of a supreme court decision often tells the whole tale. In the *Bakke* case Justice Mosk stated the question before the court and answered it in the same breath: "In this case we confront a sensitive and complex issue: whether a special admission program which benefits disadvantaged minority students who apply for admission to the medical school of the University of California at Davis offends the constitutional rights of better qualified applicants denied admission because they are not identified with a minority."

The second sentence, stating the court's conclusion, had a clearly redundant ring: "We conclude that the program, as administered by the University, violates the constitutional rights of non-minority applicants because it affords preference on the basis of race to persons who, by the University's own standards, are not as qualified for the study of medicine as non-minority applicants denied admission."

The opinion was a news reporter's dream. There was no need to read beyond the first paragraph. Mosk had dealt himself four aces, and only constitutional scholars would be interested in seeing how he played the hand. But the question he had put to himself was based on the vital but unsubstantiated premise that Bakke and other rejected white applicants were "better qualified" than the sixteen minority students who had been accepted under the Task Force program. Unless the court accepted this premise as fact, Bakke had no case. He certainly could not claim he had been subjected to discriminatory treatment if the accepted minority students were better qualified. Superior qualifications had always been an acceptable reason for preferring one person over another, and if this were true, Bakke could not argue that he was denied admission *solely* because of race.

Mosk placed responsibility for this crucial finding on the "University's own standards." But what were these standards? Bakke had claimed he was better qualified on the basis of his higher undergraduate GPA and MCAT scores. Justice Mosk used these figures in his opinion to show that special admissions students were less qualified.

Applicants considered under the regular program were automatically disqualified if their undergraduate GPA was below 2.5, but minority students were admitted with GPAs as low as 2.11. (Bakke's GPA had been 3.51.) Bakke had scored above the 90th percentile in the verbal, quantitative, and science portions of the MCAT, while the average scores of the task force students were below the 50th percentile. Finally, the benchmark scores of some special admissions students were 20 to 30 points lower than Bakke's.

Despite the absence of a clear explanation of how the university determined which applicant had the best qualifications, the record indicated a strong reliance on grades and scores by the admissions committee. Dr. Lowrey's testimony that the committee looked hard at other qualities was, for Mosk, just an attempt to justify racial preference after the fact. The university had not challenged the trial court's finding that whites were barred from the special admissions program. Mosk obviously believed that the scores of the two groups were comparable and that the medical school had favored lower-scoring "less qualified" minorities over higher-scoring "better qualified" whites. But many other whites had been admitted with grades and test scores lower than Bakke's. Were they also "less qualified"?

Justice Tobriner, the lone dissenter in the court's opinion, broke with the majority at this initial stage of the analysis of the facts. ". . . the majority incorrectly asserts that the minority students accepted under the special admission program are 'less qualified'—under the medical school's own standards— than non-minority applicants rejected by the medical school. This simply is not the case. The record establishes that all the students accepted by the medical school are *fully qualified* for the study of medicine." By this assertion, Tobriner argued, the court was giving greater significance to grades and test scores "than the medical school attributes to them or than independent studies have shown they will bear."

Tobriner did not believe the court could discuss qualifications until it understood the goals of the medical school. If the school wanted to produce general practitioners as well as specialists, individuals who would practice in rural as well as urban settings, then it would have to seek a variety of skills, backgrounds, motives, and personalities for each class. In his view, the court could not speak as if there were one single, inflexible standard. The record showed that the medical school wanted an integrated student body that would lead to better services for the state's minority population. To fulfill this important goal, the school had judged the minority applicants "better qualified" than applicants like Bakke, who had been turned down.

Mosk's majority opinion moved on to a discussion of the constitutional ground rules the court would follow in considering the legality of the Task Force program. He posed two questions for the court to consider. The first was what test should be used in determining whether or not the program violated the equal protection clause, and the second was whether the program met the requirements of that test.

In considering a constitutional question, appellate courts follow the precedents established by earlier cases. When enough cases have been decided according to the same legal principle, a constitutional doctrine or rule develops. The process by which a court determines if a principle is being complied with is called a test.

"The general rule," wrote Mosk, "is that classifications made by government regulations are valid if any state of facts reasonably may be conceived in their justification. . . . This yardstick, generally called the 'rational basis' test, is employed in a variety of contexts to determine the validity of government action and its use signifies that a reviewing court will strain to find any legitimate purpose in order to uphold the propriety of the State's conduct." In this brief paragraph of legal jargon, intelligible only to the initiated, Mosk reminded his audience of lawyers how appellate courts most often looked at equal protection cases. While the terms of the equal protection clause were absolute, this did not mean that every law must apply to every person in the same way. After all, laws would serve no purpose if they could not treat people in different circumstances differently. For example, a law designed to ensure highway safety could grant a driver's license to a sighted person and refuse one to a blind man or woman. A state could provide welfare assistance to a disabled person and deny it to one who was physically able. Criminal laws treat violators and nonviolators differently, just as tax laws have different impact on rich and poor. Laws by their nature involve unequal treatment and often favor one group or individual over another.

How was this apparent paradox resolved? As two law professors had written in the *California Law Journal* forty years earlier, different treatment is not unequal treatment unless there is no good reason for the difference. In other words, a state has to show a need to make laws that treat people differently. In legal language, this is called the minimal rationality or rational basis test, and the Supreme Court of the United States told the states that different treatment had to be rationally related to some state purpose. The word *minimal* allows a state some flexibility in attempting to reach its goal. For example, a state might set the minimum drinking age at eighteen, although some people might be mature enough to drink at a younger age.

In all such cases the courts assume the wisdom of legislators and defer to them as long as the law is not clearly arbitrary or irrational. Under this practice of "minimal scrutiny," the courts do not require states to justify their motives or means.

It was clear that under this minimal scrutiny approach Allan Bakke would not have much of a chance. The state's purpose of integrating the medical school, providing better medical care in minority neighborhoods, and remedying past effects of discrimination all were legitimate societal goals. The court would not have had to "strain" to uphold the university's conduct.

But, as Mosk's opinion continued, in some cases a stricter standard of review is imposed: "Classification by race is subject to strict scrutiny, at least where the classification results in detriment to a person because of his race." Not only did the state have to show a "compelling interest," Mosk went on, but it also had to show there were no other ways to achieve this goal, and the burden of proof rested, in this case, on the university. Mosk was proposing to apply the strict scrutiny test, a different standard for looking at a state law's purposes and the means chosen to achieve them.

In this situation the court would require the state to show that the different treatment of different groups or classes of people was *both* necessary and rational. This test had been applied by the courts in situations that involved especially important or "fundamental" constitutional rights: the right to vote, to travel, to privacy, or to a fair trial. Strict scrutiny was applied in these situations because it was felt that states had to have a damned good reason to deny these important rights to an individual. The second major area where this test was applied involved laws that singled out a class of persons— blacks, aliens, or illegitimate children, for example—for less favorable treatment. The courts had recognized that in such cases the power of the majority was often used to oppress unpopular or politically powerless groups. The U.S. Supreme Court has referred to such groups as "suspect classifications."

Mosk had selected the strict scrutiny test because he believed that Bakke's exclusion from the medical school at Davis was based on the fact that he was white. The U.S. Supreme Court, he noted, had consistently held that racial classifications were suspect and should be subjected to strict scrutiny. His choice of this test was crucial to the outcome of the case.

Under the rational basis test, Bakke's lawyers would have faced the impossible task of convincing the court that the Task Force program was related to no legitimate state purpose. Under strict scrutiny the burden was now on the university to prove that there was no other way to achieve its goals.

Mosk rejected the university's contention that racial classifications were suspect only if they isolated or stigmatized a minority. He argued that racial discrimination could not be justified against one race but not another. Whites suffered a disadvantage by their exclusion from the university on racial grounds, and this discrimination could not be allowed.

Again, Mathew Tobriner chose to differ from his colleague. He noted that in previous cases the court had distinguished between invidious racial classifications and remedial classifications. Tobriner could not accept the argument that there was no difference between laws that used race to stigmatize minorities and laws intended to overcome the effects of past discrimination. Once again, the argument had reached the issue of victimization. Mosk was saying the program at Davis was illegal because it made victims of whites. Tobriner was arguing that the law attempted to halt the victimization of minorities and that it was inevitable that some whites would lose in the process.

To support his argument that there was a difference, Tobriner went to the history and purpose of the Fourteenth Amendment. The amendment had been intended to prevent states from discriminating against blacks and had gradually been extended by the U.S. Supreme Court to cover other minority groups in similar circumstances. But, Tobriner went on, nothing in the history of the Fourteenth Amendment suggested that the federal government or the states were prevented from attempting to meet the peculiar needs of minority groups.

In addition, said Tobriner, there was good reason for differentiating between invidious and benign racial classifications: "prejudice against discrete, insular minorities may be a special condition which tends to seriously curtail the political process." His argument, supported by a long list of cases, was that the strict scrutiny test was inappropriate for reviewing laws intended to benefit minorities because the majority had the protection of the normal political process and minorities did not.

"It is indeed a very sad irony," Tobriner said, that the "first admissions program aimed at promoting diversity ever to be struck down under the 14th Amendment is the program most consonant with the underlying purposes of the 14th Amendment."

Again the California court's two most liberal and intellectual judges had looked at the same set of facts and come to different conclusions. Was the strict scrutiny standard the correct one for this case? Was any governmental action that took race into account "suspect" and therefore subject to "strict scrutiny"? Or were there, as Tobriner argued, certain "benign" racial classifications that did not require the court to be suspicious? This was the crucial issue being debated. Not only would it determine the outcome of the case, but it would also affect the ways in which the modern manifestations of racial discrimination would be addressed.

The larger issue underlying the *Bakke* case was whether a school, an employer, a union, or a government agency should be allowed to notice who was black and who was white in an attempt to overcome a past that had made many of these institutions all-white. The majority opinion of the California Supreme Court was that the Constitution is color-blind and that race could never be considered.

Mosk's opinion implied that minorities were asking for more than their share of equal protection by asking for a higher degree of protection. This attitude was reminiscent of the view of a U.S. Supreme Court justice in another era. In 1883 Justice

Joseph P. Bradley struck down an act of Congress outlawing segregation in public places. Speaking of the black man who had been recently freed, Bradley said that "there must be some stage in the progress of his elevation when he takes the rank of mere citizen, and ceases to be a special favorite of the laws, and when his rights, as a citizen or man, are to be protected in the ordinary modes by which other men's rights are protected."

Tobriner's lengthy and scholarly exposition of the case law supporting the use of race as a remedial tool was virtually ignored by the majority. The dissenting opinion had pointed out that the U.S. Supreme Court had found remedial racial classifications essential in desegregation and employment cases. How else could a desegregation or hiring plan be implemented without paying attention to race? If the U.S. Supreme Court upheld such practices in overcoming past discrimination, why couldn't the medical school use them to overcome minority underrepresentation? Mosk responded to Tobriner's twenty-page analysis in several footnotes. The cases cited by Tobriner were not applicable, he said, because desegregation remedies did not "grant benefits to one race at the expense of another." Also, in all the employment cases cited "there was a finding by either a court or an administrative agency that the employer had engaged in racial discrimination in the past."

Tobriner had anticipated Mosk's first objection by pointing out that desegregation often excluded whites from the best schools in a district in order that the basic goal of integration could be achieved. Mosk's second argument assumed the absence of past discrimination in the *Bakke* case. Earlier Mosk had written that there was no evidence in the record to indicate past discrimination by the university. Neither party had argued that such discrimination had existed; therefore, the court had to presume that no past discrimination existed.

Then, in an inexplicable burst of candor, Mosk added in a footnote: "Admittedly, neither the University nor Bakke would have an interest in raising such a claim. But this fact alone would not justify us making a finding on a factual matter not presented below." This segment of the majority opinion was perhaps the best example of Mosk's ambivalence about the case. He had used the judicial fiction that an appellate judge may see only what is in the record to avoid seeing the reality of state-imposed discrimination, and in the next breath, he confessed that his blindness was artificial and self-imposed.

Just a few months earlier the California Supreme Court had found, in *Crawford* v. *L.A. Unified School District,* that the city of Los Angeles was still operating an unconstitutionally segregated school system. A few years earlier the U.S. Supreme Court had ruled in *Lau* v. *Nichols* that the San Francisco school district was violating the rights of Chinese children by failing to provide them with a bilingual education. There were numerous instances of documented discrimination against minority children in California, and this continued unequal treatment surely affected the ability of minorities to compete for admission to the university. But since none of this was in the trial record, Mosk and the other justices in the majority could choose to ignore the world around them.

Once the strict scrutiny test was adopted, Mosk went on to determine whether the university had met the heavy burden of demonstrating that the special admissions program was necessary for a compelling state interest and that its objectives could not be achieved without imposing a lesser burden on the majority. The university had made three arguments. One, integration of the school and profession would provide diversity and make both students and faculty members more sensitive to the needs of minority communities; two, an increase in minority doctors would provide needed medical services for minority communities; and three, minority doctors would have more rapport with patients of their own race and a greater interest in and sensitivity to their problems.

Considering how rarely the U.S. Supreme Court had upheld laws under the strict scrutiny test, the university's argument might seem futile, but these were the same grounds the Washington Supreme Court had used in upholding the state in *DeFunis*. Justice Mosk rejected these arguments. Quoting from Justice Douglas's dissent in *DeFunis*, he said, "The Equal Protection Clause commands the elimination of racial barriers, not their creation in order to satisfy our theory as to how society ought to be organized. The purpose of the University of Washington cannot be to produce black lawyers for blacks, Polish lawyers for Poles, Jewish lawyers for Jews, Irish lawyers for Irish. It should be to produce good lawyers for Americans. . . .'"

The sentiment was noble, but it ignored the fact that in many communities the alternative to a black doctor was none at all. It ignored the reality that in Chicano or Chinese neighborhoods the choice might be between a doctor who could communicate with his or her patients and a doctor who couldn't understand them at all. Underlying this argument were also a rejection of any societal responsibility for the nearly total absence of black and Chicano physicians and the implied assumption that paying attention to race naturally meant a lowering of quality.

Mosk was willing to assume that the other goals of the special admissions program were legitimate. But the goal of integrating the student body and improving medical care, even if legitimate, had failed the strict scrutiny test because the university had not proved to his satisfaction that they could not be achieved by other means. Mosk rejected the university's argument that the program was necessary because before the Task Force was created, only two blacks and one Mexican-American had been admitted to the medical school.

He offered three "less restrictive" alternatives for achieving the university's aims. He suggested the university increase minority enrollment by instituting aggressive programs to identify, recruit, and provide remedial schooling for disadvantaged students of all races. He suggested the university expand its enrollment. And finally, he recommended the introduction of more flexible admissions standards that relied less heavily on quantitative factors such as test scores and grade point averages.

If the majority opinion seemed somewhat less than compelling in its consistency and logic up to this point, it had now crossed the threshold into the disingenuous. Recruitment and remedial programs aimed only at minorities would involve the same race consciousness Mosk considered unconstitutional. Furthermore, while racial minorities are disproportionately disadvantaged, when one looks at the absolute numbers there are more disadvantaged whites than blacks. Racially neutral recruiting might bring about a needed change in the economic structure of the profession but drastically reduce the number of minority students in the process.

As for increasing medical school enrollment, Mosk must have thought he was offering a hypothetical solution. But the increase had already taken place. Between 1968 and 1976 medical school enrollment had nearly doubled, with first-year medical school registration up from 9,479 to 15,351 during that period. The new opportunities had been swallowed up in the surge of competition for places in medical school. Tobriner had dismissed his friend's suggestions caustically. "It is a cruel hoax to deny minorities participation in the medical profession on the basis of such clearly fanciful speculation," he said.

But Mosk's third alternative did offer a ray of hope for continued minority presence in the medical school. The use of flexible standards was surely the best of his suggestions. But this was precisely what the medical school had tried to do in its somewhat clumsy fashion. Mosk would not accept Tobriner's assertion that his opinion compelled the university to use only "the highest objective academic credentials" as the criteria for admission. Yet he had used these same academic credentials to determine that Allan Bakke was more qualified than the minority students.

Mosk offered similar alternatives for meeting the need for more doctors to serve the minority community. He suggested that applicants be selected by evidence of demonstrated concern for minorities and by declarations of intent to practice in such communities. How ironic that this "alternative" standard sounded precisely like the method the Task Force said it had used in selecting applicants. Two former Task Force chairmen, Dr. Kumagai and Dr. Gray, insisted they had interviewed a number of whites and minority students and rejected them because of a lack of demonstrated commitment to minority communities. But of course, neither Gray nor Kumagai had been given the opportunity to present this evidence to thè trial court. On the basis of the evidence in the record, Mosk could only conclude that whites were excluded from the program. Once again the formality of court proceedings had done little to uncover the reality of what had actually taken place.

"Few legal issues in recent years have troubled and divided legal commentators as much as that we decide today," wrote Justice Mosk. He was convinced that his position was correct, and he would not apologize for it; but he felt a need to share the difficulties he had experienced in reaching his decision. Mosk outlined the major arguments made by proponents of special admissions. Preferential treatment is essential in order to give minorities the opportunity to enjoy the benefits that would have been theirs but for more than a century of exploitation and discrimination. Although racially discriminatory laws have been removed by the courts and the Congress, minorities still are faced with severe handicaps. To achieve the American goal of equal opportunity for all races, more is required than the mere removal of the shackles of past formal restrictions.

These were strong arguments, but Mosk had not referred to them because he considered them credible. His purpose was to contrast them with other "more forceful policy reasons against preferential admissions based on race." "The divisive effect of such preferences needs no explication," declared Mosk, "and raises serious doubt whether the advantages obtained by the few preferred are worth the inevitable costs to racial harmony." Once again he was not seeing the victims created by the status quo. Two decades earlier, judges in the South had argued that school desegregation would upset the harmony between the races. Now Mosk was speaking as if racial divisions had been eliminated in our society and we were in danger of creating new ones. As long as our society favored its white members, resentment came from minorities. If steps were taken to adjust these preferences, it was inevitable that some whites, finding themselves in a less advantageous position, would react disharmoniously. By leaving things as they were, Mosk was only making sure that the resentment would stay on the minority side of the racial line, as witness the angry pickets he resented.

Mosk argued that an overemphasis on race would be counterproductive. Once again Justice Mosk had identified the crime, but he had blamed the wrong culprit. It is not because of preferential treatment that the mention of Arthur Ashe, Thurgood Marshall, Edward Brooke, or Stevie Wonder brings race to mind. Mosk was rejecting racism as an entity that lingered despite the best intentions of judges and politicians.

Mosk listed several additional drawbacks. There would be pragmatic problems in deciding which groups should be preferred and in identifying who belonged to those groups. Once a preference was established it would be difficult to get rid of it. "Human nature suggests a preferred minority will be no more willing than others to relinquish an advantage once it is bestowed," Mosk warned.

A number of critics had raised the problem of identification after small numbers of white males attempted to list themselves as "Cherokee Indian" or "Spanish-surnamed" in an effort to reap the benefits of affirmative action. But were the pragmatic problems of correctly identifying these individuals more difficult than spotting welfare cheats or tax swindlers? Few whites were willing to accept full-time minority status despite their complaints that minorities were being given unfair advantage. The prediction that preferred minorities would want to retain their advantages was no doubt an accurate assessment of human nature. But advantages bestowed by the majority on a minority can easily be taken away. The specter of a permanent black ruling class was reminiscent of the nightmares of Klansmen, not the basis for a reasoned judicial decision.

"Perhaps most important," said Mosk, summing up, "the principle that the Constitution sanctions racial discrimination against a race—any race—is a dangerous concept fraught with potential for misuse in situations which involve far less laudatory objectives than are manifest in the present case." Had the university asked the court to sanction "racial discrimination," or was it asking, as Justice Tobriner had argued, only for the sanction of the use of race to correct the effects of prior discrimination? If such classifications were misused, the court could easily enough identify and outlaw such practices.

In closing, Mosk, who suspected that his son had once been subjected to an anti-Semitic quota at an Ivy League college, spoke of the evil he feared most: the "revival of quotas." "No college admissions policy in history has been so thoroughly discredited in contemporary times as the use of racial percentages," he said, now convinced that his decision was both legally and morally correct. "Originated as a means of exclusion of racial and religious minorities from higher education, a quota becomes no less offensive when it seeks to exclude a racial majority. No form of discrimination should be opposed more vigorously than the quota system."

Mosk argued that to decide in the university's favor would be to "sacrifice principle for the sake of dubious expediency" and would represent a retreat from recent court decisions removing legal barriers to racial equality. The Davis special admissions program was unconstitutional "because it violate[d] the rights guaranteed to the majority by the equal protection clause of the 14th Amendment and of the United States Constitution."

Justice Tobriner did not choose to respond to Mosk's argument that the burdens of special admissions outweighed the benefits except to say that such considerations were out of place. Mosk and his colleagues in the majority were perfectly free to agree with those persons who felt it was preferable to avoid any use of racial classifications as a matter of policy. But they were wrong to equate their own personal views of appropriate policy with what the Constitution required.

Once again Tobriner's conclusions differed sharply from those of his colleague and friend. Mosk perceived a society that had nearly won the battle for equality and was on the brink of retreat at the expense of whites. Tobriner saw a world where whites were still dominant and discrimination against minorities was still the rule. Where Mosk feared "principle sacrificed for the sake of dubious expediency," Tobriner saw a clumsy but necessary step in the right direction. "Two centuries of slavery and racial discrimination have left our nation an awful legacy, a largely separated society in which wealth, educational resources, employment opportunities—indeed all of society's benefits—remain largely the preserve of the white-Anglo majority. Until recently, most attempts to overcome the effects of this heritage of discrimination have proven unavailing. In the past decade, however, the implementation of numerous 'affirmative action' programs, much like the program challenged in this case, have resulted in at least some degree of integration in many of our institutions." Citing a series of decisions by the court of which he and Mosk were members, Tobriner summed up: "It is anomalous that the 14th Amendment that served as the basis for the requirement that elementary and secondary schools be *compelled* to integrate should now be turned around to *forbid* graduate schools from voluntarily seeking that very objective."

In the end, it was clear that what had most influenced these two men in reaching their conclusions was their vision of the world around them. Justice Mosk and those who agreed with him saw the movement toward equality progressing without need of special protection and intervention on behalf of groups and individuals whose status at the lower end of the social scale was the result of centuries of unequal and often brutal treatment. In fact, they believed fervently that racial prejudice had ceased to be a major factor in determining opportunity. Such a theory was attractive to a majority that had lost faith in the ability of the nation to provide for all its citizens. Philosophies that proposed to limit expectations among those on the bottom were comforting to the segment of the population that already had its share or could reasonably expect to acquire it. The flaw in such theories and in legal opinions that gave support to such attitudes was the lack of an alternative. Mosk's opinion was an elegant exercise in legal theory, but his attempt to present solutions failed because it ended up preserving the arrangements that had failed to work for so many for so long.

From the same bench, Justice Tobriner had a startlingly different view. He saw a country that had taken small, tentative steps toward the ideals it had ignored for so long but was now backing off because it had lost the courage to pursue its objectives. Those who chose the most comfortable solution, he was warning, would reap the harvest of their shortsightedness.

The California Supreme Court's surprising decision was

announced on September 16, 1976. Within hours, Reidhaar held a news conference to predict the regents would appeal the case to the U.S. Supreme Court. But many of the organizations that had been united in their opposition to *Bakke* and to the court's decision were not in agreement about what the next step should be. On the basis of the record and the university's defense, many believed there was little chance of obtaining a favorable ruling before a body with a decidedly less liberal reputation than the California court. Ralph Smith, a law professor at the University of Pennsylvania and adviser to the National Conference of Black Lawyers, declared, "We are trying to tell the university, 'You do not have a good case. You did not do all that could have been done in this case. Let's not compound the error.'" The NAACP Legal Defense Fund, the Mexican-American Legal Defense Fund, and several other organizations joined in opposing an appeal. In their view, the decision affected public institutions in the state but left considerable leeway for private institutions in California and for affirmative action throughout the country.

However, Nathaniel Colley, the general counsel of the NAACP's Western Region, took the view that the damage had been done. Because of the California Supreme Court's prestige, he predicted, many courts in other states would use Mosk's opinion as a precedent in similar cases. Without an appeal, affirmative action would not recover from this crippling blow. In addition, Colley argued, the issue was not strictly a matter of liberal or conservative ideologies. He believed there was a good chance of winning at the U.S. Supreme Court. While Colley's position was not popular among the minority organizations, it had some influence on the university. One of his closest friends was William Coblentz, an influential San Francisco attorney and former Yale classmate, who was chairman of the Board of Regents. The regents met in Los Angeles a week after the state supreme court decision. In a closed-door meeting, they decided to petition the state court for a rehearing and, failing that, to go ahead with the appeal to the U.S. Supreme Court.

Once again the university's attorneys made a move that fueled the controversy surrounding the defense. In declaring the special admissions program at Davis illegal, the California Supreme Court had ordered the case sent back to Yolo to determine if Bakke should be admitted. But in the petition for rehearing, Reidhaar said the university had already produced all the available evidence on the admissions process and, therefore, could not prove that Bakke would have been rejected if there were no special admissions program.

"Mr. Bakke was a highly qualified applicant and came extremely close to admission in 1973 even with the special admission program being in operation," said the university. "It cannot be clearly demonstrated that the special admission program did not operate to deny Mr. Bakke admission in that year."

The turnaround in the university's position was peculiar. Two years earlier Reidhaar had argued that Bakke had done "fairly well" in the admissions process. In his deposition Dr. Lowrey had gone to great pains to enumerate the number of rejected applicants with higher scores than Bakke's who had not been accepted by the medical school. Lowrey's arguments, used again and again in university briefs, stated that when Bakke applied in 1973, most of the places in the class were already filled. Of the 160 letters of acceptance sent out to fill the 100 places, only 37 remained to be sent when Bakke's application was completed. According to Lowrey, there were at least nineteen applicants with Bakke's identical score of 468 and fifteen others with scores of 469. Throughout, the university had insisted that the statistics simply did not warrant Bakke's contention that he was discriminated against.

In an effort to explain this reversal to the California Supreme

Court, Reidhaar admitted that the university had "a strong interest in obtaining review by the U.S. Supreme Court" to determine whether the special admissions program at the Davis Medical School and other similar programs were unconstitutional. "It is far more important for the University to obtain the most authoritative decision possible of the legality of its admission process than to argue over whether Mr. Bakke would or would not have been admitted in the absence of the special admission program," he wrote.

Later Reidhaar would give two reasons for the shift. One, he admitted that the university could simply not meet the burden of proof asked by the court. "It simply could not be demonstrated with any assurance that he would or would not have been admitted in the absence of the Task Force program," he said. The second reason, of course, was the desire for quick resolution that had always affected the defensive strategy of the university.

But these explanations did not quell the skepticism. At no time in two years had the university ever indicated that there was any doubt about Bakke's lack of standing. Lowrey had specifically pointed out that he would have been excluded even without the special admissions program. As for the desire for a definitive ruling, the state supreme court had split the case into two parts, and it seemed that the university could have pursued the issue of affirmative action while Bakke's application was reconsidered.

But to determine Bakke's right to attend Davis, the entire admissions process would have to be examined again, and this time it was likely that the Yolo County court would have wanted much more information about the methods used at Davis. While the university argued it had provided all the information available, this was simply not true. In *DeFunis* the university had been required to submit a complete list of students, their grades, test scores, and benchmark ratings. The

Davis Medical School had provided only a range of grades and an average of student test scores. At no time did it ever provide the benchmark ratings that were so crucial to the admissions process.

While the case was making its way through the courts, an important political event occurred on the Davis campus. During the 1975–76 school year, George Sutherland, a student at the Davis Medical School, investigated the admissions practices at the school and raised questions about Dean Tupper's special authority to admit students. When faculty members discovered that Tupper's authority to overrule the admissions committee was not clear, a running battle erupted over the practice. The flames were fueled by the disclosure that one white student whose grade point average was 2.19, well below the 2.5 cutoff for regular admissions, had been admitted by Tupper. The controversy was picked up by the local Davis newspaper and by the *Los Angeles Times* in the summer of 1976.

For the first time the dean's admissions procedure was in the minds of faculty members and administrators at the medical school. A review of the admissions process would inevitably disclose the gaps in the university's defense of the case. Sutherland, who was still a student at Davis at the time, believes the decision not to review Bakke's application was strictly political. "They sacrificed the minority admissions program rather than the dean," he says. "They made the choice."

On October 28, 1976, the state court denied the university's request for a rehearing of the issues, despite a new study showing that the number of minorities admitted to the university would decline sharply without race-sensitive admissions procedures. On October 28, 1976, the California Supreme Court issued its final decision: "On appeal the University has conceded it cannot meet the burden of proving that the special admission program did not result in Bakke's exclusion. Therefore, he is entitled to an order that he be admitted to the

University." The Yolo County Superior Court was directed to "enter judgment ordering Bakke to be admitted."

Reidhaar went back to the California Supreme Court on November 15 and obtained a thirty-day stay of the ruling so that the university could decide whether to appeal. The state court agreed to delay enforcement of its decision indefinitely if the United States Supreme Court agreed to hear the case. Four days later the regents met again in a private session and voted 11 to 1 to appeal to the nation's highest court despite pressure from minority and civil rights groups to abandon the pursuit of a final decision.

The university counsel remained optimistic about the chances of getting the California decision overturned. "There is a very genuine prospect we can win the case," he argued. "It is not a foregone conclusion we will lose it." By the time the regents gave him the go-ahead, Reidhaar had already hired two specialists to help prepare the university's case: constitutional scholar Paul Mishkin and former U.S. Supreme Court clerk Jack Owens.

The university filed its first brief with the U.S. Supreme Court on December 14, 1976, pleading that the urgency of the problem and the fundamental questions raised by the California Supreme Court's decision made a decision at the highest level an essential one. At the same time a number of the organizations that had opposed the university's plan to appeal the decision filed briefs asking the U.S. Supreme Court to deny the writ of certiorari. Most of the critics argued that the case lacked the kind of record necessary for resolution of such an important issue and that the university had failed to make a vigorous defense. Despite these charges, it was clear that the nation's highest court had finally decided to take on a controversy that gave no sign of disappearing. On February 22, 1977, the U.S. Supreme Court agreed to hear *Regents of the University of California* v. *Allan Bakke*.

Five

THE CONTINUING
SIGNIFICANCE OF RACE

Ultimately, all the arguments about strict scrutiny and state interest and equality lead back to race. Why *is* race such a dangerous and troublesome issue in the *Bakke* case? A common argument made in discussions of the case takes this tack: "Bakke should be judged as an individual when the medical school decides whether to take him or not. He should not be denied admission just because he is a member of a particular group." The legal version of this argument was made by the American Jewish Committee's brief: "It is well settled that the right to equal protection granted by the 14th Amendment is an individual and personal one, not a group right. . . . If an individual is denied admission to a state institution even though he is better qualified than others who have been accepted, and if the denial is due to the fact that he is not a member of a particular racial or ethnic group, his personal and individual right to be free from discrimination has been infringed."

There is a strong respect for the individual in many of our traditions. America is a nation whose founders came to a wilderness to escape the poverty, classism, and religious intolerance of Europe. The Declaration of Independence and the Constitution document the ideal of the equality of individuals and the concern for protecting the rights of the individual against government. In a frontier land with infinite resources to be shared, the only limits on an individual's opportunities and development were his own.

But through a remarkable self-serving schizophrenia, American whites were able to define nonwhites as subhuman and exclude them from this value system that held the individual in such high regard. Despite the contradictions, the ideal of the individual grew and flourished with America. And although this ideal has never overcome the restrictions of race, class, and religion, Americans have continued to view their society as an open one, where a poor boy can become a millionaire and a woodcutter can one day sit in the White House. All this, of course, runs in the face of evidence that a poor man's son is as likely to be as poor as his father and probably more so now than 100 years ago. Still, we continue to believe that success in this society comes by virtue of hard work and superior ability.

In an amicus brief for the Anti-Defamation League in the *DeFunis* case, the late Alexander Bickel argued that special admissions programs subverted the ideal of individualism. Bickel, an eloquent opponent of race-conscious programs, wrote: "In a society in which men and women expect to succeed by hard work and to better themselves by making themselves better, it is no trivial moral wrong to proceed systematically to defeat this expectation." But is Bickel's concern about the subversion of individualism warranted in this case? When it is suggested that Bakke has not been treated as an individual, there is a danger that oversimplification has led us to a righteous but erroneous conclusion.

There are many situations in which individuals are identified and treated differently because of membership in a group we find perfectly acceptable. If Allan Bakke had not been graduated from college, we would not be outraged if he were denied admission to medical school. If he had never taken a chemistry course or had been turned down at Davis because he planned to practice plastic surgery in Hollywood, the case would have never reached the California or U.S. Supreme Courts. Two medical schools had no qualms about telling Allan Bakke he was too old. Yet each of these reasons for denying a student is based on a generalization about members of a group. Any admissions procedure relies on standards or generalizations about groups which may not be true for every individual in that group.

When the regular admissions committee at Davis set a cut-off point of 2.5 for GPAs, applicants who fell below that figure were automatically rejected and never interviewed. An applicant whose average was one-tenth of a point below the cutoff might well have demonstrated qualities of dedication, motivation, and sensitivity in an interview which would have made that person a better candidate for medical school than an applicant whose grade point average was above the cutoff. But inclusion with the group below the 2.5 minimum prevents the individual from being considered on individual merits. Few would argue that such an arbitrary grouping deprives that person of a constitutional right.

However, identification by racial group is seen as very different because we are told that Bakke can't do anything about his race and because skin color has nothing to do with his ability to be a good doctor. It is true that individuals do not control their color and their sex. But we also have little control of our intelligence, mechanical aptitude, athletic ability, or place of birth. Our inability to change these personal attributes does not make them an improper basis for awarding scholarships or diversifying a student body.

Race seems a more bothersome immutable personal trait than intelligence or athletic ability, not because it is harder to change but because we like to think of race as irrelevant. Those who oppose minority admissions programs say they take a superficial characteristic like race and turn it into something important. Professor Philip Kurland of the University of Chicago Law School made this argument when he condemned any use of race as a criterion for admission in a brief on Bakke's behalf for the Anti-Defamation League. "A racial quota cannot be benign," he wrote, echoing Justice Mosk, "it must always be malignant because it defies the constitutional pronouncement of equal protection of the law; malignant because it reduces individuals to a single attribute, *skin color*, and this is the very antithesis of equal opportunity."

Kurland's argument is seductive because it is familiar. How often have we heard people say, "I don't care if he's black or blue or green and from Mars as long as he's competent." The relevance of race to qualifications is often compared to the relevance of hair color or skin color. The consistent substitution of *skin color* for *race* in this debate makes it clear how misunderstood the issue is in this society and why we need to remain conscious of race until its meaning is changed.

One of the most persuasive arguments for the use of race in admission and employment has been made by Richard Wasserstrom in a UCLA *Law Review* article entitled "Racism, Sexism and Preferential Treatment: An Approach to the Topics." Wasserstrom, who teaches law and philosophy at UCLA, had witnessed the debate within his own faculty over the propriety of race-conscious admissions and hiring. He had heard his colleagues profess the irrelevance of race, arguing that they didn't care whether their students and colleagues were green and from a red planet. "It is truly possible to imagine a culture in which race would be an unimportant insignificant characteristic of individuals," he wrote. "In such a culture race would be largely if not exclusively a matter of superficial physiology; a matter, we might say, simply of the way one looked."

But that imagined culture is not this culture, said Wasserstrom, pointing to the phenomenon of "passing" as evidence of that fact. "Passing" is the practice among some blacks of identifying themselves as "white" because they look white. Many black Americans recall stories of family members who used their light skins temporarily to get access to jobs reserved for whites or permanently to gain the benefits afforded the white race in our society. This phenomenon has been packaged for popular consumption in Sinclair Lewis's novel *Kingsblood Royal* and in films such as *Imitation of Life* and *I Passed for White*.

In Wasserstrom's imaginary culture, in which race is just a matter of the way one looks, the concept of "passing" would make no sense. The phenomenon can be understood in our own culture because race is much more than physical appearance. The fact that a person may look white and still be defined and treated as black makes it obvious that race is not the same thing as skin color and that although skin color may be irrelevant, race is not.

In America to be nonwhite—and especially to be black—is to be treated as a member of a group that is viewed by the dominant group as different and—in too many instances—as inferior. Despite the gains made by a segment of the black population in recent years, membership in this minority is membership in a disliked and oppressed group.

Wasserstrom examined the apparently trivial practice of segregated bathrooms that was so common some years ago: "The point of maintaining racially segregated bathrooms was not in any simple or direct sense to keep both whites and blacks from using each other's bathrooms; it was to make sure that blacks would not contaminate bathrooms used by whites. The practice also taught both whites and blacks that certain kinds of contacts were forbidden because whites would be degraded by contact with blacks.

". . . The ideology was [not only] that blacks were . . . less than fully developed humans, but that they were also dirty and impure. This ideology was intimately related to a set of institutional arrangements and power relationships in which whites were politically, economically and socially dominant. The ideology supported the institutional arrangements and the institutional arrangements reinforced the ideology."

The primary evil of racial classifications in cases cited by supporters of Bakke as evidence that race should be suspect involved the designation of black persons as degraded, dirty, less than fully developed persons who were unfit for full membership in the political, social, and moral community. Many of the opponents of race consciousness cite court decisions in miscegenation cases to support their arguments, but these laws did not operate equally against blacks and whites any more than laws that segregated trolley cars and toilets. Their purpose was not to keep blacks and whites from marrying each other but to label blacks as unfit to marry whites. The argument that Bakke was being subjected to practices that had been outlawed some years earlier obviously was not true because he was not being stigmatized or marked as inferior.

The "race is irrelevant" argument confuses another important point. Those who argue that race is a superficial characteristic that should not be considered inevitably fall back on the argument that grades and test scores are the only proper criteria for evaluating applicants. By claiming that individuals applying for professional schools and employment should be judged only according to this specific "merit" system, they ignore the entire scope of crucial human factors that also measure an individual's qualifications.

Although skin color may be a legitimate factor in choosing Richard Burton to play Richard III or James Earl Jones for Othello, it is clearly not a legitimate factor in choosing who should attend medical school. But by equating race with skin color, the critics imply that the experience of being black or a member of another minority group has no value. There are few who would dare tell survivors of the Nazi Holocaust that their experiences have given them no special insight, no special compassion, and no special qualification.

Once we begin to understand that the significance of race is not color but experience, then it is no longer an irrelevant or superficial characteristic. After all, an individual's experience has traditionally been considered an important criterion in determining qualifications for employment or school admission. While this racial experience may not automatically qualify an individual as a member of a group, neither does the requirement that this individual complete a number of courses in biology, physics, and organic chemistry.

The goal of the University of California of integrating the medical school and the medical profession did not come out of an aesthetic preference for a variety of skin color in its classrooms and hospital wards. The purpose was to bring a wider variety of backgrounds and experiences to the school and profession. Bringing in these experiences would help eliminate the causes and effects of past and present discrimination.

Individuals who had experienced racial discrimination shared a common qualification that would help achieve the university's goal. Persons who had not been subjected to racial oppression lacked that experience and were likely to be less qualified for pursuing that goal. Once race was viewed as an important criterion, like successful completion of a college degree or a number of science prerequisites, then it could become an appropriate and constitutional criterion.

Another reason for so much reservation about government's paying attention to race is that racial classifications have historically been used as a tool of oppression. By certifying racial classifications in the law, racial groups without power have been defined as inferior and denied equal access to the benefits of society. In this way a permanent underclass, defined by race, is created, and the racial group in power is assured of permanent and superior status. Official race consciousness reminds us of Nazi Germany, South Africa, and our own history of slavery segregation and legalized apartheid.

The Fourteenth Amendment was adopted for the specific purpose of putting an end to distinctions based on race. The Thirteenth Amendment had abolished slavery, but the former slaveholder refused to surrender. He enacted the Black Codes in the years after the Civil War to maintain the arrangements that had existed before Emancipation. These codes severely restricted the movement of freedmen under vagrancy and apprenticeship laws. In some states blacks were forbidden to practice any occupations but farming and menial service; a special license was required to do other work. In other states blacks could be punished for "insulting gestures," "seditious speech," or walking off the job.

This new form of slavery led the Congress, under the guidance of Charles Sumner and Thaddeus Stevens, to enact the Freedmen's Bureau Bill and the first Civil Rights Act. Both these bills were passed under the mandate given to the Congress by the Thirteenth Amendment to enforce the right of freedom. These laws were drafted to protect the "civil rights" and "immunities" of freedom, making clear that Congress believed there could be no liberty without equality. Blacks were given the right to make and enforce contracts; to buy, sell, and own real and personal property; to sue and be parties to legal action; and to have "full and equal protection of all laws."

But congressional conservatives argued that these laws were illegal because the Thirteenth Amendment required not the equal treatment of blacks and whites but only the end of the legal relationship that had existed between the master and his African slave. Stevens and his fellow Radical Reconstructionists saw the necessity of placing the new rights of the freedmen

beyond the reach of future congressional majorities and conservative courts which might interpret the Thirteenth Amendment more narrowly. The Fourteenth Amendment was the
answer, spelling out the rights of black Americans in explicit
and sweeping language.

Much of the debate about the *Bakke* case in the legal community has focused on the purpose of the Fourteenth Amendment. The Supreme Court often attempts to assess the intent
of the framers of the Constitution in order to determine the
scope and meaning of particular provisions of that vaguely
worded document. In the landmark desegregation case of
Brown v. *Board of Education,* the Court had asked for additional briefs and a second oral argument on the issue of
whether the framers of the amendment intended to abolish
segregation. Supporters of minority admissions have argued
that the history of the amendment proves beyond doubt that its
purpose was to secure full citizenship for the newly freed
slaves and that remedial policies designed to upgrade the status
of blacks by providing special services and programs were not
only permissible but specifically contemplated by the congressmen who drafted the Fourteenth Amendment.

Legal scholars who oppose minority admissions argue that
the framers intended to abolish *all* distinctions based on race.
They argue that the evil or mischief that the Fourteenth
Amendment was intended to abolish was not just the particular
oppression of slaves by whites but all oppression based on race
and other arbitrary characteristics.

The first position was extensively documented in an amicus
brief filed with the U.S. Supreme Court by the NAACP Legal
Defense Fund, Inc. The Fund chose to focus on the history of
the adoption of the amendment, partly because this had not
been explored by other briefs and partly because the Fund
had a good head start on collecting the evidence. When the
Brown case had been argued in 1952 and 1953, Thurgood

Marshall, then the Fund's chief attorney, had organized a massive effort to answer questions put by the U.S. Supreme Court on the intentions of the framers of the Fourteenth Amendment.

The Fund's brief argued that while the amendment's history is often unclear, it is neither ambiguous nor inconclusive on the issues presented by the *Bakke* case.

". . . the precise question at issue in this case—the permissibility of providing educational benefits to blacks but not whites—was heatedly debated and self-consciously resolved by the same Congress which approved the 14th Amendment," the Fund argued. The Congress that fashioned the amendment believed that race-conscious remedial programs were not only permissible but necessary. The brief examines the legislative history of eight different social welfare laws adopted during that time. Each of these laws expressly delineated the racial groups entitled to benefit from its programs, and each of these race-specific measures was adopted over strong and vocal objections by a minority of Congress and President Andrew Johnson, who opposed special assistance to a single racial group as "class-conscious legislation discriminating against whites."

The most far-reaching of these programs, the 1866 Freedmen's Bureau Act, was enacted less than a month after Congress approved the Fourteenth Amendment. The bureau not only was authorized to provide land, buildings, and funds for "the education of the freed people" but could also provide such aid to refugees and other whites. The act also conveyed some disputed lands to "heads of families of the African races." A report from the commissioner of the Freedmen's Bureau provided a long list of programs intended to benefit only the freed slaves. Both the 1865 and 1866 Freedmen's Bureau bills were opposed on the grounds that they applied only to blacks. The arguments sound uncannily familiar to those we have heard in recent debates over the *Bakke* case. Most opponents of the bills complained that they made a distinction between the two races. Some congressmen contended that the bills would result in two separate governments, "one government for one race and another for another." These measures were adopted despite this opposition, and the Fund argued that the Congress that passed the Fourteenth Amendment deliberately enacted race-conscious remedies.

But opponents of race-conscious admissions have not been persuaded by the Legal Defense Fund's exhaustive account of the history of these amendments. The courts, they say, should not make their decisions according to what some men in the Thirty-ninth Congress thought necessary and proper in 1866. The only history that is binding on the courts is legal precedent. They argue that the Constitution is not a static document and that its purposes and principles must be adaptable to new conditions beyond the specific evils that gave them birth.

"There is no evidence that the equal protection clause can still be interpreted to protect only blacks," argued the brief of the Anti-Defamation League, "for such a construction has the Orwellian flavor of requiring that blacks be treated as equals to members of all other races, but no persons of another race would be constitutionally entitled to equality with blacks. Surely it is too late in the day for such an interpretation of the equal protection clause." Bakke's supporters saw race consciousness as the more general evil to which the Fourteenth Amendment must be directed. They turned to the language of the U.S. Supreme Court's own decisions to support their arguments that the amendment required the Constitution to be "color-blind."

"While the principal purpose of the 14th Amendment was to protect persons of color, the broad language used was deemed sufficient to protect all persons, white or black, against discriminatory legislation by the state," the brief went on to say. "The Equal Protection Clause, like the Civil Rights Act from which it derives, in the words of Senator Trumbull, 'applies to white men as well as black men.' "

There is no argument about the fact that the equal protection clause protects all persons regardless of race. The real issue is whether race consciousness, in every instance, denies whites equal protection. Certainly, the equal protection clause protects whites, as it does everyone, from arbitrary and irrational treatment by government. It protects them from being treated differently for no good reason. The question before the Court, however, was not whether whites received the benefits of the equal protection clause but whether, in applying the clause, the Court has any reason to suspect foul play on the part of government, whether there is any need to apply the strict-scrutiny test.

All the cases cited in the Anti-Defamation League brief to support the proposition that the amendment applied to "white men as well as black men" involved groups that had traditionally been subjected to discrimination for no other reason than oppression. *Yick Wo* v. *Hopkins* and *Oyama* v. *California* found the use of race unconstitutional because Asians (in California), like blacks (in the South), had historically been the objects of discrimination and oppression. Likewise, *Graham* v. *Richardson, Sugarman* v. *Dougal,* and *In re Griffiths* found discrimination against aliens unconstitutional because they were a traditionally disfavored and relatively powerless group. Discrimination against illegitimate children was struck down in *Levy* v. *Louisiana* and *Gomez* v. *Perez* for the same reason. The laws in these cases received more careful attention, not because the plaintiffs were white, as the authors of the Anti-Defamation brief would have us believe, but because they were members of disadvantaged minority groups. In addition, the government could offer no good reason for the discrepancy in treatment that was not related to hostilities toward those groups.

In *Yick Wo,* for example, the city of San Francisco had systematically denied licenses to Chinese laundries that were built of wood. Wood laundries owned by whites were granted licenses. The rationale was safety, but the white-owned laundries were clearly no safer. The obvious purpose was to put the Chinese out of business.

Other cases used to argue that race consciousness is always unconstitutional include *Memorial Hospital* v. *Maricopa County* and *Shapiro* v. *Thompson,* but these cases involved residency requirements, and the Supreme Court applied strict scrutiny because the issues involved the important right to travel.

Similar arguments were made in a brief to the U.S. Supreme Court from the American Jewish Committee, the American Jewish Congress, and several white ethnic organizations. The brief argued that the Supreme Court has held that application of the Fourteenth Amendment "has not been restricted to those forms of racial discrimination that are regarded as 'invidious' because they stigmatize and denote the inferiority of a minority group. Racial classifications which oppress members of the minority and majority racial groups with equal force have been found constitutionally defective without reference to the issue of stigma." The cases cited—*McLaughlin* v. *Florida* and *Loving* v. *Virginia*—were cases in which the Court ruled antimiscegenation laws unconstitutional. Once again we are back to the distortions of the original intent of such laws as pointed out by Wasserstrom. The oppression suffered by whites under such laws was clearly less than that suffered by blacks. To argue that the laws involved in these cases did not "stigmatize and denote the inferiority of a minority group" is simply dishonest.

Other popular references in this line of argument are *Shelley* v. *Kraemer* and *Buchanan* v. *Warley,* which involved racially restrictive housing. Again the argument is that such laws hurt both whites and blacks equally. But the purpose of housing segregation, like other forms of racial separation, is to demean and stigmatize the excluded group, and that group suffers in a wholly different way from those who are doing the excluding.

Bakke's supporters have argued that it is judicial precedent, not congressional history, which should control the issues in this case. If there was a strong precedent to support their position, it was not found in the cases they have relied upon.

Once again we come face-to-face with the differing perceptions of the issues and problems involved in the *Bakke* case. The argument that no special consideration need be given to race or racial groups is based on the view that these groups no longer need the special protection of the Fourteenth Amendment. One line of argument in this debate suggests that race is no longer an issue in the success or degree of opportunity available to Americans.

In its annual report, "The State of Black America 1978," the National Urban League presents a very different picture. The League points to the growing divergence of perceptions of discrimination between whites and blacks. Most whites have come to believe that bigotry is no longer an important factor in the progress of minorities in this country. But, as the report points out, there are twice as many blacks out of work in 1978 as there were ten years earlier. The number of unemployed black men tripled between 1967 and 1977, and the unemployment rate among black teenagers increased from 26.5 to 38.6 percent in that decade. "There are just as many poor black families today as there were ten years ago, although the number of poor white families has dropped over that period. . . .

Black families are still four times more likely to be poor than white families."

The report concedes that much progress has been made, especially among black middle-class families, who have narrowed the gap with the rest of the middle class. "Still, the harsh truth remains . . . that the majority of blacks have not seen their status materially improved over the past decade, and that for many, their lives are still lived out in despair and deprivation."

Six

THE BEST DOCTORS

When a great deal is at stake in a struggle of ideas and principles, words become weapons, loaded with connotations designed to trigger an emotional response that will benefit a specific point of view. Many words have achieved this status in the *Bakke* case but probably none more than *qualifications.* Allan Bakke launched his campaign for admission to Davis on the grounds that minority students selected by the medical school did not have the "best qualifications, both academic and personal." In writing the majority opinion of the California Supreme Court, Stanley Mosk cast the issue as a choice between "better qualified whites" and "less qualified minorities." The University of California insisted that all its students were "fully qualified," but opponents of special admissions saw the difference between the grades and test scores of the two groups as evidence that standards were being perilously lowered. One formerly liberal magazine concluded that affirmative action succeeded only in replacing "mediocre whites with mediocre blacks."

These comments seem gentle when compared to statements in a brief filed with the U.S. Supreme Court by a group of prominent scholars and academicians who supported Allan Bakke: ". . . it is a distinct disservice to these young people to admit them to schools where they cannot succeed, and where their poor performance confirms rather than dispels the false stereotypes about minority abilities." Of course, it takes an admirable manipulation of the facts to reach a position that strengthens a stereotype of minority students under the guise of protecting them from humiliation.

The brief by the Committee on Academic Nondiscrimination and Integrity and the Mid-America Legal Foundation is one of the most fascinating documents submitted to the Supreme Court. Important figures such as Bruno Bettelheim, Sidney Hook, Daniel Boorstin, and Nathan Glazer have endorsed a document that concludes that a choice has to be made between excellence and race-conscious admissions practices. Bakke's situation is compared to that of blacks before the passage of the Fourteenth Amendment, and the authors assert that Bakke "is far better qualified than most if not all of the preferentially admitted minority applicants."

What is worth remembering is that the distinguished members of this committee are surely aware that their position is not supported by the facts, which clearly show that the great majority of special admissions students complete their studies successfully. In some cases, despite their lower grades and test scores, special admissions students have surpassed the achievements of their white classmates. According to the Association of American Medical Colleges, "for the 1970 and 1971 entering classes, the retention rates for blacks were 95 and 91 percent respectively, as compared to 98 and 97 percent for white students."

Obviously, some affirmative action students have not done as well as students selected by traditional methods. But special admissions is relatively new, and school officials have had to work on a trial-and-error basis. In nearly every year since these programs were instituted, the retention and achievement rates of special admissions students have improved. According to the American Medical Association, 11 percent of blacks and 9 percent of Mexican-Americans admitted to medical schools in 1976 had to repeat their first year, against 1.2 percent of whites. The critics use these figures to attack special admissions, but proponents point out that these programs involve a calculated risk that is paid off when nine out of ten blacks and Chicanos are promoted with their classmates. In addition, the higher repeat rate is a sign that schools are not promoting students until they successfully complete the requirements.

But in making a choice between a class that is one-tenth empty or nine-tenths full, the critics have persisted in their attacks on minority students, their abilities and credentials. To some, the ease with which these attacks have been embraced tells much about a new form of racial McCarthyism which deliberately ignores and distorts the truth. But then, the perception of minorities as less competent and less qualified than the majority whites is hardly a new concept in America.

One reason, of course, was the image of the Task Force students created by the vague use of terms such as *less qualified* during the litigation of the case. If the Task Force students existed at all, they were an amorphous, undeserving, and unqualified group hardly likely to find understanding in the new, less compassionate racial atmosphere of the 1970s. It was easier for most of the public to sympathize with Allan Bakke—blond, blue-eyed, hard-working, individual—the victim of a misdirected sense of social obligation. Considering the vague and ambiguous quality of most of the issues in the case, the numbers had a comforting solidity. Bakke's 3.51 GPA was higher than the 3.49 and 3.29 average of regular students admitted to Davis in 1973 and 1974. The averages for Task Force students in those years were 2.88 and 2.62. Some had GPAs as low as 2.11 in 1973, and 2.21 in 1974, well below the school's cutoff point of 2.5. On the MCAT, Bakke scored in the 90th percentiles in the verbal, quantitative, and scientific categories, higher than most of the regular students and far higher than the Task Force students.

Of course, as we pointed out earlier, some of the Task Force students had higher grades than some of the whites admitted (and higher than Bakke and other whites rejected). A number of regular students also had grades and test scores lower than those of Allan Bakke. The most consistent area of difference was in the MCAT scores. In this area, however, there is an impressive body of research to show that these scores, while useful in predicting student performance in the first two years of medical school, have little value in assessing talent in the clinical aspects of medicine (the last two years of school) or performance as medical professionals. To improve the situation, medical schools asked the AAMC, which administers the test, to "explore the development of additional instruments to measure personal qualities deemed necessary for the practice of medicine."

It would seem that personal qualities had much to do with the selection of Task Force students and regular students with lower scores and grades. Such exceptions reflect the growing recognition of the limits of numbers in the admissions process throughout the country. The AAMC reports that nearly a third of white applicants to medical school in 1976 had undergraduate GPAs of 3.30 or better and MCAT science scores above 600 (on a 205–795 scale). "Yet," says the association, "31 percent of these applicants were not accepted to any medical school, while 882 white applicants whose grades and MCAT science scores were *both* lower than these levels were accepted. Therefore it is clear that admissions committees have looked beyond grades and test scores in selecting students to be admitted."

But arguments persist that separate standards of selection were unfair to white applicants because minorities with lower "qualifications" were picked. If human qualities, character, and motivation are as important as officials say, then the method of selection is unfair for different reasons. If as much emphasis were placed on commitment as on academic qualifications, medical schools would choose white students who are more humane and more compassionate individuals and provide better doctors for everybody.

When Allan Bakke was turned down by the University of California at Davis in 1973, sixteen minority students were chosen who, in his estimation, did not deserve places in the medical school. Once these students were admitted, the only special treatment they received was a three-week tutorial before the start of classes. The special program was designed to familiarize them with study and examination procedures in medical school and to help them identify their areas of weakness. After completing the program, they were plunged into the same highly competitive and intense atmosphere that their other classmates had faced from the first day of school. Four years later, thirteen of the original sixteen were graduated from Davis, and their accomplishments do much to undermine the stereotypes promoted by groups like the Committee on Academic Nondiscrimination and Integrity. No figures are available for the success rate of regular admissions students at Davis, but the national rate is close to 99 percent.

Orel Knight would probably have enjoyed a discussion of "qualifications" and "standards" with Bruno Bettelheim and Sidney Hook. Knight was completing his first year at Davis when Allan Bakke sued the university for letting in "less qualified" minorities. When Knight was graduated in 1977, he had won the medical school's most coveted prize: the senior class award for the qualities most likely to produce an out-standing physician. The vote by the Class of 1977 paid tribute to Knight's outstanding academic and clinical record by desig-nating him the best doctor in the class.

Like some of the most ardent opponents of special admis-sions, Knight was a poor immigrant who made good in Amer-ica. He was born on October 18, 1944, in Georgetown, Guyana, a former British colony on the northern rim of South America. Knight's father supported his wife and six children by working as an accountant. Like many of his fellow countrymen, Orel dreamed of emigrating to a country where he would have greater opportunities. After being graduated from high school, he went to work and began saving his money. After four years he had enough for his passage, tuition, and, he hoped, a year of living expenses in the United States.

In 1966 Knight settled in the predominantly Hispanic com-munity of East Los Angeles, where he rented a room for $25 a month and stretched his meager savings by riding a bicycle to classes at East Los Angeles College. "I was living on close to $7.50 a week," he recalled. "I was riding a bicycle when they weren't 'in' yet. I looked funny, an adult, riding down Brook-lyn Avenue." Knight's wry sense of humor comes through easily in conversation. He is an impressive six-footer, a *café au lait* Clark Gable with a square jaw, prominent cheekbones, a thin mustache, and a wave of black hair. "It was a cultural shock, coming from a poor, underdeveloped country to the richest nation in the world. East L.A. was a sort of buffer. My main goal was to do as well as I could in school."

In his first year in America, his social life was "next to nil," but his concentration on studies paid off. He had close to a straight A average in junior college and won a scholarship to the University of Southern California. He retains fond mem-ories of his early days in East Los Angeles: "The people were my own kind." After taking a class in biological sciences, Knight decided to study medicine. "I realized if I wanted to become a doctor, the time shouldn't matter."

But after a year of full-time study, his funds were running low. He had found a job at Blue Cross of Southern California, where he worked as a claims examiner while carrying a full load of courses at USC. "It was fortunate the job was related to the medical field," he said. "You learn a lot of [medical] terms. I also learned there are ways a physician can bill to get more money for his patients."

The years at USC did not have the warmth and comfort of his days in East Los Angeles. He was in a highly competitive environment, where premedical students sometimes sabotaged each other's laboratory experiments in the furious struggle for places in medical school. "I was the only black premed in 1968, and in the entire time I was there, I took one science class with another black. There was only one professor whom I thought might have been prejudiced. Once he mentioned William Shockley [the Nobel Prize–winning physicist who is an advocate of white genetic superiority] in a class on genetics. I never really felt comfortable in his class. But there were a lot of professors who were quite anxious to help."

In 1971 Knight sent out his first applications to medical schools, but he found that few slots were available for foreign students. By the time he was graduated in 1972, he had obtained permanent resident status—the first step toward U.S. citizenship—and he was admitted to Davis through the Task Force. Knight says he enjoyed his years in medical school. He says he worked hard and feels he was rewarded for his efforts. In his first medical school exam he had the highest score. "I remember the chairman of the Task Force coming to congratulate me, as if to say, 'I told them so.'" Knight feels he had advantages in getting through medical school because he was older than most of his classmates and because his background in Guyana had spared him the history of racial discrimination experienced by most black Americans. "In Guyana there were six races and we united against the common enemy: the British."

Knight strongly supports programs like the Task Force. "While I was at Davis, only one black came through the regular admissions, but there were [Task Force] students in my classes whose grades were just as good as the whites'. If you're trying to pick people with 3.9s, you don't need interviews. You can use a computer." He says grades are misleading because they don't take other circumstances into account. He says he didn't do as well at USC as he did in junior college because he had to work. In his last year at Davis, Knight scored "honors" (on a fail/pass/honors grading system) in all but one of his courses. "People get the impression minority students barely get through medical school and that minority physicians can only deal with minorities. I didn't need the Task Force to get my commitment. I want to treat minorities, but it's my own choice. I feel somebody has to take care of my own."

After leaving Davis, Knight got his first choice for his internship, the nationally recognized obstetrics and gynecology program at the USC–Los Angeles County Medical Center. He plans to practice in an area of Northern California with a large minority population, possibly Oakland or Sacramento.

Patrick Chavis and his wife, Toni Johnson-Chavis, were also among the sixteen Task Force students admitted in 1973. Pat Chavis decided to become a doctor when he was still a junior high student in Watts. He was one of five children in a poor family, and he stuck by his ambition despite an uncle's warning that he would be a financial burden on his mother. He earned a bachelor's degree in human biology at Albion College in Michigan, and a GPA of close to 3.5 helped him get into Davis. According to members of the medical school faculty, Chavis did well academically and even earned a master's degree in public health at UCLA "on the side" while completing his last year of medical school.

Like Orel Knight, Chavis's high ranking in medical school helped him get his first choice, the OB-GYN program at L.A. County. In the spring of 1978 he took a National Board exam in his specialty and had the highest score among the interns at L.A. County. "All the efforts people have made over the years to advance the cause of minorities are going down the drain with Bakke," Chavis said. "It's more than just a color issue. We're talking about affirmative action, about trying to make things better and giving people who are poor and oppressed a chance for a better life."

Toni Johnson-Chavis is an even more ardent advocate of special admissions. Her father worked on the Santa Fe Railroad for twenty-seven years. She was the oldest of five children reared in the poor black enclave of Compton, just outside Los Angeles. "Ever since I can remember, all my life, I wanted to be a doctor," she said. "My father was an extremely intelligent man, but he had to do demeaning jobs because he came from a poor family and never got a chance for a good education. Through his children, my father felt he had his chance to do something."

At Compton High School her education included hand-me-down books from Beverly Hills High School and science classes in poorly equipped laboratories. "I had to do double time to keep up when I went to Stanford [on a scholarship], not knowing even how to use a slide rule, not having basic chemistry, competing with people from top prep schools in the nation. In addition to the educational disadvantages that poor students face when they get to college, I lived with white people burning crosses on my dormitory lawn and putting swastikas on my dormitory door. Nobody did anything special for me. I finished in three years to get the hell out of that kind of environment." After being graduated from Stanford in 1972, she completed a master's degree in public health at UCLA before going to Davis.

"There's a whole public misconception about the Task Force program. The thinking is that somehow the people who came in through the program are different from the rest of the class. They can't understand why we weren't admitted through regular admissions. That's why I'm angry. The people who came through special admissions programs were as qualified or more qualified because, believe me, I feel more qualified than the average person who came in. I have done more. There have been no favors, no corner cutting. They've only addressed themselves to the fact that there are not enough black physicians and we must make some kind of goal and commitment to get more people in."

She and three other Task Force students set up a weight reduction clinic in Del Paso Heights, a poor area of Sacramento, and found that more poor whites than blacks came to the clinic. But she says she was never able to recruit her white classmates to help. "One of the students told me straight. He told me he wanted a nice Wilshire Boulevard practice and didn't want to be bothered with poor people, white or black.

"Twenty percent of the white students who came into the class at Davis had grade point averages less than Bakke's. The dean was able to let people in for straight political reasons. There are three applicants for every spot in medical school. There are just not enough medical school spots, and unfortunately someone gets the shaft. It's unfair to everyone. People have never complained about nepotism being a way of getting into medical school or about having a lot of money giving you an advantage. But now that they're considering affirmative action programs, it's a big deal. People can't tolerate the idea that you're going to let that spot be filled by a black person and a poor black person at that. The people who were let in for special reasons were rich white people who had poorer grades than Bakke. Why not complain about these people? Why single out the sixteen in the Task Force?"

The treatment of Task Force students by the news media is one reason Vivian Legette refused to be interviewed until after she was graduated from Davis. She had seen reporters storm the campus after the California Supreme Court decision, stick microphones in the path of minority students, and ask how it felt to be "less qualified." According to Allan Bakke's logic, Vivian Legette was one of the students who deprived him of a place the second time he applied to the medical school in 1974.

Vivian's grandparents were farmers in the hamlet of Hemingway, South Carolina. Her parents owned a "fish joint" until her mother refused to say "sir" to a local sheriff in 1951. The Legettes were advised that their lives would be safer in Charleston, and their father joined the Air Force to support his family. Military assignments took the Legettes all over the country and to the Far East, but whenever possible Vivian and her two brothers spent the summers with relatives in Hemingway, picking cotton and tying tobacco. Her father stayed in California after retiring from the Air Force and bought a modest house in a black area of Sacramento.

Vivian had considered becoming a lawyer or a writer; but circumstances made her go to business school, and she found a job as a secretary for Planned Parenthood in Sacramento. Her efficiency and initiative prompted some of the doctors she met through her work to encourage her to go back to school. She took some courses at Sacramento State before transferring to the University of California in San Diego. She did so well academically that she was able to apply to medical schools as a junior. She was accepted at Howard, Northwestern, and UC–San Francisco, but she chose Davis to be near her parents.

"I was really afraid. I didn't have the background of students with master's degrees, Ph.D.'s or even B.A.'s," she said of her early days in medical school. She believes there was a great deal of hostility because of racist and sexist attitudes among the faculty. "During the basic science years we only had to contend with attitudes because the tests were objective. How much help you received from faculty depended on how they felt about the Task Force. I sought very little help." On one occasion she went to a professor to discuss some material she was having trouble with. He was condescending, unfriendly, and dismissed her after five minutes. A white classmate who went to the same instructor was given ninety minutes. She shared her notes on the subject with Vivian.

After two years in the basic science curriculum, students at Davis move into the clinical courses more closely related to medical practice. Here, said Legette, attitudes were more difficult to judge because ratings and grades were extremely subjective. She believed that in many instances minority students were given lower scores than they deserved. "It depended not only on scores and exams but on impressions." When she became interested in surgery as a specialty, she discovered a great deal of resistance to women in this traditionally male preserve. During a fourth-year clerkship at a hospital in the Midwest, a staff physican started his evaluation of her work by describing her "sweet and charming disposition." In another instance a surgical resident kept "forgetting" to call her when important cases came to the hospital. "They barely tolerate women in surgery," she concluded. Despite the obstacles, Legette's work impressed the hospital staff so much that they offered her a residency in surgery at the hospital. Eventually she hopes to become an ear, nose, and throat specialist on the South Side of Chicago. Despite her successes, her memories of Davis remain bittersweet. "I wish I could have had more than I got. If I could do it over again, I would go to another school that had more experience with minorities and women."

•

Understandably, Task Force students who did well at Davis spend little time dwelling on the kind of atmosphere they encountered at Davis. The sudden plunge into the intense academic grind of the first two years is intimidating enough for all students. Those Task Force students who had early academic successes found the burden of their roles as minority group representatives easier to bear. But many of the others had to contend with negative attitudes as well as the pressures of the curriculum. As could be expected, faculty opinions on special admissions reflected the entire spectrum of public opinion. Small segments of the faculty were strongly for or against affirmative action. The great majority fell into the middle and shifted with the prevailing winds. Many former and present Task Force students say the polarization increased once the *Bakke* case became a national issue.

In 1975 one medical school faculty member circulated a memo suggesting that Task Force students had lowered the standards of the medical school. "By introduction of Task Force students into the student body," he wrote, "we have invalidated this mechanism of determination of quality. It is my contention that the presence of Task Force students has resulted in a decrease of the mean and an increase in the standard deviation [a statistical measure] of virtually all of our examinations." The memo concluded by suggesting that the introduction of twenty first graders into the class would have had the same impact as the sixteen Task Force students. The medical school administration did a statistical study that refuted the memo's suggestions, but many Task Force students say the incident reinforced their feeling that they were simply not wanted at the medical school.

While admissions officials may have put less emphasis on grades, these remained the main determinants of excellence in the minds of most faculty and students. Arthur Chen, an Asian student admitted through the regular committee with a 3.0 GPA and average MCAT scores, remembered fearing conversations with his classmates. "I was always feeling my statistics were nothing to brag about. I was happy they didn't ask me what my GPA was because they'd make the judgment that 'you probably got in through the Task Force' or 'Oh. I have a friend with a 3.5, and *he* didn't get in.' I can admit I was influenced by that, and I tended to stifle talk about it." Ironically, when Chen was graduated, he was chosen by his classmates to deliver the valedictory speech at commencement exercises.

Some students felt a stricter standard was in effect for Task Force students because of faculty doubts about their ability. They believed that passing marks in courses were often set arbitrarily to eliminate Task Force students at the bottom of classes and that makeup exams were often given to whites but denied to blacks and Chicanos. There are many stories of racist and sexist remarks made by professors not accustomed to dealing with women and minorities. In one course on human reproduction, the instructor said he would concentrate only on male orgasm and leave female orgasm for the course on psychiatry. When half the class was absent from a seminar during the spring, the instructor asked, "Where are the Task Force students? That's why they don't do well here." Such remarks prompted one class to file a petition in protest.

Donald Parks, a student admitted through the Task Force in 1974 and dropped in 1976, said these incidents underlined the hostility of faculty members who had not been educated to understand the process used in picking students in nontraditional fashion. Since he was dismissed for academic reasons, Parks has waged a private war for readmission to Davis. A native of New York City, Parks was the first member of his family to go to college. He majored in education at New York University and went into the Air Force in 1965 to serve an

ROTC obligation. He worked in race relations and counseling in the Far East and became interested in medicine after working for a base psychiatrist.

Parks admits his grades were "average" and his MCAT scores mediocre, but he believes he was accepted at Davis because interviewers took into consideration his eight-year absence from school as well as his background in the military. But soon after the start of classes in 1974, Parks developed eye trouble. He says the eye problems and the side effects of steroids used in treating him contributed to his failing a course in his second year. He was put on probation and asked to repeat the entire year. When his eye problems started again, he was refused a chance to drop a course and reduce his load. He failed the course and was dismissed. His appeals were turned down, and he has been trying ever since to get readmitted.

Parks, who gets a captain's disability retirement pay from the Air Force, has compiled a foot-thick file of memos, transcripts, and letters to document his charges of discrimination and arbitrary treatment by the medical school. Even officials who are skeptical about Parks's claims admit that he has forced the medical school to reform many of its disciplinary and review procedures, which were often vague and arbitrary. After seeing the carefully cross-indexed file, some people half-jokingly suggest that Parks switch to law. But he is determined to get reinstated. "What I want to do," he says, "is get my record straight. I don't have a choice. If I don't get back in here, I can't get into an accredited medical school anywhere. What I'm trying to do is set a model, not just for minority students, but for all students to know their rights. I want to feel that I'm accomplishing something." Charges brought up by Don Parks and other students are difficult to prove. But they do expose the vulnerability of students who are admitted to medical schools with academic deficiencies and who get little help in correcting those shortcomings. In an atmosphere where there is serious doubt about their talents and abilities, the fact that most Task Force students are able to do well, and that some do outstanding work, must serve as testimony to their drive and determination. As for those who fail, one has to conclude that they were simply too far behind, that they had too many deficiencies and difficulties to overcome, and that, in their own way, they will continue to be victims.

If there is one area that both critics and proponents of affirmative action can agree about, it is the fact that students admitted through such programs often suffer from stigmatization. But while all may agree about the effect of such programs, the solutions offered are much different. For critics of special admissions, the final authority on the subject is Thomas Sowell, an economist at UCLA, who, they are careful to point out, is black:

"What the arguments and campaigns for quotas are really saying, loud and clear, is that black people just don't have it, and that they will have to be given something in order to have something. The devastating impact of this message on black people—particularly young black people—will outweigh any extra few jobs that may result from this strategy. Those black people who are already competent, and who could be instrumental in producing more competence among the rising generation, will be completely undermined, as black becomes synonymous—in the minds of black and white alike—with incompetence, and black achievement becomes synonymous with charity payoffs."

One flaw in the "Sowell Defense" is the assumption that special admissions (here called quotas) must always be associated with inferiority. If the majority perceives members of minority groups as less competent because of affirmative action, isn't there a choice other than ending all such programs? A more fruitful solution might be to educate the public about the false logic of such associations. The same might be said of charges that affirmative action polarizes ethnic and racial groups. This suggests that racial harmony is the responsibility of the victim of racial harmony—the excluded minorities. This logic is not much different from that which blamed racial unrest in the 1960s on outside agitators. The truth is that the impact of minorities on the competitive pool has been minor. The makeup of professional and graduate schools has been drastically changed by the presence of women, and they are the real competition for white males. The percentage of women in medical schools has risen sharply from 5.7 in 1959 to 22.4 in 1977. The total enrollment of minorities in U.S. medical schools was 8.2 percent in 1977, and because of the limited pool of minority applicants with training in sciences, the number is expected to decline in the next few years.

What the critics of special admissions try to do is to substitute one myth for another. Viewing blacks as incompetent, which Professor Sowell fears, did not begin with affirmative action and would not end if minorities were excluded. Caught between the rock and the hard place, minority groups have no choice but to continue to push for a fair share of opportunities and hope that at some point they will be accepted on their own merits. The crucial fact remains that special admissions is not as revolutionary as some would like to believe. Consider this report from the admissions committee to the Faculty of Arts and Science at Harvard University, a recognized bastion of the meritocracy:

"Faced with the dilemma of choosing among a large number of qualified candidates, the Committee on Admissions could use the single criterion of scholarly excellence and attempt to determine who among the candidates were likely to perform best academically. But for the past 30 years the Committee on Admissions has never adopted this approach. The belief has been that if scholarly excellence were the sole or even predominant criterion, Harvard College would lose a great deal of its vitality and intellectual excellence and that the quality of the educational experience offered to all students would suffer. Consequently, after selecting those students whose intellectual potential will seem extraordinary to the faculty—perhaps 150 or so out of an entering class of 1100—the committee seeks . . . variety in making its choices."

What is remarkable is that this report was written in 1960, long before the advent of affirmative action. It makes clear that in their zeal to discredit programs that would bring members of minority groups into the mainstream, the critics create precedents that never existed. The ancient meritocratic process that is being so valiantly defended simply never existed. Of course, many of the ardent foes of special admissions were themselves victims of quotas and admissions policies that didn't see members of certain ethnic groups as adding "vitality" to the Harvard experience. But it surely is a commendable sign of progress that the definition of diversity has been expanding to encompass all groups and segments of society. Once again, because of the large pool, many qualified individuals will be excluded, as they were in the past for an infinite variety of reasons over which they had no control. The apparent "fairness" of this approach would lead Justice Powell to laud the "Harvard Plan" when he grappled with a decision in *Bakke*. From the minority point of view, the injustice of quotas is not difficult to understand, but their benefits are also obvious. To a group that was subjected to a quota of zero, a quota of 10 percent was a distinct advantage of opportunity, helping form a core of highly educated individuals over several decades. Had racial minorities been recipients of this essentially perverse paternalism, the makeup of our society in the last quarter of this century would be fundamentally different from what it has turned out to be.

•

The crush of competition for places in professional and graduate schools today obscures the historical fact that just twenty years ago the opportunities for whites were much greater than they are today. Until 1961 the Boalt Hall Law School automatically admitted any college graduate with a B average. The LSAT was required only for those with less than a B who could not talk an admissions official into admitting them without it. And in those days a score of 500 was enough for admission. According to a brief filed by the deans of several law schools, in 1960, 708 persons applied to Boalt and 517 were admitted. In the fall of that year, 268 or 53 percent of those admitted enrolled in the first-year class.

The postwar boom of babies impacted on admissions in the 1960s, and applications rose sharply. In 1966, 1,500 applied for 278 places at Boalt Hall. In 1972, 5,000 applied and 271 were enrolled—5 percent of all the applicants. The LSAT was now required of all applicants, and the median scores were 638 in 1967 and 712 in 1976. The grade point average of entering law students in 1976 was 3.66. "It is quite clear," said the law school deans, "that the level of record achievement required to gain admission to Boalt Hall is far in excess of the level which would be required if the sole criterion were a record sufficient to justify a confident prediction that the applicant could successfully complete the program and become a competent member of the bar."

The history of medical school during the last two decades is similar. In the early 1960s some schools complained they could not fill all their available places. The Medical College Aptitude Test was introduced in the 1950s to help reduce the attrition rate "by providing a standardized measurement of knowledge and ability in order to predict success in the basic science curriculum, which usually comprises the first two years of medical school." The high attrition rate of the time was the result of a basically "open admissions" policy at many medical schools. The mean MCAT science score of accepted students was 516 in 1957 and 615 in 1975. The quantitative score on the test went from 517 to 620 in that period. "Because of the larger pool of academically qualified students," said the AAMC, "medical schools have raised their admissions standards well beyond the minimum level necessary to ensure completion of the course of study leading to the M.D. degree."

In these cases the pressure of competition has raised the level of academic qualifications far beyond what is needed to succeed. The medical schools point out that minority applicants are scoring at the level of whites who were admitted to medical schools twenty years ago. "The qualified minority applicant, who is perhaps just catching up to the level of educational ability and achievement attained by the qualified white applicant of twenty years ago, cannot compete with the even more highly academically qualified white applicant of today," the AAMC concludes. The additional irony may be that some of those who complain loudly about lowered standards are complaining about students who match and even surpass the "qualifications" they used to get into professional schools just a generation ago.

Still, the argument about the "better qualified" would be valid if a connection could be made between the MCAT scores and the quality of physicians produced. If a science score of 700 meant a better doctor than one of 500, it would be immoral to choose a student with the lower score. But extensive studies over the last two decades simply do not support such conclusions. In 1972 Ralph Friedan and several other medical investigators reported: "Several investigators have observed that the criteria for selecting medical applicants correlate poorly with the student's performance in medical school and not at all with their performance as physicians. In particular, investigators have not been able to predict physician performance by college grade point average, a criterion greatly emphasized by medical school admissions committees. Similarly, the grade point average obtained as a medical student, considered an important factor in acceptance in internship-residency programs, has been found to have a zero correlation with a physician's clinical performance."

Robert Montoya, a California health official, cites a 1975 study of twenty-three minority students admitted in 1970 and 1971 to the medical school at the University of California in San Diego. "Under traditional admissions criteria," said Montoya, "only one of these 23 would have been accepted; 22 out of 23 would have been rejected." On the first part of the National Board Examination, which physicians must pass to be able to practice medicine, 17 of these students passed on the first try, and all the rest eventually completed the test successfully. "In terms of clinical performance, the minority students have been performing at an average level. All 23 passed pediatrics and surgery clerkships on their first attempt, but two had to repeat the medicine clerkship. A randomly selected group of 21 of their traditionally selected cohorts showed one had to repeat the medicine clerkship and one had to repeat the surgery clerkship." The average GPA of the minority students in the study was 2.93 overall and 2.84 in science. Their average MCAT scores were in the 45th percentile in science and in the 37th percentile in the quantitative segment.

What these studies confirm is what the medical school administrators have been saying: minority students do less well on standardized tests, but this does not imply they are any less able. In fact, a 1967 study of 180 physicians working in Public Health Service hospitals (most of them white, we can safely assume) showed a *negative* correlation between their MCAT scores and rating of their work by supervisors. "If an admissions committee were to follow literally the implications of studies relating MCAT scores to physician performance," facetiously suggests a brief in support of special admissions, filed in the *Bakke* case by an organization of black law students, "it should prefer candidates with lower scores."

There is a clear link between race and rating in the MCAT test. Even within the same income range, minorities do worse on the test than white applicants. Since performance cannot be related to MCAT scores or ethnic identification, it becomes clear that, in a purely objective sense, the MCAT discriminates racially. David White, an authority on testing at the University of California at Berkeley, has pointed out similar problems with the LSAT. His solution: "If admissions had been determined on undergraduate grades without the LSAT, there would be more minority students in law school than there are with the LSAT and special admissions." White found that 10 percent of black applicants to law school had an academic average over 3.2, while only 3 percent had an LSAT over 600 and only 1 percent had both. But the grades and test scores of white applicants were more evenly matched. "This is the most dramatic, persuasive evidence ever of the independent racial bias of the LSAT," White concluded.

If the evidence is so overwhelming about the irrelevance and racial bias of standardized tests, why do officials continue to use them? Primarily because they are a convenient tool for paring down an overwhelming number of applicants. A semblance of fairness is created by having every applicant take the same examination, although the test itself has virtually no value in predicting what contribution the student will make to the profession he or she is about to enter. Also, the basic reforms in medical education, begun in the early part of the century after Abraham Flexner's seminal report on the state of medicine in America, have escalated to a point where most schools in the United States train scientific researchers rather than physicians. Demands for better primary care are not being met because doctors are taught to depend on a high level of technology that ties them to major urban research centers.

Dr. George Silver, professor of public health at the Yale University School of Medicine, who takes the position that *all* current admissions methods are unfair, suggests an admissions policy that admits all applicants. Silver believes the costs could be met by shifting funds away from biomedical research to the preparation of physicians. The essential research could be done at a few key institutions, and attrition would eliminate the unqualified from medical programs. But Silver admits that the medical establishment is not likely to adopt his proposals, which point out that faculty-heavy medical schools in the United States drive up the costs of training doctors far beyond those of other industrialized countries.

But as long as major reforms are resisted by the majority, special admissions and other similar programs are the only alternatives to total exclusion from professions that have profound impact on the economic, professional, and social well-being of all citizens. In an atmosphere of growing conservatism and self-interest, opportunistic scholars and intellectuals, who have access to all the research on testing and achievement, can callously assert that attempts to select minorities more fairly are a form of discrimination.

The practice of using numbers to exclude racial groups is not at all new. In his book *The Legacy of Malthus: The Social Costs of the New Scientific Racism,* Allen Chase traces the development of intelligence tests and their enthusiastic use by the eugenics movement in the early part of the twentieth century. The eugenicists, who had in their ranks some of the world's most prominent scientists, believed in the superiority of Northern Europeans over all other racial groups. They believed in limiting the propagation of "undesirable" genes by limiting immigration and forced sterilization.

Racial and anti-Semitic prejudices predated the eugenics movement, but testing seemed to provide an "objective" tool for confirming these prejudices. One of the many ironies of the battles around the *Bakke* case is the willingness of ethnic groups that were once the victims of testing procedures to line up in support of examinations that work to exclude certain minorities. The language of the early intelligence testers reflected the ancient historical prejudices against those who were not white, Anglo-Saxon, and Protestant.

In 1912 psychologist Henry Herbert Goddard used a version of the intelligence test invented by Frenchman Alfred Binet to "prove" the inferiority of immigrant Jews, Italians, Hungarians, Poles, Russians, and others. Lewis M. Terman of Stanford University developed the Revised Stanford-Binet IQ test and concluded: "Common observation would itself suggest that the social class to which the family belongs depends less on chance than on the parents' native [hereditary] qualities of intellect and character." After testing Indian, Chicano, and black children in the Southwest and California, Terman and his associates concluded from their IQ tests: "Their dullness seems to be racial, or at least inherent in the family stocks from which they come. . . . They cannot master abstractions, but they can often be made efficient workers, able to look out for themselves."

Their theories would be amusing except for the fact that these scientists exerted considerable influence on government and social policy. The restrictive immigration laws passed by Congress in 1924 followed almost exactly the ranking of ethnic European groups devised by the eugenicists. Northern Europeans were the most desirable immigrants; Jews and Eastern Europeans were the least welcome. One impact of these tests, said Chase, was the exclusion from sanctuary in the United States of millions who would become victims of the Nazi Holocaust. Not surprisingly, the theories of the eugenicists had great influence on the development of Nazi racial theories.

The influence of IQ and World War I intelligence tests declined sharply in the 1930s, when more thorough analyses of their findings pointed out the discrepancies of education and environment that provided racial differentials in the scores. But the use of the tests had a resurgence in the 1950s after the U.S. Supreme Court ordered an end to school segregation. Politicians and educators in the South used IQ scores and studies that deliberately distorted the findings of prominent researchers to meet their political needs. But the eugenicists had a second rebirth in 1969, when Arthur Jensen's landmark article on race and IQ was published in the *Harvard Education Review*. "Is there a danger that current welfare policies," Jensen wrote, "unaided by eugenic foresight, could lead to the genetic enslavement of a substantial segment of our population?"

Jensen was clearly aware of the political repercussions of his research. "Since much of the current thinking behind civil rights, fair employment, and equality of educational opportunity appeals to the fact that there is a disproportionate representation of different racial groups in the various levels of the educational, occupational and socioeconomic hierarchy, we are forced to examine all the possible reasons for this inequality among racial groups in the attainments and rewards generally valued by all groups within our society."

After reviewing the literature, Jensen suggested that black and white children had different learning abilities and that black children could not easily grasp abstractions. He concluded that compensatory education programs had failed because they tried to achieve too much. He suggested they concentrate on the basic skills minority children would find most useful in their eventual low status as adults. *Newsweek*'s summary of his ideas reflected the prevalent interpretation by mass media. "Since intelligence is fixed at birth anyway, he claims, it is senseless to waste vast sums of money and resources on such remedial programs as Head Start, which assumes that a child's intellect is malleable and can be improved."

Jensen's ideas were immediately challenged by an influential segment of experts in the fields of genetics and intelligence research, and even those who praised his methods disagreed strongly with his conclusions. In a subsequent issue of the *Review,* Martin Deutsch, who had co-authored a book with Jensen in 1968, took issue with his associate: ". . . I believe the impact of Jensen's article was destructive; that it had negative implication for the struggle against racism and for the improvement of the educational system," said Deutsch. "The conclusions he draws are, I believe, unwarranted by the existing data, and reflect a consistent bias toward a racist hypothesis."

Deutsch's understandable concern about the political implications was reflected in the attention given to Jensen's ideas by the press. A nation torn by the war in Southeast Asia and racial confrontation had its purse strained by military expenditures and the vestiges of the Great Society programs. A rationale for eliminating compensatory programs was extremely attractive. Jensen's theories were extended by Richard Herrnstein, Edward Banfield, and others into programs for political action that found acceptability in political and journalistic circles.

Historians of science have noted the common practice among promoters of racial superiority of distorting the facts and ignoring the research that contradicts their findings. Recently, much of the work of Dr. Cyril Burt on intelligence has been discredited because of evidence that he made up many of his figures. Burt's work was an important source for Jensen's research, as he conceded in his *Harvard Education Review* article: "Probably the most distinguished exponent of the application of these methods to the study of intelligence is Sir Cyril Burt, whose major writings on the subject are a 'must' for students of individual differences." But when other researchers went back to Burt's original data and found serious discrepancies, Jensen was forced to retreat from his reliance on the work of the man he admired so much.

The new scientific racism comes full circle when one finds that some of its most ardent advocates hail from racial and ethnic groups that were targets of the early eugenicists. William Green, an early president of the American Federation of Labor, argued that "our republican institutions are the outgrowth of ten centuries of the same people in England and America. They can only be preserved if the country contains at all times a great preponderance of those of British descent." The concept of preservation against an onslaught of outsiders can still be found in the positions of many opponents of special admissions. The concept of pure racial stock has now been converted into the preservation of "high standards" in the meritocratic argument. This argument dwells on the dangers to the institutions of democracy of programs of affirmative action and race consciousness. Yet, since these fragile institutions survived the inequities of slavery and racial segregation, why must they collapse under efforts to achieve an end that even the critics admit to be admirable?

The most disturbing aspect of the opposition is that it offers no real alternatives to special admissions programs. Numerical apportionment is attacked as a dangerous quota. Race sensitivity is described as "reverse discrimination," and the rejection of rigid numerical standards is seen as a serious assault on standards. The best alternatives that can be offered are increased recruiting and special tutoring. But the deans of medical and law schools have made it clear: without special programs, most professional and graduate schools would once again become virtually lily-white. And most of these officials, who surely have to be concerned about the reputations of their institutions, insist that the quality of education and training provided has not been harmed by the presence of minority students.

Considering the body of independent evidence to support these arguments, one has next to consider the motivation of the critics. What they end up saying to minority groups is that they need to wait longer for equality—not the equality of paper and law, but the real equality that reflects the random distribution of skills and talents through all ethnic and racial groups, Jensen notwithstanding. In the end, the issue becomes one of the preparedness of the majority to accept minorities in unaccustomed roles as lawyers and doctors, supervisors and university intellectuals. In the effort to measure black progress in recent years, little attention has been paid to white progress toward acceptance of a racially diverse society.

Black Americans especially find bitter humor in the new concern that special admissions casts doubt on the talents and abilities of members of minority groups. Somewhere in the folklore of every black family is the story of the relative or ancestor who suffered under the burden of this doubt. There are enough stories about black doctors who couldn't practice at local hospitals because the American Medical Association excluded them, about black Ph.D.'s who spent their lives working in the Post Office, about black college graduates who were messengers and stock clerks on Wall Street. Yet distinguished scholars feel comfortable enough in rewriting history to argue that the treatment of blacks earlier in American history was equivalent to the treatment of Jews and ethnic whites. To refuse to differentiate between partial and total exclusion becomes the highest form of demagoguery.

The basic assumption adopted by the opponents of corrective programs is that American society has suddenly become generous and open in a free market of talent and initiative.

Even the most ardent advocates of the free enterprise economy would be embarrassed to suggest that such a state of openness exists. Somehow the creeping economic socialism about which Milton Friedman complains has not yet corrupted the intellectual meritocracy. The doors are allegedly open to all, and the complaints of minority groups that they are not getting their fair share are interpreted as evidence of their unwillingness and inability to compete.

In 1976, 42,155 applicants competed for 15,774 positions in medical schools. Of these applicants, 33,762 were white and 9,393 were from minority groups. In that year 8.3 percent of those accepted, or about 1,300 of the students accepted, were from minorities. If these 1,300 were excluded, 25,000 applicants would still be left out of medical school, many of them highly qualified applicants.

In arguments about qualifications race serves as a mechanism for avoiding an analysis of the broader issues. If minority demands, and confrontations like the *Bakke* case, serve to expose broad injustices, those with the least to gain from such disclosures are those who already benefit from privilege and whose chances for access are highest. One lesson of the civil rights movement was that many of the victories won by blacks benefited not only other minority groups but many whites. The doubling of class sizes in medical schools under pressure for minority access is one example of unexpected benefits to the majority.

In truth affirmative action, special admissions, and other such devices are imperfect remedies. Many of the basic problems of American society have been exposed by racial confrontation because the discomfort of confronting color leads to an examination of other factors that are not at all racial. There was little dialogue about the exclusion of disadvantaged whites from professional schools until the *Bakke* case. But if a solution is limited to a racial basis, one basic inequity is resolved at the expense of another. This would not be the first time that race has been used to preserve privilege. Racial issues are easier to confront than broad philosophical problems about the inequality of classes in America.

Opponents of broad political and social reform can retreat into the glass house of their own standards without having to listen to dissidents who insist on bringing up issues of race, color, and opportunity. If there ever is a confrontation in America over these issues, as there was in the 1960s, it will probably not have the cloaking in morality that existed in the last decade. At this point the shaping of moral indignation is too firmly in the hands of those who reap the benefits of this alleged meritocracy. That is one reason that recent efforts by black leaders to appeal to moral and ethical obligations have failed. These leaders have been wedded to the traditions of Martin Luther King, Jr., and others who forged the civil rights movement. But this emphasis on morality ignores a definite shift in the movement's strategy that was cut off by Dr. King's death. In 1968 he was attempting to form a coalition along class lines that would counter the impact of the growing conservative movement that was to put Nixon in office.

It is becoming increasingly clear as the nation approaches a new decade that there is little hope of creating a movement along racial lines. Advocates of equality have the unenviable task of broadening their struggle so the majority will understand that the underdogs are not only black and brown but often white as well. The main obstacle to such a political movement is a lack of access to the information industry. Given a choice between "better" and "less" qualified individuals, the public has little doubt about who should be picked. The function of minority groups has always been to serve as point men in ferreting out the contradictions of American democracy. They begin by noticing the color-coded aspects of privilege, and they end up raising questions about fundamental issues of rights and the distribution of benefits. It becomes extremely difficult to convince minorities that the present order of things is the just result of the Medical College Aptitude Test or God's will.

Seven

A CHANGE OF MOOD

On a Sunday afternoon a small group of young and successful black professionals sat around the remains of a sumptuous
dinner and engaged in a ritual that had accompanied many of
the Sunday dinners of their parents and grandparents before
them. After covering the latest developments in foreign policy,
presidential politics, and the arts, the conversation drifted into
what used to be called "the state of the race." Under the influence of several bottles of fine California wine and the hyp-
notic flicker of the fireplace, they shared their views of the one
issue that separated them from other groups of young American
professionals.

One of the diners was excited about a new venture in television. He had planned meticulously, brought in the best minds
to help him develop his project, and had obtained the funding
for an ambitious program aimed at teenagers. In retracing his
steps, he described in a matter-of-fact tone his struggle against
an indifference caused partly by the bureaucratic inertia that
can be found in any institution and partly by the fact that he,
like everyone else in the room, was black. He was not complaining about the racism he had encountered, for he would
have been surprised if it had been absent. After a decade in
white organizations he had simply learned to isolate and out-

flank that peculiar irrationality in the thinking of his white colleagues.

The reporter nodded in sympathy and launched into a convoluted and hilarious story about a confrontation with an editor who could not understand why a magazine article derogated the abilities and the competence of blacks. The journalist had lost the argument, but he hoped that the fuss he raised would raise the consciousness of the editor. He had learned along the line that his influence on the prestigious publication he worked for was only incremental.

The others around the table agreed and recalled their own experiences. In each case there was that instant of conflict which revealed a chasm between their own perception of the world and that of the people they worked with. None of them would have been classified as militants in the 1960s, and they all had impressive credentials to verify their ability to compete successfully in the mainstream of society. Yet they had no doubt that the color of their skin still set them apart and to some degree increased the odds against achieving their goals.

Just as their individual accomplishments would be used as evidence of black progress in the years since the civil rights era, their collective view of the world would just as vehemently be denied by the majority of Americans. For the irony of the time is that the views of blacks and whites about the nature of racism in American society are now probably more in conflict than they have been since the Supreme Court ruled that separate was not necessarily equal. When Stanford University professor Seymour Martin Lipset analyzed polls of racial attitudes recently, he concluded that "most whites do not believe discrimination is the principal cause of black inequality." But the majority of blacks, on the other hand, even those who are relatively affluent, continue to believe that their opportunities are still circumscribed by hostile racial attitudes. This differ-

142

ence of opinion is important in assessing the meaning and impact of the *Bakke* case.

On the tenth anniversary of the assassination of Martin Luther King, Jr., there was the predictable flurry of reports on black progress in America. The neat pile of statistics documented the gains made by the middle class and warned about the continued existence of an "underclass" that had not benefited from the victories of the civil rights movement. But these reports told more about the changes in race relations in the country through their style than through their content. After decades of moral indignation, fear, protest, and hostility, the dialog on race had been reduced to dry economic terms that could be charted on graph paper.

Clearly, race no longer had the fire or importance it demanded in the last decade. A 1978 Gallup poll found that whites ranked "the problems of black Americans" last on a list of thirty-one concerns. The issue may not have gone completely away, but it could not hold the national attention in the same manner as demonstrations, protests, and riots. Even *Bakke*, with all the hoopla about its landmark status, failed to provoke much of a debate on race relations. Most of the discussions centered on the legal and ethical issues raised by affirmative action and peripherally on the relative economic status of the races.

But there were other indications that white attitudes had not changed so fundamentally as to warrant this kind of complacency. The case itself could not have reached such prominence without a national sentiment for reassessing the obligations of the majority toward minority groups. And for the first time in history most whites were willing to believe that equality had been achieved and that programs to improve the status of minorities were giving these groups an unfair—and possibly an unnecessary—advantage. This was clearly the appeal of a term like *reverse discrimination*.

This shift in attitude was not isolated from other political and economic issues that had developed in the aftermath of the economic recession and the end of the Vietnam War. The resurgence of political conservatism could be attributed to the profound disappointment of the middle class in government and the growing sense of economic insecurity. Inflation and "making ends meet" were the major concerns of Americans, and the fear of economic competition from minorities had always intensified racial antagonism.

The difference in the 1970s was that this antagonism was not as simple as it had been in the past. A much more complicated set of ideas and assumptions had replaced the old arguments for racial superiority. As late as 1970 a Louis Harris survey showed that 76 percent of whites believed that blacks experienced discrimination in trying to achieve full equality. The majority of whites also believed that there was discrimination in housing, employment, and education. But in 1977 another Harris poll showed the extent of the change in attitude. Only one out of three whites believed that discrimination existed, and even fewer thought racism to be a factor in housing, education, and employment. At the same time 55 percent of whites believed blacks were pushing "too fast" for equality.

Since the majority of whites had concluded that race was no longer an important issue, they could turn their attention to other problems without feeling guilty. If blacks were at the bottom, most of them believed, it was because of their own shortcomings. Since minorities were dependent on the good-will of the majority, this new attitude could have a strong impact on their struggle for parity.

This change of mind was a result of many factors. For one, the world of most whites was no longer racially exclusive. They might still live in segregated neighborhoods, but minorities appeared in most of the other areas of their lives. Blacks were more prominent than ever on television, in entertainment, and on the playing field. Whites had to work with blacks, ride public transportation with them, and generally adjust to a multiethnic world. The fact that change had taken place was easier to assess than the degree of change. The layman's gut reaction was reinforced by an intellectual and political campaign that touted black progress. Nixon adviser Daniel P. Moynihan's infamous "benign neglect" memo suggested that enough progress had been made to warrant a pause in government efforts on behalf of minorities. As early as 1965 Moynihan suggested that 50 percent of black families were in the middle class. *Commentary* made the same argument in 1973 with an additional suggestion that black leaders were covering up these gains for their own political ends. A few months later *Time* devoted a cover to the black middle class, and CBS News did a one-hour special on four black "middle-class" families, including one with an income of $8,000 a year. Although the figures and charges were disputed by other experts, the image of middle-class advancement dominated the 1970s.

The statistics on black progress were impressive. Between 1966 and 1976 the proportion of black families with incomes of $15,000 or more increased from 19 to 30 percent. Black families with incomes of $25,000 or more went from 3 to 8 percent. There were more white families, 53 and 19 percent respectively, in these categories, but the rate of change among blacks was faster. During that decade black college enrollment increased from 4.6 to 10.7 percent of the total, although the majority of blacks were enrolled in two-year and vocational schools.

But there were other numbers that did not bode well. Between 1967 and 1977 black unemployment doubled from 638,000 to 1.5 million. The black unemployment rate went from 7.4 to 13.2 percent, and black teenage unemployment soared from 26.5 to 38.5 percent. As one economist put it, the financial profile of the black community was being transformed from a pyramid to an hourglass. While the number of affluent blacks was increasing, the number of poor families was also growing. One sign of the impact of the poor was that despite the gains of the middle class, the median income for blacks in 1977 was 59 percent of white income—just one point higher than it was in 1966. The Kerner Commission's warning that America was moving toward two separate and unequal societies was being reflected in the black population. And beyond the numbers was the toll of human waste: the infant mortality rate matched only by Third World countries; the third and fourth generations of families on welfare; homicide as the greatest cause of death among young black men. The negative statistics were all higher than they had been during the era of urban violence.

The new class division among blacks was a reflection of what economists were calling the dual labor market. Young, educated blacks were reaping the benefits of affirmative action and moving into the middle-class income group while the poor were entering a job market of dead-end jobs which often did not pay enough to support the worker. Reflecting the values of the larger society, many of the poor were refusing to enter this lower track with no promise of advancement and dropping out of the labor market.

A University of Michigan study of 5,000 families showed that in 1967, after working six years, blacks between twenty and twenty-nine earned $2.40 an hour while whites were paid $3.30. Over the next eight years, the study found, the disparity in income grew from three-fourths to two-thirds. University of Chicago sociologist William J. Wilson suggests that middle-class blacks were able to move into white-collar and management positions because that sector of the economy was expanding during the past decade. But the economic recession of the mid-1970s slowed growth in this area and was reflected in the intense competition for places in professional schools. Already

more than 1 million college graduates were classified as unemployed or underemployed, and the U.S. Census Bureau
warned about intense competition over the next few decades
as the baby boom of the 1940s played out its actuarial course.

The financial stresses on the middle class, caught between
inflation and their own rising expectations, were reflected by
the passage of California's Proposition 13, which attempted to
limit government spending to relieve the tax burden of property owners. But this act, apparently lacking in strong political
ideology, had strong class and race implications. Some 72 percent of those who voted for the proposition said they hoped
the cuts would be made in welfare costs. No wonder that many
minorities were skeptical about arguments that race was no
longer a factor in the social equation. For many, *Bakke* was
nothing less than a reaction to competition from minorities at
the middle-class level.

Other studies of the labor market showed that blacks made
the greatest gains in areas where there was not much competition from whites. In fact, when the recession drove large numbers of white women into the employment area, the number
of blacks in the service workers' category declined significantly.
As Wharton School economist Bernard Anderson described it,
blacks were still in the caboose of the train that was the economy, and they stayed at the rear whether the train speeded up
or slowed down.

Despite this evidence, the concept of a racially neutral society was too attractive to give up easily. When the Department of Housing and Urban Development did a study of housing discrimination in 1978, it found that only a fraction of
blacks received equal treatment. The study said that blacks had
a 62 percent chance of being discriminated against in buying a
house and a 75 percent chance in trying to rent. "Even I am
surprised at the figures," said HUD assistant secretary Donna
E. Shalala. "We made every effort to be on the conservative

side. We're talking about turning away people, the most overt form." Recent surveys of white attitudes showed most of them believed that housing was one area where blacks were least likely to encounter racism.

To many observers of the civil rights movement, the shift of national attitudes was signaled by the election of Richard Milhous Nixon in 1968. Urban violence was very much in the minds of most Americans, and the new administration moved quickly to establish some distance between the White House and the black masses whose militancy was so disturbing. The antipoverty and legal assistance programs which were seen as centers of provocation were quickly dismantled. The Republicans shifted government activities on behalf of equality to the middle class under the guise of "Black Capitalism." Not only was this kind of activity appealing to a conservative electorate, but the images it projected were much less threatening. Commerce secretary Maurice Stans made cameo appearances in black communities in striped pants and homburg to shake hands with black bank presidents and company executives.

Nixon's master stroke was his transformation of the civil rights movement from a moral to a political issue. Blacks were simply another special interest group deserving of no more— and often much less—attention than other competing interests. This practice of reducing all issues to their basic political essence would ultimately reach its fatal conclusion in Watergate, but that was still some years away. There was a war in Southeast Asia, and the young whites who had waged a holy crusade in Selma, Oxford, and Tupelo were redirecting their efforts on Saigon, Washington, and the Pentagon.

In the eyes of many whites the essential issues of race had been resolved by passage of the Civil Rights and Voting Rights acts. In addition, the demands made by blacks demanded more than the benevolent acquiescence of liberalism. The coalitions that had lobbied for equality in the 1960s were breaking down, and the black movement was becoming more isolated.

Thomas Blair observes that the militant organizations which evolved out of the Student Nonviolent Coordinating Committee and CORE "introduced new imperatives into the process of race relations and turned black protest organizations toward a concern with economic and social problems of the masses." In the summer of 1966, Stokely Carmichael's outline for Black Power called for the formation of political organizations outside the traditional political parties to speak and act for blacks. The most effective instrument for change was not moral judgment, he said, but the exercise of power. What drew national attention was Carmichael's rejection of the philosophy of nonviolence, the need for strong black organizations before the formation of coalitions with whites, and his suggestion that whites go work within their own communities on racial issues. "Black Power is not black supremacy," said Floyd McKissick, "it is a unified black voice reflecting racial pride in the tradition of our heterogeneous nation."

But the positive aspects of the Black Power message never reached the white majority. "The thrust of Black Power into national politics sounded the death knell of the civil rights alliance," says Blair in *Retreat to the Ghetto*. "It brought the black masses into what Frederick Douglass called the 'awful roar of the struggle.'" The mild-mannered civil rights leader was displaced in the public mind by the fiery young men calling for the overthrow of the system. The new generation of activists melded easily into the stereotype of the dangerous black male that still lurked in the psyches of white America.

There is a tendency now to forget how much fear was a catalyst in race relations. In major cities whites barricaded themselves in their homes or fled to the suburbs on the weekend following the death of King. Many of the reforms made in the wake of King's death were prompted as much by the aura of martyrdom as by the concern that militancy would gain credibility among blacks. In 1968 J. Edgar Hoover declared the Black Panther party the "number one threat to national security" and launched a plan to destroy it that would be the envy of any totalitarian government. But what was taking place was a division along class lines that had been dramatized by King's failure to extend his campaign in northern cities. The movement that had shifted from protest to politics was now making another crucial shift to economics and to much more fundamental questions about American society.

The Black Political Convention in Gary, Indiana, in 1972 was a momentous event in the evolution of black political thought. Throughout the country, grass-roots organizations brought into the political debate blacks who had never before participated; they voted on the issues and elected delegates to the convention. But it soon became clear that the growing class divisions within the black community had also spread to the political ideologies. Middle-class delegates wanted to strengthen their hand for the Democratic National Convention in Miami. Blacks from inner-city organizations and rural areas were committed to a black nationalist perspective and wanted to create an independent entity with no commitment to either party. There were several thousand delegates to the convention and as many observers and curiosity seekers. Every major news organization as well as many smaller journals and black newspapers staffed the convention.

Only a masterful diplomatic effort by the convention organizers prevented a full-scale debacle, but in one last defiant slap at the elected officials the nationalist groups forced through a resolution condemning Israel's policies in the Middle East. Most of the elected officials, dependent on Jewish support, retreated from the organization, and without the administrative superstructure they could have provided, the convention lost an opportunity to develop a cohesive black political organization.

The right to vote was one of the great victories of the civil rights era, but the impact of the black electorate remains marginal because of inconsistent turnouts and the lack of unified views on many issues. Blacks have been elected in unprecedented numbers at the local, county, and municipal levels, but black elected officials consist of just one-half of 1 percent of the nation's total.

At the national level, blacks have depended on coalition politics to strengthen their impact. The sixteen black House members are loosely organized into the Congressional Black Caucus and through political pressure have been able to acquire key positions on committees and subcommittees. But their most effective tool has been their ability to persuade white members with large black constituencies to support legislation that serves black interests. This strategy was used to win home rule for the District of Columbia and to extend the life of the Office of Equal Opportunity. "As individuals," says Howard University political scientist Marguerite Barnett, "most CBC members are 'good liberals'; as a collectivity, they hold the possibility of joint effective action for the beleaguered black community."

But because most members have different aims and different constituencies, they are more a symbol of black political aspirations than a real force in the Congress. The often tense relationship between President Carter and black leaders during the early days of his presidency reflected doubts about the real political clout of blacks at the polls. Until blacks demonstrate the same ability as other ethnic groups to switch their loyalties according to the issues and to deliver more than an average election turnout, they will not have much of an impact on the political process.

The political clout of blacks was diminished to a large degree by the breakup of traditional alliances. Many important pieces of civil rights legislation were supported by a triumvirate of blacks, labor, and Jews. But once the civil rights struggle turned to economic issues, this alliance was seriously weakened. The kind of economic reordering demanded by affirmative action, quotas, and efforts to overturn seniority systems put blacks and labor at odds. When the *Bakke* case went to the Supreme Court, neither the AFL-CIO nor the once-powerful Leadership Conference on Civil Rights filed a brief because of strong internal disagreements about a position.

Perhaps the most widely publicized split involved the long and honorable alliance between blacks and American Jews. In *Bakke* most of the major Jewish organizations filed briefs on behalf of Allan Bakke. Some commentators suggested that the black-Jewish conflict was unimportant in the larger context of the black-white struggle, but the civil rights movement had grown up depending on Jewish support, and the withdrawal of that support was extremely harmful. American Jews, with their disproportionate impact on national sentiment, intellectual debate, and journalism, had been a valuable ally.

Many northern liberals had doubts from early on about the tactics of the civil rights movement, and *Commentary*, the influential publication of the American Jewish Committee, reflected these concerns early. An early supporter of the civil rights movement, the magazine's shift to the right preceded a similar shift of the national sentiment. Many of the positions its editors and authors now hold can be safely considered to be in the mainstream of current thought.

In 1961 Tom Brooks wrote a prophetic article entitled "Negro Militants, Jewish Liberals and the Unions," which examined the conflict that erupted when black unionist A. Philip Randolph attempted to organize a Negro American Labor Council along the lines of the powerful Jewish Labor Council.

"One wonders if the growing antagonism between Jewish and Negro labor camps is a precursor of strained relations between the larger Jewish and Negro defense agencies," Brooks asked, "and ultimately between the two minority communities in general."

In March 1964 *Commentary* sponsored a round-table discussion on "Liberalism and the New Negro," featuring James Baldwin, Nathan Glazer, Sidney Hook, and Gunnar Myrdal. Editor Norman Podhoretz defined traditional liberalism as "society being made up not of competing economic classes and ethnic groups but rather of competing individuals who confront a neutral body of law and a neutral institutional complex." Podhoretz called "radical" the thought that "the Negro community *as a whole* has been crippled by 300 years of slavery and persecution and that the simple removal of legal and other barriers to the advancement of individual Negroes can therefore only result in what is derisively called 'tokenism.'"

Hook, who would later come to embrace Podhoretz's concerns about the inviolability of the individual, said he saw "no conflict with the traditional principles of liberalism, as I understand them, in the idea of *temporary* crash programs to improve the position of the Negro community." He compared this kind of effort to aid for earthquake victims but warned that he was opposed to any lowering of standards. Later on he would equate crash programs with lower standards in becoming a prominent neoconservative.

Glazer, who was still a liberal, admitted that "formal equality simply hasn't worked to produce actual equality, or rather, it has been working too slowly." To counter inequalities that had existed in the past, Glazer cited the use of such mechanisms as the ethnically balanced political ticket, a sensitivity to ethnicity which he would later renounce. Hook pressed for continuing efforts by arguing, "There's a difference between collective guilt and collective responsibility in the present for such responsibility can ultimately be brought home to each individual's door."

Professor Hook's casual statement during the discussion that there were few racial problems on university faculties drew a perceptive letter from a reader who wondered if "there would still be no problem if those same academic communities were suddenly to acquire a proper proportion of Negroes . . . enough indeed to threaten faculty jobs." At that point the concept of whites competing with blacks was just beginning to trouble the white liberals who had supported equality as an ideal.

In December 1964 Glazer wrote that the demands of black organizations for "preferential union membership" and "preferential hiring" simply could not serve as a basis for a common effort by blacks and Jews. Minority pressures for busing and school integration, he warned, would cause conflict. "The insistence on the primacy of integration over all other educational objectives breeds antagonism among former Negro allies." The black push for inclusion, Glazer concluded, was "a serious threat to the ability of other groups to maintain their communities."

The first serious conflict between blacks and their allies had been defined. As long as whites had been able to direct the thrust of the struggle for liberation, it had posed no threat to their self-interest. But blacks were beginning to see that laws were not enough to bring about equality. Bayard Rustin noted this shift in February 1965: "At issue, after all, is not civil rights, strictly speaking, but social and economic conditions." The liberal admonitions "of moderation are, for all practical purposes, admonitions to the Negro to adjust to the status quo and are therefore immoral."

But the concept of morality had died with Martin Luther King, Jr.'s, disastrous Chicago campaign. His inability to affect complex social, economic, and political issues in the urban ghettos gave credence to the nationalist militants and hastened the retreat of liberals from the battle. *Commentary* carried a running debate over the value and danger of Black Power. When Moynihan analyzed the 1966 elections, he concluded that "the electorate is fed up to the teeth with demonstrations and riots and perhaps more particularly with the assertion of the right to resist open threats of violence." A year later Moynihan would admit the failure of Congress to enact real economic reforms, but in 1968 he observed that "plain physical fear of the Negro is now a political fact of American life and not a happy one for liberals."

Moynihan's assessment of the national mood was reflected by the changing character of the magazine. After the confrontations over community control of education in New York, many Jews concluded that blacks were anti-Semitic and began to reconsider their involvement in civil rights. Earl Rabb's "The Black Revolution and the Jewish Question" reemphasized the Jewish commitment to a pluralistic society (which black nationalism seemed to threaten) and concluded that the key question had to be: "Is it good for Jews?" Over the next few years *Commentary* and its editors would usually conclude that it wasn't. The magazine published attacks on government intervention in social problems, affirmative action, and school integration. Arthur Jensen and other advocates of black genetic deficiency were given space to defend their right to express their views. Understandably, after the Jewish experience with Nazism, the magazine was somewhat uncomfortable about giving outright support to genetic theories. A few years later the magazine would not be so anxious to support the First Amendment rights of American Nazis.

The initial retreat from the alliance with blacks was primarily emotional, over charges of black anti-Semitism which had been greatly exaggerated. But the efforts to shift the civil rights struggle to economic issues were a much more real threat. Jews were an ethnic group that continued to live in proximity to blacks in large cities. Demands for quotas and affirmative action threatened Jewish jobs that were most directly accessible to black pressure: civil service, education, city government. The pressure for community control posed a direct threat to the base of Jewish political power in the cities. Many blacks saw this movement as the inevitable result of expectations raised by the newly acquired freedoms, but they had underestimated Jewish insecurity.

The love-hate relationship between blacks and Jews grew out of a combination of admiration and envy. The influence of Jews on American institutions and their representation in the most desirable professions was viewed as a guide for the development of black communities and political organizations. But the pressure of black competition was aimed at the very group blacks most admired. There were serious discussions in *Commentary* and other publications about possible linkups between black militants and the white Anglo-Saxon establishment. The concept of the meritocracy was refurbished for use in cases like *Bakke*.

But the Jewish establishment found unexpected support in its uneasy battle against minority demands. Many Gentiles were also threatened by pressures for massive structural readjustments and economic redistribution. The neoconservative line honed in *Commentary* and *Social Policy* was well received in *Harper's, The Atlantic,* and the newsweeklies. The reservations about minority demands no longer had to be the Jewish position. The Jewish establishment's concern about the image of Jews as radicals, Communists, and civil rights advocates as a possible trigger to anti-Semitism could be alleviated. Milton Friedman, Glazer, and Podhoretz could help Jews merge with the mainstream while they still preserved the group's interest. After all, their work was full of reaffirmations of American institutions and American ideals. The neoconservatives could wrap their views in the flag and reject demands for equality on patriotic grounds.

The New Racism was not a resurrection of the old ideas of racial superiority but a much more sophisticated attack on the abilities and motivations of minority groups. By rewriting the history of white ethnics in America, the neoconservatives could resolve the ticklish problem of societal obligation (or guilt). Glazer's *Affirmative Discrimination* outlined the argument for the washing of hands by white ethnics: "These groups were not particularly involved in the enslavement of the Negro or the creation of the Jim Crow pattern in the South, the conquest of part of Mexico, or the near extermination of the American Indian. They came to a country which provided them with [fewer] benefits than it now provides the protected groups. There is little reason for them to feel they should bear the burden of the redress of a past in which they had no or little part, or to assist those who presently receive more assistance than they did. We are indeed a nation of minorities; to enshrine some minorities as deserving of special benefits means not to defend minority rights against a discriminating majority but to favor some of these minorities over others."

This version of history, reprinted in the B'nai B'rith brief in support of Bakke, ignores the active role of ethnic whites in excluding blacks from the city political patronage machines they developed at the turn of the century, in excluding blacks from the labor movement from its inception to World War II, all acts that can be linked directly to the high unemployment figures and the relatively low economic and political status of blacks and other minorities today. These "favored minorities" need assistance today because they were denied the basic human rights of political power and full-time employment that gave other ethnic groups their first step into the economic mainstream.

But if guilt could be eliminated, the subordinate role of minorities still had to be explained. The new eugenicists stepped in with refurbished versions of nineteenth-century Social Darwinism to explain the oppression of blacks in terms of the "culture of poverty" and the genetic deficiencies promoted by Jensen, Shockley, and others. "The lower class individual lives in the slum and sees no reason to complain," wrote Edward C. Banfield, an adviser to Nixon and Rockefeller. "He does not care how dirty and dilapidated his housing is either inside or out, nor does he mind the inadequacy of such public facilities as schools, parks, libraries: indeed where such things exist, he destroys them by acts of vandalism if he can. Features that make the slum repellent to others actually please him." Banfield's *The Unheavenly City* became a popular college textbook in the 1970s by reviving ideas of motivation among the poor that had been abandoned thirty or forty years earlier.

But while these theories were enough to hold back the hordes in the inner city, ways had to be found to justify the retreat on affirmative action, which involved middle-class jobs. New code words came into use: *qualifications, competence, reverse discrimination, inarticulate.* All these fed into the new consensus that minority groups were making unreasonable demands. The initial rush into affirmative action had brought hundreds, even thousands, of minorities into jobs that put them into direct contact and competition with whites. Inevitably, some did not do well. Others could not cope with the pressures or lacked the proper preparation. The people doing the hiring meant well, but they often lacked experience to select members of these minority groups. Still, failures were used to justify the claims of lowered standards and unqualification.

But if minorities were not moved by such rationalizations, it was because an entire generation had gone to school and worked with whites. There no longer was any mystique about white superiority. Minorities saw whites who were competent and others who were not. They saw those who succeeded and those who failed, and many began to suspect that a double standard was in operation.

Dr. Price Cobbs, a San Francisco psychiatrist and management consultant for large corporations, has studied the dynamics of racial interaction at the middle-class level. "I don't have any question," says Cobbs, "that racism is alive and well." The coauthor of *Black Rage*, a 1960s best-seller on race relations, Cobbs says the subtlety of the New Racism makes it no less real. "A primary manifestation of this is the perception that white middle and top managers have about blacks. We are dealing with a range of preconscious assumptions about the relative competence of blacks, about the intelligence of blacks. You run into good, well-motivated people who think they are fair, who feel they have turned around attitudes and beliefs of ten to fifteen years ago but who continue to view blacks in a deficit model: 'less than,' 'not as good as,' 'if we could only do so-and-so to bring them up to speed.'

"If you look back," Cobbs goes on, "much of what passed for benign race relations was some kind of social comfort on the part of whites who were dealing with blacks. There are many whites who can be comfortable socially but who don't have any idea of the depth and degree of their remaining negative assumptions about people who are different."

Many of these preconscious assumptions can be found in the reporting on the *Bakke* case. *Less qualified minorities* is a term that was not supported by any evidence in the *Bakke* case, but the term followed the case from its early days to the morning of the Supreme Court's decision. These same assumptions make Allan Bakke a sympathetic victim but fail to see the minorities who are victims on a much greater scale and in far greater numbers.

The greatest danger that the New Racism poses to minority efforts at equality is its assumption that racism no longer exists, that whites have finally overcome several hundred years of cultural reinforcement, and that they can make objective judgments about the ability and performance of minority-group individuals. Neither history nor experience gives minorities reason to believe that is so. It is extremely difficult to develop mutual trust in a relationship where power is shared so unequally.

The racism that has been a virulent and violent force through most of our history has been changed greatly in the last two or three decades. Just the fact that open racism is no longer socially acceptable is one measure of the tremendous progress that has been made. But there is a danger as well in assuming that it is not there at all. What is less tangible is no less real.

The neoconservative catechism preaches assimilation of those who have gained entry into the middle class and isolation and punishment of those who have been unfortunate enough to become victims of society. Putting aside considerations of race, one has to wonder if such a dispassionate vision can appeal to the majority of Americans. Even the most ardent liberals would admit that there were failures and excesses in the Great Society experiment of the last decade, but rather than reject wholesale the concept of a helping hand, isn't there a way to build on this experience for a better future?

The desire of Americans for simple solutions to complicated problems has made them susceptible to demagoguery. The experience of minorities has always been dichotomous and has often been a catalyst for appealing to the better instincts of the majority. For a group of young blacks discussing the state of the race on a Sunday afternoon, there is no contradiction between their individual successes and their concern about the fate of those who have not been fortunate.

The duality of the minority experience in America helps them understand why a struggle for equality can often appear to be a threat to individual liberties. This experience helps explain why laws intended to protect minorities from oppression can be turned against them in convoluted debates over legal technicalities.

But there are people who understand that the *Bakke* case does not exist in a vacuum, that it is not isolated from the shifting political and economic winds of its time. But because the idea of justice has long been debated by men, they will not let this complicated process be reduced into a kind of athletic competition where the bottom line is the question of whether Allan Bakke wins or loses.

Eight

THE SOLICITOR'S
BRIEF

The Carter administration had been in office only a month when the U.S. Supreme Court agreed to hear the *Bakke* case. The various groups that claimed responsibility for Jimmy Carter's victory looked to his political appointments for evidence of his gratitude, and they were difficult to keep happy. Blacks complained about tokenism. Women were upset about the paucity of top-level appointments. Hispanics and labor expressed concern about the direction of selections. It was just about what could be expected in a new Democratic administration.

Carter's nomination of his good friend Griffin Bell to be attorney general of the United States provoked bitter complaints from some liberal and black groups, and they remained unhappy after his confirmation. Bell's selection of two blacks for top posts in the Justice Department was clearly intended to appease the critics. Wade McCree, a judge on the Sixth Circuit Court of Appeals, was named solicitor general. Drew Days, an attorney with the NAACP Legal Defense Fund, was appointed assistant attorney general for civil rights. Both men had impeccable establishment credentials and strong ties in the black political community, and their selection was universally hailed. But the case of the white aerospace engineer would become a controversial issue in their lives and demonstrate that the divisions over the *Bakke* case were not strictly along racial lines.

On the day the Supreme Court agreed to hear the case, attorneys for the University of California were in Washington soliciting the support of McCree and Days. Under federal law, the attorney general or the solicitor general can file a brief or appear before the Supreme Court in almost any case in which the government feels it has an interest. By tradition, parties in a suit are allowed to seek support from the government, which can often influence the decision of the Court. But the meeting was not very productive. University constitutional expert Paul Mishkin and Harvard Law professor Archibald Cox, who had been chosen to argue the case before the Court, urged the government to support their side of the case. They told the two Justice Department officials that the case was going to be a constitutional landmark which would have direct impact on the many federal programs that used affirmative action. But McCree and Days would make no firm commitment. They pointed to the weaknesses in the case record and gave Mishkin and Cox the impression they were not anxious to become involved.

Soon afterward Days, as the government's chief civil attorney, asked the major federal agencies whether the government should intervene as a friend of the court in *Bakke*. Often the Court will ask the government to participate in a case that has obvious federal interest. But the Supreme Court had not asked the government's input in *DeFunis*, nor, for reasons known only to the nine justices, had this invitation been extended in *Bakke*.

Over the next few months all the major federal agencies and departments informed Days that they would support intervention. In June, Days and McCree met with representatives of the various agencies to work out a basic position for the solicitor general's brief. The discussion was in general terms, but it was understood that the government would come out against fixed quotas but in favor of affirmative action.

At this point the process seemed to be moving along smoothly. The importance of the *Bakke* case was clear to both sides, and all the parties concerned were busy preparing and filing the 160 amicus briefs that presented their views. When a group of black attorneys made an informal inquiry through a White House aide, Griffin Bell said he would go along with whatever Days and McCree decided. The cause of affirmative action seemed to be in safe hands.

The first disturbance to the somewhat somnolent atmosphere around the government's brief took place on June 5, 1977, when HEW secretary Joseph Califano delivered the commencement address at the City College of New York. Califano called for a renewed commitment to an equal educational opportunity for all Americans. "We cannot rest as a society—and we will not rest as a government—until full minority participation in American education is a fact rather than a dream," Califano told his audience, which included a *New York Times* reporter. "And if we are serious about doing that, we must have a way of measuring our progress.

"I know the dangers and potential for injustice that are inherent in any system of arbitrary, long-term quotas. For in our efforts to eliminate differences and inequalities, quotas may actually aggravate them. Arbitrary quotas will not be a part of our enforcement programs; we want to rely on the good faith and special effort of all who join us in the final march against discrimination. But we will also rely—because we must rely—on numerical goals as a benchmark of progress."

The headline on the next day's *Times* read: "Califano Asks 'Goals' Not 'Quotas.'" Many Jewish organizations, which were already uneasy about the new administration, were outraged by the speech and demanded a retraction. One group took a full-page advertisement in the *Times* calling for Califano's resignation. The president was in trouble with an important group of supporters. He extracted a retreat from Califano and issued a somewhat ambiguous statement condemning rigid quotas but affirming his commitment to equal opportunity.

Maybe because it was summer in Washington or maybe because no direct link had been made between the president's position and the government's brief in the *Bakke* case, the tempest died down almost as rapidly as it had erupted. One additional factor was also the fact that the two top officials in the government's brief were black.

Both Days and McCree could have been called representatives of the talented tenth by W. E. B. Du Bois. Despite their differences in age, they were examples of the best of the black "old guard," men who had achieved success long before affirmative action came to be the vogue. McCree was a native of Iowa who had attended the exclusive Boston Latin School, Fisk University, and Harvard Law School, where former Transportation secretary William Coleman had been a classmate. McCree had been an elected judge in Michigan, and he had earned a reputation on the court of appeals for his finely crafted opinions.

Days, a decade younger than McCree, was the first black assistant attorney general to head any division of the Justice Department in its 187-year history. Born in Tampa, Florida, and reared in suburban New Rochelle, New York, Days had his share of memories of blatant discrimination. But he had clearly overcome the obstacles. In the 1960s he was one of five blacks in his Yale Law School class. His involvement with the Yale Russian Chorus led him to meet his wife, Ann Ramsey Langdon, a direct descendant of Sarah Ball, a cousin of George Washington's. In addition to working for the Legal Defense Fund, Days had spent two years teaching at the Temple University Law School.

The first draft of the government's brief was written by Days and two attorneys on his staff. The draft went to McCree, who gave it to an assistant to revise. Beyond that, responsibility for the contents become vague. Until it went to the government printer, the different versions would appear to be the work of many hands. Sections were pasted up, cut, crossed out, and corrected by hand.

Toward the end of August the White House gave the first signs of concern about the brief. There were some casual inquiries, but the message from McCree's office made it clear that it thought it none of the White House's business. Traditionally, the attorney general was considered the top political job in the Justice Department. The solicitor general had a more scholarly and abstract image, and McCree clearly wanted to keep that aura of independence. When a newspaper story appeared suggesting that the government would support the university, the White House renewed its efforts to determine the contents of the brief. White House aides extracted a concession from McCree's assistants that the president had the right to have his views expressed in the government's brief, but they were told to route their suggestions through Bell.

Finally, a draft was delivered to President Carter by the attorney general on September 1. Carter turned it over to the chief of his domestic policy staff, Stuart Eizenstat. The brief was obviously in preparation, Eizenstat noted from the corrections, additions, and revisions. He criticized its style, organization, and tone. But the content was even more important, and Eizenstat considered that a political disaster. The brief supported the admission of Bakke, declared the admissions program at Davis unconstitutional, and gave tentative support to the use of race in admissions.

In a long memo to the president, Eizenstat warned that the brief would be regarded as the administration's definitive statement on affirmative action. He said the language of the brief would harm the government's affirmative action programs and added that the trial record was too thin to warrant support for Bakke's admission. The memo was passed to Bell, who once again had it transmitted to the solicitor general.

By this time the rumors about the Justice Department's position had alarmed civil rights advocates enough that the Congressional Black Caucus arranged for University of Pennsylvania professor Ralph Smith and several other attorneys to discuss the case with them. Many had been involved in Capitol Hill politics and had paid little attention to the controversy surrounding *Bakke*. The lawyers warned them that it was important that the Justice Department take a strong position on the issues or affirmative action would be jeopardized. The caucus was scheduled to meet with President Carter on September 7, and before that meeting they discussed their concern about *Bakke* with Vice-President Mondale. Mondale said he had not read the brief, but he arranged a meeting with Bell and other Justice Department officials for that afternoon. But the meeting was not very productive. The legislators knew very little about the facts of the case, and they did not know what was in the government's brief. In the words of one participant, "McCree just whipped them."

By now the controversy had spilled into the public arena. The *New York Times* published a story on September 8 declaring "Justice Dept. Brief Opposes Race Quotas at Coast University." At a second meeting between the caucus and the Justice Department officials the next day, it became clear that there were profound disagreements between the politicians' concern about political repercussions and McCree's intellectual approach to the law.

The politicians and their lawyers decided that political action was the next step, and they made plans to stop the brief at the White House. They found an unexpected ally. There was an anonymous telephone call to one of the concerned officials. If he went outside, he would meet a taxicab with a copy of the brief on the backseat. Finally, the civil rights forces had a copy of the government's brief. They saw immediately that their concerns had been well founded.

The brief was not a political document at all. It was written in a scholarly, neutral tone reminiscent of a law review discussion. In discussing "minority-sensitive" programs, the brief said: "We conclude that the case for such programs, although not one-sided, is compelling. We discuss all the arguments not because we doubt the constitutionality of such programs but because they are serious arguments and not all arguments advanced in support of such programs are persuasive."

In different type the argument continued: "It is better, we conclude, to face the difficulties and to identify the arguments on which we do not rely here."

The brief criticized programs like the one at Davis, which only compared minority applicants to one another. This would result in the selection of "those minority applicants who have suffered the least from discrimination. The pertinent comparison should be between the most highly qualified whites and the most highly qualified blacks, Chicanos and Asian-Americans." The concern about quality could be attributed to McCree and Days, two men who had met the best standards of excellence and who clearly resented any implication that minorities could not compete with whites, but the ponderous style did not seem to be the work of McCree, with his reputation as a legal stylist.

The problems with the argument were clear. Opponents of affirmative action had used the most strident and extreme arguments to support Allan Bakke. The proponents of affirmative action could not afford the tentative and hesitant tone of the brief as the government's position on the issues. Through the weekend a group of black attorneys shut themselves up in a hotel room with "fried chicken and Chivas Regal" and prepared an analysis and critique for a third meeting with McCree and Days the following Monday. The lawyers tried to get in touch with McCree, but they were told he had gone to Detroit. They reached through the small network of black professionals and had contacts in Detroit corner McCree.

They expressed their concern about the offending passages in the brief. How could they know? he asked; they hadn't read the brief. They quoted some of the most disturbing passages. The solicitor general was furious about the breach of confidentiality. But copies of the draft were already circulating among members of the president's Cabinet, which would also meet on the following Monday. Califano was outraged and ordered an assistant to prepare an alternative brief. Eizenstat and other White House officials were dissatisfied with this latest version and expressed their displeasure to Justice Department officials. Caucus members approached HUD secretary Patricia Harris and UN ambassador Andrew Young about the problem. That Saturday, September 10, McCree, under heavy political pressure, called his office from Detroit and dictated four points that would become the core of government's brief. The ambiguous and tentative language of the earlier drafts was replaced with a call for strong support of affirmative action that allowed the use of race, opposed rigid racial quotas, declared there was an inadequate finding of facts, and urged the case be sent back to California. The new brief also made it clear that the government's interest was primarily in affirmative action—not in Allan Bakke.

On Monday the political assault on the Justice Department's brief was two-pronged. At the Cabinet meeting Califano, Harris, and Young made a spirited defense of affirmative action and deplored the strong position against quotas. The meeting between the caucus members, their legal advisers, and the Justice Department officials was better orchestrated. Representative Parren Mitchell of Maryland, the Democratic chairman of the caucus, made some brief opening remarks and gave the floor to Representative Louis Stokes, who talked about the need for partnership between the legislative and executive branches of government. James Nabrit, Jr., an attorney with the NAACP Legal Defense Fund, traced the historical basis of the Fourteenth Amendment in protecting the rights of blacks. University of Pennsylvania Law School dean Louis Pollak talked about the role of the solicitor general as the attorney representing the interests of all the people. Mc-Cree's predecessor, Robert Bork, a conservative Yale law professor, had argued forcefully for the consideration of race in drawing legislative district lines to strengthen the vote of minorities. Pollak quoted Bork's argument that to be color-blind was to be blind to reality. Smith pointed to the shortcomings of the court record and argued against support for Bakke.

The second hour of the meeting was given over to questions, and again, there seemed to be a curious gap between McCree's assertion about the brief and what it actually contained. On one occasion Days seemed surprised when one of the attorneys read from the document. The confusion remained, but it seemed clear that the political pressures would have an impact. After the meeting the caucus warned that President Carter would "discredit his presidency in the eyes of history" if he endorsed the existing version of the brief. "The brief's legal positions pronounce a death sentence for programs which use race or ethnicity to achieve integration or equality," the caucus said in a position paper issued after the meeting with McCree and Days.

After this latest salvo of criticism, McCree and Days took personal charge of the final drafting of the government's position and took a line much closer to what the caucus and the Cabinet members had advocated. The brief supported the use of race for affirmative action and urged the Supreme Court to send the case back to California to determine if Bakke's rights had been violated. The influence that the black and liberal forces were able to exert on the White House was testimony to the structural changes that had taken place within the country's political system. Minority groups had complained that they had no input into the defense of the case, but they had been able to change the direction of government in the preparation of its position on the issue.

But the sequence of events also reflected on the peculiar situation of blacks who find themselves in positions of power. At one point in the discussions, McCree rejected the suggestion that he should be true to "the black community." "I have to be true to myself," he asserted. His concerns probably did reflect the fears among some blacks that affirmative action programs would be used to cheapen the achievements of minorities. In addition, what was the obligation of a member of a minority group to his or her community and what was his obligation to his own deep-seated convictions? The problem for the solicitor general was that his position was much more political than he wanted it to be. Maybe there would be a time when men and women like McCree could carry out the duties of their office without giving consideration to race and ethnic origin. But as with the argument about color blindness, it would be some time still before that ideal could be translated into a reality.

Nine

A DISCUSSION
AMONG GENTLEMEN

The intensity of the game the night before had been excep-
tional, a classic confrontation of athletes at the peak of ability.
The arguments over contracts, free agents, and salaries were
set aside for a moment, and it was just baseball again, that
synthesis of body and mind that raises sport to the level of art.
At the White House, General Olusegun Obasanjo, the Nigerian
head of state, warned President Carter that armed conflict was
inevitable in southern Africa and would result in black rule.
His statements were a reminder that the balance of power in
the world had shifted to a point where black Africa could
chart its own course with destiny and simply inform the
world's most powerful nation out of simple courtesy.

Against the background of conflicts in sports and world
politics, the nine justices of the United States Supreme Court
prepared to hear the case of *Regents of the University of California* v. *Allan Bakke*. At Yankee Stadium, Paul Blair's sharp
single in the twelfth inning gave the home team a 4–3 victory
over the Los Angeles Dodgers in the hundredth World Series
game played in the House That Ruth Built. No one had kept
count, but confrontations over race were as common to the
Supreme Court as extra-inning victories in the South Bronx.
The dilemma of discrimination in a democracy had been discussed often in this imposing building with the words *Equal*

Justice Under Law carved over the entrance. Once more the application of this slogan would play to a full house on a bright, sunny day full of the golds and reds that mark the end of the baseball season.

Certain news items on that October 12, 1977, made the day more familiar than might be expected. In New York two white policemen were accused of killing a black postal worker, resulting in a meeting between the police commissioner and a group of angry black citizens, led by a Baptist minister from Brooklyn. The *Washington Post,* basking in the afterglow of Watergate, devoted considerable space to a sociological study of pimps—complete with a vocabulary list that was closer to Iceberg Slim than Pulitzer Prize–quality journalism. It all made a tableau of autumnal *déjà vu,* American style: diplomacy, racial conflict, and now a debate on inequality with a peculiar O. Henry twist. The complainant this time was white, the defendants were white, and the most affected parties, the blacks and browns who still sought to have the generous motto of equality apply to them, sat on the sidelines like spectators along the first-base line.

Few bothered to discuss baseball as the long line of people wound its way toward the building that had prompted Charles Evans Hughes to proclaim, "The Republic endures and this is the symbol of its faith," when the cornerstone was laid in 1932. In hope of seeing the process of democracy unfold, the most determined had camped at four o'clock the day before in the shadow of this Greek temple to American law. Such all-night vigils were not uncommon outside baseball stadiums at World Series time, but here they served as testimony to the intensity of this confrontation. Across the street from the court, several hundred demonstrators raised placards and banners they hoped would influence the events taking place inside.

Court officials could not accommodate the crush of spectators, so they finally decided to rotate groups through the courtroom, limiting their participation in history to three-minute intervals. Most would have to wait for eyewitness reports and news stories from the media representatives who had competed fiercely for the 100 ringside seats. For once, representatives of print and electronic media would operate under the same handicaps because the Court allowed no intrusion of modern technology. All the reporters would have to depend on pad and pen to record the event. Even as the crowds waited, Court employees placed ten-inch white quill pens on writing pads at the counsel tables in the courtroom. All these gestures were in keeping with the image of tradition promoted by the sixteen Corinthian columns of the Court's facade, the black robes of the justices, and the red velvet curtains around the courtroom's perimeter. The mystique of tradition and formality gave the Court its power, and this power was guarded jealously.

The guards began admitting spectators at about nine-thirty, guiding them through the metal detectors that were one concession to the political realities of the time. Members of the press were shuffled off to the packed narrow alcove on the left side of the courtroom, where their view of the events would be partially obscured by the red curtains and the proliferation of Greek columns. Admission to the press area and the main courtroom were, in fact, reasons for triumph, for access to tickets had been at least as difficult as to seats for the World Series.

This was a select audience of government officials, attorneys, and interested parties. The men wore the vested suits of dark blue and gray that were the uniform of the legal profession, and they greeted each other with the enthusiasm of old classmates at the Harvard-Yale game. In fact, most of them were graduates of the best law schools: Harvard, Yale, Stanford, Columbia. This was the eastern legal establishment, divided now by this troublesome issue but still united by their common experiences in education and society. The scarcity of women was testimony to the years when they were exceptions in this professional elite of law. There were a number of blacks, but few if one considered the special interest this case had for them. In 1952, when the Court had heard *Brown*, almost half the audience was black. The lack of a strong black presence here illustrated the peculiar sideline role that minority groups had played in this case and the divergence of the propaganda of equality from the reality of justice that was at the heart of this case.

Those blacks who had gained admission to this session had survived the rigorous process of selection by the establishment. They held many "firsts" at important schools and prestigious law firms, the peculiar honorific measure that had somewhere distorted advancements in the attitudes of whites into a measure of progress for blacks. The men and women who were now members of this club had struggled for their equality before the advent of affirmative action, quotas, and special programs, and while they were at ease with their white colleagues, their presence here was an indication that they had not abandoned their struggle for equality.

Despite the tensions surrounding this case, the mood of the courtroom was clearly festive as the crowd filed in. This was a social event divorced from the real-life passions that enveloped the case. Like opening night at the theater, the show was not limited to the stage. The attorneys—Archibald Cox and Donald Reidhaar for the university, Wade McCree for the United States government, Colvin and Robert Links for Bakke —took their places at the long tables below the elevated mahogany bench. Out of sight of the audience, the justices performed one final ritual, the round of handshakes, each justice with every other, a reminder of common purpose despite serious differences.

The sharp rap of the gavel brought an end to the rumble

of conversation, and the audience stood in the traditional display of respect for authority. The justices took their seats according to the custom of seniority: Chief Justice Warren Burger at the center, the most senior members of the Court at his immediate right and left, the newest justices, William Rehnquist and John Paul Stevens, at the far ends of the bench. Burger read the docket number of the first case on the day's calendar and nodded toward the university counsel's table. "Mr. Cox, you may proceed whenever you're ready."

Cox, a tall, thin, and scholarly man who had been chosen to argue for the university, rose to address the court. He was no stranger to the nine men seated in a half circle before him. Like three of the justices, he was a Harvard man. He had argued many cases before this Court, first as solicitor general during the Kennedy administration and later as the first Watergate special prosecutor. He had been fired after five months by President Nixon in the infamous "Saturday Night Massacre" which ended with the resignations of Attorney General Elliot Richardson and Deputy Attorney General William Ruckelshaus. Cox had gone back to Harvard to be Williston Professor of Law. He was more peer than supplicant, and the justices understood this. He was formal enough to buoy the traditions of the Court, yet familiar enough to participate in a discussion among gentlemen.

There had been much speculation in California about who would argue for the university before the Supreme Court. No one doubted the university would follow the common practice in such cases and hire an outside counsel. The regents were concerned about the charges of collusion and incompetence generated by the early handling of the case. To rehabilitate its image, the university needed an attorney whose integrity and reputation were at least as impressive as his ability and credentials.

Paul Mishkin, a respected constitutional scholar on the Berkeley campus, was given primary responsibility for preparing the university's brief, but his reputation was limited to scholarly circles. Nathaniel Colley, a Yale graduate who was probably the most successful and prominent black attorney in California, was recommended by minority organizations, along with William Coleman, the secretary of transportation in the Ford administration, whose academic and professional credentials few white attorneys could match. But neither Colley nor Coleman was approached. The regents wanted to make it clear that their lawyer represented the university and higher education and not the interests of minority groups. By this curious turn of logic, Cox became the obvious choice.

Cox made the traditional opening statement: "Mr. Chief Justice, and may it please the Court." He spoke deliberately and conversationally. He might have been conducting a seminar at the Harvard Law School, picking his words carefully but with the full assurance of a man among his peers. That unspoken kinship would assert itself throughout the day.

This case, here on certiorari from the Supreme Court of California, presents a single vital question: whether a State university, which is forced by limited resources to select a relatively small number of students from a much larger number of well-qualified applicants, is free, voluntarily, to take into account the fact that a qualified applicant is black, Chicano, Asian or Native American in order to increase the number of qualified members of those minority groups trained for the educated professions and participating in them, professions from which minorities were long excluded because of generations of pervasive racial discrimination.

Cox's opening had been carefully drafted, with each word selected for a purpose. He had condensed the vital elements of the case he was about to make into one forceful sentence. He told the Court that the California Supreme Court had answered the wrong question. This was not a matter of whether the university could prefer less qualified minorities over better qualified whites, but a question of whether the university could consider race as a factor in selecting from a large pool of qualified applicants. He reminded the Court that the university's choice in allocating these resources was a *voluntary* decision by a responsible (white) policy-making body. It was a choice no different from many other choices made at functioning academic institutions. The Court had to choose whether the states would remain "free" to make such choices. And finally, he pointed out that the decision to consider race was made not in order to discriminate against whites but to remedy the effects of "generations of pervasive discrimination against minorities."

Cox's argument was aimed at the conservative wing of the Court. Justices Rehnquist, Burger, Harry Blackmun, and Lewis Powell, all Nixon appointees, were often joined by Potter Stewart and Byron White in a majority that took a jaundiced view of Supreme Court intervention in state efforts to resolve social problems. This Burger Court had begun to reverse a trend toward government by judiciary that had been the hallmark of the Court under Earl Warren but that this group viewed as constitutionally suspect.

The Court's record on racial issues was mixed. Many of its decisions involving minority plaintiffs had actually aimed at limiting federal protection of individual rights. In *International Brotherhood of Teamsters* v. *U.S.*, a case with profound implications that received little media attention, the Supreme Court had refused to overturn union seniority systems that continued favored privilege for whites despite evidence of past discrimination against blacks. What it had done was doom an entire generation of black workers to permanent inequality. Yet, in a case involving voting rights in New York, the Court had allowed the creation of a predominantly black election district despite white protests that their political power was being diluted.

Cox outlined the "three facts or realities" dominating the situation at the Davis Medical School which he felt the Court had to consider:

The first is that the number of qualified applicants for the nation's professional schools is vastly greater than the number of places available. This is a fact and an inescapable fact. In 1975–76, for example, there were roughly 30,000 qualified applicants for admission to medical school, a much greater number of actual applicants, and there were only about 14,000 places. At Davis, there were 25 applicants for every seat in 1973; in 1974, the ratio had risen to 37 to 1. So the problem is one of selection among qualified applicants, not of ability to gain from a professional education.

The second fact, on which there is no need for me to elaborate, but it is a fact, for generations racial discrimination in the United States, much of it stimulated by unconstitutional State action, isolated certain minorities, condemned them to inferior education, and shut them out of the most important and satisfying aspects of American life, including higher education and the professions.

And then there is one third fact. There is no racially blind method of selection which will enroll today more than a trickle of minority students in the nation's colleges and professions. These are the realities which the University of California at Davis faced in 1968, and which, I say, I think the Court must face when it comes to its decision.

It was a succinct and forceful opening. Cox's pace quickened somewhat, and he began to outline the history of the Task Force program at Davis. He was interrupted by Justice White, who asked if there was something in the record to indicate *who* proposed or adopted the Task Force program.

COX: It's indicated that it was adopted by the faculty of the school or was voted by the faculty. That appears in Dr. Lowrey's testimony. And it also appears——

WHITE: Of course he [Dr. Lowrey] wasn't there then, was he?

COX: No, I guess he must have learned when he came some-what later. There is nothing more than his testimony gained on—I may say I have seen minutes that——

WHITE: Is there anything on the record indicating the approval of the Regents [of the Task Force program] other than the fact that they are defendants in the suit?

COX: No, because the Regents had delegated to each faculty of the school the responsibility for admissions.

WHITE: Thank you.

Cox seemed to be floundering. He was arguing from a trial court record not of his own making, and although he had studied it well, he could not correct its deficiencies. His answers appeared evasive and detracted from the impact of his opening statement. He tried to regain his ground by adding his personal endorsement of the decision by the regents to delegate admission standards to each college.

"So that this was left to the different colleges, and very wisely I think because autonomous institutions, each trying to solve this problem in their own way, may give all of us the benefit of the experience of trial and error, creativity. That's the virtue of not constitutionalizing problems of this kind."

Cox was relying on his own personal status to lend weight to his argument. He was also reinforcing his theme of judicial restraint and nonintervention. At this point Cox unexpectedly opened the Pandora's box of the quota issue: "I want to empha-size that the designation of 16 places was not a quota, at least as I would use that word. Certainly it was not a quota in the older sense of an arbitrary limit put on the number of mem-bers of a nonpopular group who would be admitted to an institution which was looking down its nose at them."

The fact that a certain number of places was set aside for minority students was the most vulnerable aspect of the program Cox had been hired to defend. The California Supreme Court had flatly rejected the practice of setting aside sixteen places. The quota issue had, more than anything else in the *Bakke* case, aroused the passion of traditionally liberal Jewish and labor organizations in supporting Bakke's position. Much of the discussion of the case in the media had focused on quotas. Apparently, Cox had decided to take the issue head-on. The Court would raise it sooner or later, and by starting the discussion himself, he could choose his ground in making a defense. The justices were not about to let him off easily.

STEWART: It did put a limit on the number of white people, didn't it?

COX: I think that it limited the number of non-minority, and therefore, essentially white[s], yes. But there are two things to be said about that. One is that this was not pointing the finger at a group which had been marked as inferior in any sense and it was undifferentiated. It operated against a wide variety of people. So I think it was not stigmatizing in the sense of the old quota against Jews was stigmatizing, in any way.

STEWART: But it did put a limit on their number in each class?

COX: I'm sorry?

STEWART: But it did put a limit on the number of non-minority people in each class?

COX: It did put a limit, no question about that, and I don't mean to infer that. And I will direct myself to it a little later, if I may.

STEVENS: Do you agree, then, that there was a quota of 84?

COX: Well, I would deny that it was a quota. We agree that there were 16 places set aside for qualified disadvantaged minority students. Now, if that number—if setting aside a number, if the amount of resources——

STEVENS: No, the question is not whether the 16 is a quota. The question is whether the 84 is a quota. And what is your answer to that?

COX: I would say that neither is properly defined as a quota.

STEVENS: And then, why not?

COX: Because, in the first place—because of my understanding of the meaning of "quota." And I think the decisive things are the facts. And the operative facts are: this is not something imposed from outside, as the quotas are in employment, or the targets are in employment sometimes, today. It was not a limit on the number of minority students. Other minority students were in fact accepted through the regular admissions program. It was not a guarantee of a minimum number of minority students, because all of them had to be—and the testimony is that all of them were—fully qualified . . .

It did say that if there are 16 qualified minority students, and they were also disadvantaged, then 16 places shall be filled by them and only 84 places will be available to others.

POWELL: Mr. Cox, the facts are not in dispute. Does it really matter what we call this program?

COX: No. I quite agree with you, Mr. Justice. I was trying to emphasize that the facts here have none of the aspects . . . that lead us to think of "quota" as a bad word. What we call this doesn't matter, and if we call it a quota, knowing the facts and deciding according to the operative facts and [we are] not influenced by the semantics, it couldn't matter less.

In asking the Court to look beyond the connotations of the word, Cox was saying the system did not stigmatize whites.

But again the facts he and Justice Powell wanted so much to agree on did not exist. The number sixteen had become established in the case as the goal or quota or whatever for the Task Force, and the university was stuck with it. But a later search had shown that only fifteen minority students had been admitted in 1974. One place had been given back to the regular admissions committee, apparently because the Task Force felt the sixteenth minority candidate was not strong enough. But because this fact was not in the trial record, it could not rescue Cox in his effort to convince the justices that the process was not unconstitutional. He tried to clarify his point by using an analogy.

cox: Justice Stevens, let us suppose that . . . the school was much concerned by the lack of qualified general practitioners in Northern California, as indeed it was, . . . and it told the admissions committee: "Get people who come from rural communities, if they are qualified, and who express the intention of going back there." And the Dean of Admissions might well say: "Well, how much importance do you give this?" And the members of the faculty might say, by vote or otherwise, "We think it's terribly important. As long as they are qualified, try and get ten in that group." I don't think I would say that it was a quota of 90 students for others. And I think this, while it involves race, of course, that's why we're here, or color, really it is essentially the same thing. The decision of the University was that there are social purposes, or purposes aimed in the end at eliminating racial injustice in this country and in bringing equality of opportunity, there will be purposes served by including minority students.

BLACKMUN: Is it the same as an athletic scholarship?

cox: Well, I——

BLACKMUN: So many places reserved for athletic scholarships.

Cox hesitated. The analogy was correct, but there was the unflattering comparison of minority students with athletes whose intellectual abilities were questionable.

COX: In the sense—I don't like to liken it to that in terms of its importance, but I think there are a number of places that may be set aside for an institution's different aims, and the aim of some institutions does seem to be to have athletic prowess. So that in that sense this is a choice made to promote the schools, the faculty's choice of educational and professional objectives.

With a sarcastic note in his voice, Blackmun asked Cox if it were not true that athletic prowess was the aim of most institutions.

COX: Well, I come from Harvard, sir.

A ripple of laughter swept through the courtroom.

COX: I don't know whether it's our aim, but we don't do very well.

BLACKMUN: But I can remember a time when—Mr. Cox. I can remember a time when you did . . .

COX: Yes. Yes. You're quite right.

This time the laughter in the courtroom was unrestrained as the audience shared the joke between two Harvard men. The tension had been unbearable as Cox negotiated the thicket of the quota issue without too much success, in the eyes of most observers. But the banter broke the suspense while restoring the special kinship of those on the bench and the attorney for the university in this lament for Harvard football and their common interest in preserving the quality of higher education.

One exception to the laughter was Justice Thurgood Marshall. The black justice found it difficult to share in the levity of the moment when so much was at stake. As chief counsel of the NAACP Marshall had acquired a reputation for a good sense of humor he used well to get out of difficult situations. But now, as a Supreme Court justice, he needed to laugh only when he thought something was funny. A veteran of ten years on the Court, he was junior only to Brennan, Stewart, and White. At age sixty-nine, the toll of his thirty years as chief counsel of the NAACP was visible in his pale complexion and his puffy, jowly features. He must have thought of the day twenty-five years earlier, when he still cut a matinee idol figure, when he stood on the other side of this high bench, arguing a case that was the culmination of the most extensive master plan for litigation ever devised.

In the days that had begun with his case against the law school of the University of Maryland in his hometown, Baltimore, Marshall was a driven man: traveling long, hard miles on dirt roads in South Carolina, Mississippi, and Texas; holding strategy sessions in the back rooms of bars over fried fish and chicken; sleeping in beds too short for his six-foot-three frame. Marshall had performed a mammoth task of picking cases carefully, making the best possible record, finding expert witnesses, and taking the cases up to the Supreme Court. The task had required an incredible commitment of mind and soul against overwhelming odds.

Marshall understood that the long struggle to end the caste system of legal segregation was just a beginning in the effort to give blacks equal access to the benefits of society. But despite *Brown,* he had seen segregation in the North increase rather than decrease. He had seen the exodus of whites from the cities to the suburbs. And he had been on the Court when it overturned a Detroit desegregation order that would have bused blacks into predominantly white suburbs. Marshall did not need evidence in the record to verify past discrimination against minorities. He had lived with it for seventy years, and he could see how far the nation had to go to achieve what most of his people still dreamed about.

He remained silent through the arguments of Cox and Wade McCree, the solicitor general. He might have argued the case differently, with more emphasis on the historical and moral justifications for such programs and less on the importance of university autonomy. But he was no longer the field general of his memories, and this was not his battle to fight. His turn would come later.

Justice Rehnquist wanted to know whether Cox felt the program would still be constitutional if Davis had decided "that instead of setting aside 16 seats for minority doctors, they would set aside 50 seats until the balance was redressed and the minority population of doctors equaled that of the population as a whole." The question was a trap that Cox knew he needed to avoid. If he conceded fifty was wrong, what was right with forty, thirty, or sixteen? He also understood what troubled the Court's youngest member. If the Court allowed the university to set sixteen seats aside, what was to prevent fifty seats from being set aside, a figure most people would consider unacceptable?

Had Cox been discussing the case over a drink at the Harvard Club he might have told Rehnquist that he knew damn well that such a possibility was out of the question. But here Cox clearly floundered. He first tried to frame a constitutional principle:

cox: . . . So long as the numbers are chosen . . . and they are shown to be reasonably adaptable to the social goal . . . then there is no reason to condemn a program because a particular number is chosen.

I would say that as the number goes up, the danger of invidiousness or the danger that this is being done not for social purposes but to favor one group . . . is great.

Cox had finally hemmed and hawed his way to a firmer footing. The civil rights lawyers in the audience sighed. That was the best argument. It was simply a matter of the majority's being reasonable; after all, they were in control of the process.

Justice Powell wanted to pursue the numbers a bit longer:

POWELL: Mr. Cox, along this same line of discussion, would you relate the number in any way to population, and if so, the population of the state, the city or to what standard?

COX: Well, the number 16 here is not in any way linked to the population in California.

POWELL: It's 23 per cent, I think, for minorities.

On the surface, Powell's question was a simple request for information, but Cox recognized an issue raised in many of the amicus briefs on behalf of Bakke and took it on.

COX: Well, this was 16 . . . I'll be quite frank to say that I think one of the things which causes all of us concern about these programs is the danger that they will give rise to some notion of group entitlement to numbers regardless either of the ability of the individual . . . or of their potential contribution to society.

This conversation of gentlemen was in full bloom now. The "causes all of us concern" could not have been uttered by Nat Colley or William Coleman, no matter how suave and patrician they were. No black man could have been secure enough in the "us" to get away with that. Cox took the opportunity to talk about qualifications, another of the emotionally charged words associated with the case.

COX: The other thing I was going to say . . . is that while it is true that Mr. Bakke and some others, under conventional standards for admission, would be ranked above the minority applicant, I want to emphasize that, . . .

there's nothing that shows that after the first two years at medical school the grade point averages will make the minority students poorer medical students, and still less to show that it makes them poorer doctors or poorer citizens or poorer people.

Justice Brennan picked up the pursuit of facts. He wanted to know if the record indicated how race was taken into account in the benchmark ratings of applicants. The vaguest area of the record was under scrutiny again. Cox could speculate that race had or had not been considered, but he didn't know. Brennan wanted to know if the benchmark scores of regular and Task Force students was comparable, but there was no way to tell. During his deposition, Dr. Lowrey had suggested that benchmark scores for the Task Force might be 30 points lower, but there had never been a comparison.

cox: There wasn't any occasion to put them on the same scale. Because if you were qualified, minority and disadvantaged, then you were eligible for one of the 16 places and there was no occasion for you to be compared with anyone in the general pool.

The California Supreme Court had based its decision on the premise that "by the university's own standards Bakke was better qualified" than Task Force students. But Cox was saying that minority applicants were judged on an entirely different set of standards and that relative qualification was not anywhere in the record despite the most common characterization of the case.

Cox's time was running out. The justices asked him about alternatives. He said that minorities were but a small segment of the disadvantaged and that only by taking race into consideration could the numbers be improved. Warren Burger wanted to know about Orientals:

BURGER: Is there . . . a specific finding in this record that Orientals, as one identifiable group, have been disadvantaged?

COX: Well, I think the decisions of this Court show better than anything else that they have been the victims of de jure discrimination over the years.

The truth was that once again the record was lacking. Cox could cite several cases involving discrimination against Asians, and the Court switched to another line of questions. They would take the issue up with McCree. What about Title VI of the Civil Rights Act of 1964, they asked Cox; could they use that to make their finding and avoid a constitutional decision?

Title VI, which forbids discrimination "on the ground of race, color, or national origin," was viewed by legal scholars as an escape valve for the Court. By ruling on the basis of a statute, the Court could avoid the thundering implications of a judgment rooted in the Constitution. But asking the university to choose its battlefield put Cox in a difficult position. If he agreed that Title VI applied, the Court might avoid the issues the university wanted them to confront.

After a few hesitant thrusts at the issue, Cox suggested he be allowed to answer in written form. A week later the Court would ask for supplemental briefs and cause a rash of speculation about its decision.

Cox asked if he could save his last few minutes for rebuttal. Burger said he had little time left, but since the Court had asked an inordinate number of questions, each side would get an additional five minutes. Cox thanked the chief justice and sat down.

The only friend of the court ordinarily allowed to make an oral argument before the Supreme Court is the government of the United States. This concession is made in recognition of the fact that some cases have an impact far beyond the interests of the parties to the dispute. Often the government's presentation is only a formality, but in a case like *Bakke,* the decision could affect millions of citizens and many important federal programs. Despite Reynold Colvin's argument that this was a simple case of one man trying to get into medical school, this disagreement involved major national policy issues.

On this day the citizens of the United States were represented by Solicitor General Wade McCree, Jr., only the second black man to hold this post; Thurgood Marshall had been the first. If McCree had not been speaking for the government, he would have been in the audience. Except for the medium brown complexion and the black, wavy crop of hair, he would have blended in easily with the high-priced attorneys in the audience.

But McCree's reputation had been seriously undermined by the controversy surrounding the Justice Department brief. He had struggled with conflicting roles as representatives of the United States and as President Carter's spokesman in the Supreme Court. He would also be the only black person to address the Court on the issue. His color made him a spokesman for blacks and other minority groups whether he liked it or not. How many bright young black men had been reminded that at a crucial moment the entire race would be accountable for their actions? Few blacks could escape this demand for racial responsibility.

McCree spoke from a prepared text, deliberately, with just a touch of the resonance found among preachers and orators. By education, achievement, and position he was formally a member of this small circle of gentlemen. But his understanding of the workings of American society and the role he was to play on this day precluded any resemblance to the informality of Cox.

MC CREE: The interest of the United States as amicus curiae stems from the fact that the Congress and the Executive branch have adopted many minority-sensitive programs that take race or minority status into account in order to achieve the goal of equal opportunity.

The final version of the government's brief had substantially supported the university's position. The government supported the use of racial classifications only to correct past discrimination. But instead of asking the Supreme Court to overrule the California decision, the government wanted it sent back for more facts.

McCree's oral argument followed the central theme of the Justice Department brief but emphasized the pervasive nature of discrimination in American life that made remedial programs necessary. He traced the history of racism through the Constitution and pointed to the crowded federal dockets as evidence of continued resistance.

MC CREE: Indeed, many children born in 1954, when *Brown* was decided, are today, 23 years later, the very persons knocking on the doors of professional schools, seeking admission, about the country. They are persons who, in many instances, have been denied fulfillment of the promise of that decision because of resistance to this court's decision that was such a landmark when it was handed down.

McCree's presentation was not the most dynamic the justices had heard, but it served to remind the Court that the country was still involved in a struggle for equality and that many victims of that struggle existed outside the sheltered atmosphere of the Court and the intellectual debate now taking place. There was one of those strange juxtapositions of history and irony here. McCree quoted a phrase he had heard at the meeting with the Congressional Black Caucus, a phrase originated by his predecessor, Robert Bork.

MC CREE: To be blind to race today is to be blind to reality.

While the solicitor general urged the Court to send the case back for evidence of prior and continuing discrimination, it was clear he did not agree with the California Supreme Court's position that such evidence should be limited to acts at the Davis Medical School. McCree reminded the Court of its decisions in cases involving school discrimination in Los Angeles, Pasadena, and San Francisco. He pointed out census data indicating that as many as 40 percent of black students in California had spent some of their school years in states that had practiced legal segregation.

Chief Justice Burger wanted to know if McCree would include evidence of conduct outside California.

MC CREE: I would include conduct throughout the nation, because we are a nation without barriers to travel, and indeed California seems to have been—seems to be currently —one of the principal recipients of the flow of population from other parts of the country. And many of them bring with them the handicaps imposed upon them by conditions to which they were subjected before they went west. We suggest that it is not enough, really, to look at the visible wounds imposed by unconstitutional discrimination based upon race or ethnic status, because the very identification of race or ethnic status in America today is, itself, a handicap. And it is something that the California University at Davis Medical School could and should properly consider in affording a remedy to correct the denial of racial justice in this nation. We submit that the Fourteenth

Amendment, instead of outlawing this, indeed should welcome it as part of its intent and purpose.

After all his expressed doubts about race-conscious programs, McCree was now making an argument some justices might have considered extremely radical. If the Davis Medical School could take into account discrimination in other states, the effects of slavery, the Black Codes, and poll taxes, was there any need to send the case back for a new trial? The solicitor general's position went unchallenged, maybe because the Court was being deferential. More likely, it found McCree's statements too radical to consider seriously.

The justices picked up on the Asian issue again. If Asian-Americans were well represented in the professions, was there any point to including them in the Task Force? The government brief had suggested they shouldn't have been and wanted the case sent back to determine the reasons.

STEVENS: Supposing the evidence shows that the reason they were included was because they had in the past been the victims of discrimination. What inference should we draw from that kind of conclusion? Would that mean the program is good or bad? Is that a sufficient justification?

McCree rambled in his response. He said the government's position was not intended to suggest that Asian-Americans should be excluded but only that the continuing impact of discrimination against the group could not be learned from the record. What Stevens seemed to be asking was whether the real intent of such programs was integration rather than the correction of past discrimination. Furthermore, many other ethnic groups not considered minorities had filed briefs arguing they, too, had been subjected to discrimination.

Again, because of the paucity of the record, the Court could not know that the Task Force considered only Asians who were disadvantaged and sent applicants whom they considered middle-class to the regular admissions committee. After some commiseration over the record, McCree found the right answer. "Asian-Americans" was such a broad category that he could not determine if discrimination had impacted equally on the diverse groups within this category. McCree closed with a brief rhetorical plea.

MC CREE: I would like to conclude that this is not the kind of case that should be decided just by extrapolating from other precedents; that we are here asking the Court to give us the full dimensions of the Fourteenth Amendment that was intended to afford equal protection. And we suggest that the Fourteenth Amendment should not only require equality of treatment, but should also permit persons who were held back to be brought up to the starting line, where the opportunity for equality will be meaningful.

McCree had turned in a commendable perfomance. He had said little that would be critical to the Court's decision, but he had managed to speak for both the president and his people without doing grave injury to either.

Of the three lawyers to address the Supreme Court that day, Reynold Colvin was the least at home. He had never been before the High Court and he had been admitted to practice before this august body only the January before. He had not been to Harvard, as had three of the justices, Cox, and McCree. He had not been to Yale, as had Stewart and White. And unlike Rehnquist, he had not gone to Stanford, the western outpost of the elite circuit. He was the son of California, that distant place of rootless people, of tinsel and tourists, of strange politics and cultures that ran against, or sometimes ahead of, the mainstream. He was not a judge or a professor but a trial lawyer, a tradesman, like the majority of lawyers whom the chief justice found little reason to respect. His speech, his carriage, and his style marked him a commoner among the gentlemen assembled at court. Colvin was obviously aware of his status as an interloper. But far from being ashamed of his position, he reveled in it.

"I would be a fool to pretend I'm a great constitutional lawyer or a social philosopher. But the facts of this particular case are very, very strong facts, and as long as I remember my place, somehow I'll get through." He had made this statement to an interviewer before he went to Washington, and it ended up being his game plan. And why shouldn't it? So far the "country lawyer from San Francisco" had beaten some very sophisticated opponents.

COLVIN: It seems to me that the first thing I ought to say to this honorable court is that I am Allan Bakke's lawyer and Allan Bakke is my client. And I do not say that in any formal or perfunctory way. I say that because this is a lawsuit. It was a lawsuit brought by Allan Bakke up at Woodland in Yolo County, California, in which Allan Bakke, from the very beginning of this lawsuit in the first paper we ever filed, stated the case. And he stated the case in terms of his individual right.

Colvin was a storyteller and this talent was useful in addressing juries. After the presentations by Cox and McCree, it jarred with the atmosphere of the Court. But Colvin had a specific reason for choosing the homespun approach. By retelling Bakke's struggle for admission, he would make the justices see the individual behind all the legal arguments. He would remind them that there was a real plaintiff who only wanted to have his rights protected from the arbitrary power of government. He had used the same approach in his brief, in which twenty-two pages were devoted to the facts of the case.

COLVIN: The name of the game is not to represent Allan Bakke as a representative of a class. We are not representing Allan Bakke as a representative of some organization. This is not an exercise in a law review argument or a bar examination question. This is a question of getting Mr. Bakke into medical school—and that's the name of the game.

Now Colvin sounded more like Robert Blake selling STP than Sam Ervin pushing American Express. His reduction of the issues to the basic level made the Court impatient. When he began a description of his efforts to move the case forward, he was interrupted by Justice Rehnquist.

REHNQUIST: But no one is charging you with *laches* [neglect of duty].

Again there was laughter in the courtroom. But unlike the joke shared with Cox, Colvin had been made the brunt of the Court's humor.

POWELL: We are here—at least I am here—primarily to hear a constitutional argument. You have devoted twenty minutes to laboring the facts, if I may say so. I would like help, I really would, on the constitutional issues. Would you address that?

Colvin's tactic of focusing attention on the facts alone seemed as unlikely to succeed as Cox's attempts to ignore the facts and get an opinion on the abstract issues. Colvin cited the laws he believed had been violated in depriving Bakke "the right to admission" at Davis.

STEWART: You spoke, Mr. Colvin, of the right to admission. You don't seriously submit that he had a right to be admitted?

COLVIN: That is not Allan Bakke's position. Allan Bakke's position is that he has a right, and that right is not to be discriminated against by reason of his race. And that's what brings Allan Bakke to this court. We have the deepest difficulty in dealing with this problem of quota, and many, many questions arise. For example, there is a question of numbers. What is the appropriate quota? What is the appropriate quota for a medical school? Sixteen, eight, 32, 64, 100? On what basis is that quota determined? And there is a problem, a very serious problem of judicial determination. Does the Court leave open to the school the right to choose any number it wants in order to satisfy that quota? Would the Court be satisfied to allow an institution such as the University of California to adopt a quota of 100 per cent and thus deprive all persons who are not within selected minority groups?

Colvin had chosen an absolute position on racial classifications. The California Supreme Court had said they were unconstitutional. This position was attractive to Bakke's attorney because he did not have to worry about conceding a point to a crafty justice only to discover he had conceded too much. But the absolute position had little support in the law. Even the California court had said only that racial classifications were wrong because less restrictive alternatives had not been tried. Such a rigid position could not be attractive to the U.S. Supreme Court, always willing to postpone taking a position on a constitutional issue. Why should it declare all race classifications illegal when it didn't have to in this case? Justice White attempted to push Colvin toward a compromise position.

WHITE: Part of your submission is: Even if these are compelling interests, even if there is no alternative, the use of the race classification is unconstitutional?
COLVIN: We believe it is unconstitutional. We do.
BURGER: Because it is limited rigidly to 16?
COLVIN: No. Not because it is limited to 16, but because the

concept of race itself as a classification becomes in our history and in our understanding an unjust and improper basis on which to judge people. We do not believe that intelligence, that achievement, that ability are measured by skin pigmentation or by the last surname of an individual, whether or not it sounds Spanish.

Colvin's absolute opposition to the use of race roused Justice Marshall, and he entered the fray with a vengeance.

MARSHALL: Your client did compete for the 84 seats, didn't he?

COLVIN: Yes, he did.

MARSHALL: And he lost?

COLVIN: Yes, he did.

MARSHALL: Now, would your argument be the same if one, instead of 16 seats, were left open?

COLVIN: Most respectfully, the argument does not turn on the numbers.

MARSHALL: My question is: Would you make the same argument?

COLVIN: Yes.

MARSHALL: If it was one?

COLVIN: If it was one and if there was an agreement, as there is in this case, that he was kept out by his race. Whether it is one, one hundred, two——

MARSHALL: I said that the regulation said that one seat would be left open for an underprivileged minority person.

COLVIN: Yes. We don't think we would ever get to that point——

MARSHALL: So numbers are just unimportant?

COLVIN: Numbers are unimportant. It is the principle of keeping a man out because of his race that is important.

MARSHALL: You are arguing about keeping somebody out and the other side is arguing about getting somebody in?

COLVIN: That's right.

MARSHALL: So it depends on which way you look at it, doesn't it?

COLVIN: It depends on which way you look at the problem.

MARSHALL: It does?

COLVIN: If I may finish. The problem——

MARSHALL: You are talking about your client's rights. Don't these underprivileged people have some rights?

COLVIN: They certainly have the right to compete——

MARSHALL: To eat cake.

The black justice's remark was a visceral reaction to Colvin's magnanimous offer to allow disadvantaged minorities the "right to compete." The reaction went to the heart of the "color-blind" argument. Colvin was offering blacks who had not yet eaten the bread of equal educational opportunities promised by the *Brown* decision the right to eat cake by competing with whites who had all the advantages. Once again it was a choice of victims.

Justice Powell offered Colvin another compromise position. What if race was just one of many factors used to select students and if Bakke had been turned down under this system, which differed from the two-track process at Davis?

COLVIN: Our argument would be the same, to the extent that race itself was the crucial matter in the admissions situation.

POWELL: Well, my hypothetical listed race as one of eight or ten factors or elements the committee might fairly weigh in the interest of diversity of a student body, for example. Would that be constitutional, in your opinion?

COLVIN: In our opinion . . . race itself is an improper ground for selection or rejection for the medical school.

If, as Reynold Colvin had claimed throughout the case, his only goal was to get his client admitted, why had he refused the very argument most favorable to his cause? If the justices had given any hint of their leanings during this grueling session, it was their search for a decision on narrow grounds. If they could avoid a ruling on race classification, they might find the program at Davis illegal anyway because of the two-track admissions process. Colvin had missed the cues and plowed ahead with his absolutist argument.

The rebuttal by Cox was brief.

cox: There is no per se rule of color blindness incorporated in the Equal Protection clause . . . the educational, professional and social purposes accomplished by race conscious admissions programs are compelling objectives, or to put it practically, they are sufficient justification for those losses, those problems that are created by the use of race . . . there is no other way of accomplishing those purposes.

Once more Cox attacked the California decision. As for Colvin's position, Cox used it to counter McCree's argument for sending the case back. Colvin was either right or wrong under the law, he was saying, and no further facts were needed to make a decision.

Cox's closing remarks returned to his theme of judicial restraint. Interference by the courts would dampen creativity and take away the independence of the universities. Cox did not mention race in his last sentences. This case involved much larger issues: the creative allocation of scarce resources and the privilege of allowing state legislatures and faculties to be free to handle the sensitive area of admissions. They could be trusted because after all, their interests were not so different from the Court's. Weren't they all gentlemen?

The session ended abruptly with Justice Burger's formal closing: "Thank you, gentlemen; the case is submitted." The time was 11:58 A.M. The nine justices rose and quickly left the courtroom.

Once again the tone of the gathering reverted to the festive and social atmosphere of the morning. Reporters surrounded Cox, who had been joined by his wife, and queried him about the fine points in his argument. The press also had questions for Colvin, but they were brief and more critical. The consensus was that Bakke's attorney had not done well. Many felt that some of the justices had been clearly sympathetic to his arguments but that he had missed the cues they offered. His abrasive tone, his insistence on the facts, and his reluctance to stray into the abstractions of the law, they felt, were not only crucial errors but additional proof that the "country lawyer from San Francisco" was ignorant of the rules of gentlemanly play. The dean of an Ivy League law school joked with his friends that the event had not been a fair fight. Maybe, he said, Bakke could appeal the ruling for lack of effective counsel.

The distinguished audience filed slowly out of the courtroom: James M. Nabrit, who had argued important civil rights cases at the side of Thurgood Marshall; his son, who now worked for the NAACP Legal Defense Fund; the widow of Chief Justice Earl Warren; Eleanor Holmes Norton, a Yale Law School graduate and chair of the Equal Employment Opportunities Commission; all those who had been fortunate enough to wangle admission to this important event. They lingered in the halls of the Court, on the steps outside, in restaurants on Capitol Hill, for one moment oblivious of the politicians, whose normal standing in the Washington spotlight had been displaced by an argument over the meaning of justice.

But in the press room reporters debated the possible results of the two-hour hearing, sifting their recollections of the event much as the Greeks had read the entrails of freshly killed animals. The reporters from major publications had pooled to pay the expenses of an unofficial reporter and they chafed at the wait for a transcript. Within hours they would sit down at desks all over Washington and attempt to make sense of an event that had not yet ended.

It is easier to review plays once the curtain has come down, or to analyze baseball games because there are winners and losers. But in this case the transcript would be a box score without a final tally. The desire of the media for firm and final resolution left little tolerance for confrontations the final outcome of which was many months away.

Ten

A GENTLEMANLY

SOLUTION

More than eight months would pass between that brisk October day when Cox, Colvin, and McCree appealed to the best judgment of the nine justices and the public announcement of the Supreme Court's decision in *Regents of the University of California* v. *Bakke*. The East Coast had survived one of the worst winters in recent memory, and the successes of the New York Yankees in the autumn before had long been forgotten. The excitement of baseball fever had drifted up the coast to Boston and the Red Sox, and most of the Yankee headlines concerned the varied personality clashes of Reggie Jackson and Billy Martin.

The public had been anticipating the *Bakke* decision since early in the year, but Court experts had predicted accurately that the opinion would not come until late in the term, as was common practice in difficult cases. Sharp divisions on the Court and the tenacious commitment of individual justices to their own positions meant that the weekly judicial conferences would not be tranquil. If there was substantial agreement on the Court, there would be an effort to persuade the dissenters to join the majority. In a case where public sentiment was so sharply divided, a unanimous Court would have a moderating influence. Chief Justice Warren had spent the better part of the 1953–54 term prodding a sharply divided Court into a unified decision outlawing segregation. Warren had avoided an early vote on the case and brought it up for discussion over coffee and lunch as well as in conference. But Chief Justice Burger lacked his predecessor's skills as a statesman, and it was not apparent that either side had even a solid majority. If the Court were evenly divided, then the two sides would struggle for the vote of the uncommitted members. It would take time to find a compromise solution on which five justices could agree and to write an opinion they all could endorse. Late in the spring a Washington newspaper reported that Justice Blackmun was overheard telling a friend, "We all wish this *Bakke* case would go away." There was also some speculation that the justices would delay their release of the decision until the last possible moment in order to avoid the brunt of the inevitable political repercussions. Student groups had organized "Anti-Bakke" demonstrations all over the country, including a march by some 10,000 people past the Supreme Court building. "The Court is going to wait until school is out," predicted a student leader, "and then run for the hills."

The U.S. Supreme Court gives no advance notice of its decisions. It may well be the last institution in Washington where a secret remains secret. But as the end of the Court's term grew near, the rumors of an impending decision in *Bakke* spread like the choicest bits of Capitol Hill gossip. Weekly, from about the middle of April, the Washington grapevine reported from "sources close to the Court" that *this* would be the week. The experts purporting to have discovered the content of the decision were not quite so numerous but just as unreliable. There was a rumor that the justices had voted 9 to 0 in favor of Bakke, a report made even less plausible by the identification of Justice Marshall as the source of this information. Another story reported that the Court would duck the issue by asking the parties to reargue a particular aspect of the case in the fall. The Court had done this in *Brown* when they were still badly split at the end of the 1953 term. But in light of the sharp criticism of the Court's avoidance of *DeFunis,* this solution seemed unlikely. Still, as the Court entered the last month of the term, the reports persisted that the split was 4 to 4 with each faction courting the vote of a usually conservative justice.

On a hot muggy Wednesday, June 29, the Court was ready to announce what one reporter, sounding suspiciously like a boxing promoter, called "one of the most anxiously awaited legal decisions of the century." The Court was approaching the end of its term and was handing down several decisions each week, but the public was interested only in *Bakke.* Reporters and camera crews had been camped out at the Court since the beginning of May, and they had grown weary of the long vigil. The first hint of the long-awaited decision was the arrival of Mrs. William Brennan and Mrs. Thurgood Marshall at a side entrance to the building. When other family members and Court employees began to drift into the courtroom, there was no doubt that the time of decision had finally arrived.

At 10:01 A.M. the nine justices pushed the velvet curtains aside and took their seats on the dais. The U.S. Supreme Court is one of the last American appellate courts to announce its decisions orally, and the presentation can range from a brief summary to a verbatim rendition of the entire opinion. After quickly disposing of two minor decisions, Chief Justice Burger announced that Justice Powell would deliver the judgment of the Court in Number 76-811.

Powell, a soft-spoken Virginia aristocrat, addressed his listeners in a conversational tone. "I will now try to explain how we divided on this issue," he began with a smile. "It may not be self-evident." There was a ripple of nervous, polite laughter. Powell noted that "perhaps no case in memory has received so much attention and scholarly commentary . . . and advice." Then, acknowledging the difficulties the Court had faced in its deliberations, he said, "As we speak today, with a notable lack of unanimity, it may be evident we needed all this advice." It was apparent that those who had predicted a closely divided Court and a Delphic decision had been proved right.

Powell was the first of five justices who read excerpts from their separate opinions from the bench. The entire process took just over an hour. The full text of the opinion, which was not made public until the justices had completed their oral pronouncements, ran in excess of 40,000 words. Six separate opinions had been filed, and no single opinion commanded the majority of the votes on the Court. Powell explained how he and his fellow justices had sifted through the competing claims and gave the results of the final vote.

The arithmetic on the final scorecard was not hard to follow. Four justices (Stevens, Burger, Stewart, and Rehnquist) had voted to order Allan Bakke admitted to the medical school at Davis. They concluded that the Task Force program had treated him unlawfully under Title VI of the Civil Rights Act of 1964. They had refused to consider the constitutional question but believed the California Supreme Court decision should be affirmed. Another four (Brennan, White, Marshall, and Blackmun) had voted to uphold the Davis admissions program. They had found that it violated neither the 1964 Civil Rights Act nor the Fourteenth Amendment of the Constitution. They felt the California decision should be reversed. Justice Powell had broken the deadlock. He voted with the first four on the issue of Bakke's admission and with the second four on the constitutionality of race-conscious affirmative action. The portion of Stanley Mosk's decision ordering Bakke admitted had been upheld 5 to 4. But the part of that decision which said that race was an unconstitutional factor in admissions had been reversed. Still, the score was the only obvious aspect of the decision. As Powell, Stevens, Brennan, Blackmun, and Marshall took turns reading portions of their opinions, it was clear that the Court had left many important questions unanswered.

Lewis F. Powell, Jr., had come to the Supreme Court in 1971. A skilled and successful corporate lawyer, he had been appointed by Richard Nixon to fill the seat vacated by the late Hugo Black. Black, an Alabamian, had proved one of the Court's strongest advocates of civil rights despite a youthful flirtation with the Ku Klux Klan. Powell, a Harvard Law School graduate, millionaire, and former president of the Richmond School Board and the American Bar Association, came to the Court with a reputation as an intelligent and thoughtful southern moderate. In six years on the Court, his frequent association with the other three Nixon appointees, Burger, Blackmun, and Rehnquist, had earned him a conservative label. But Powell had also, on occasion, displayed a sensitivity and realism about racial issues that his northern brethren did not share. In a separate opinion in the Supreme Court's first northern desegregation case, Powell had pointed out that segregation had the same harmful effect on black children whether it was practiced in the North or the South. The majority of the Court seemed to miss this obvious point in differentiating between de jure and de facto segregation.

Powell's opinion straddled the two camps in the Court. He agreed with four of his colleagues that Bakke had been wronged by the Davis Medical School. But he agreed with the other four that it was legitimate to use race as a factor in selecting applicants. Powell's penchant for compromise would make his opinion the "judgment of the Court" despite the fact that no other justice chose to sign his opinion. If anything had been settled by this massive outlay of words and positions, it would be found among the carefully chosen words of Lewis Powell. Though Powell's opinion had its poetic moments, it was characteristically the work of a legal craftsman rather than a stylist. The first twelve pages were directed to a careful recitation of the facts. He then disposed of the procedural claim by the university that Bakke did not have the right to bring suit under Title VI of the Civil Rights Act. The question had not been raised until the parties reached the Supreme Court, he said, so it was unnecessary to consider it. He would assume for purposes of this case that Bakke had a right to sue under the statute.

Powell turned to the question of whether the university's admissions program violated Title VI. He noted that the language in the statute that outlawed "discrimination" in federally funded programs, such as the phrase *equal protection of the laws,* was susceptible to varying interpretations. It was not by chance that the language of Title VI and that of the equal protection clause were equally cryptic, he argued. Congressmen supporting Title VI had "repeatedly declared that the bill enacted constitutional principles," and when opponents criticized their failure to define the term *discrimination* more precisely, they had answered that the definition would be made clear by reference to the Constitution.

It was clear, he said, that the legislators were responding to the real and pressing problem of guaranteeing minority citizens equal treatment. The pronouncements of "color blindness" referred to by Justice Stevens in his dissenting argument had "occurred in the midst of extended remarks dealing with the evils of segregation in federally funded programs." "In view of the clear legislative intent," Powell concluded, "Title VI must be held to proscribe only those racial classifications that would violate the Equal Protection Clause or the Fifth Amendment."

By finding Title VI in agreement with the equal protection clause, Powell avoided further discussion of the statute. If the Davis admissions program violated the equal protection clause, it also violated Title VI. If it was constitutional, it also satisfied Title VI.

Powell moved on to the meat of his opinion. Had the Davis program violated Bakke's right under the equal protection clause? Had Justice Mosk and the majority of the California Supreme Court been correct in concluding that the clause prohibited any consideration of an individual's race in admissions programs? Powell followed the traditional approach in his analysis of the constitutional question. He began by dismissing the debate over whether the medical school had established a "goal" or a "quota." "This semantic distinction is beside the point: the special admissions program is undeniably a classification based on race and ethnic background." Powell had made the same point during the oral argument when, after a long series of questions by Justice Stevens about the meaning of "quota," he had interjected, "Does it really matter what we call this program?"

Having established that a racial classification was involved, Powell approached the question on which California justices Mosk and Tobriner had differed, the question that legal scholars had been debating since *DeFunis*. Were all racial classifications suspect and therefore subject to the Court's highest level of scrutiny? Powell's answer was yes. "Racial and ethnic distinctions of *any sort* are suspect," he said. The fact that Bakke was not a member of a "discrete insular minority" was of no consequence. Borrowing from the reasoning of Justice Mosk and former U.S. Supreme Court justice Douglas, he argued that the United States had become "a nation of minorities." Powell rejected Tobriner's notion that racial classifications that operated against the white majority might be benign. "The concepts of majority and minority necessarily reflect temporary arrangements and political judgments," he said. "There is no principled basis for deciding which groups would merit heightened judicial solicitude and which would not." American blacks would surely question Powell's use of the word *temporary* to refer to the 300-year arrangement that continued to keep them at the bottom of the ladder. They might well argue that their struggle against discrimination had differed in both quality and quantity from that of white "minorities."

Powell went on to apply the strict scrutiny test to the case. Since the test required the state to show a purpose or interest that was both substantial and necessary, he listed the goals that the special admissions program was designed to serve. They were (1) increasing the number of traditionally disfavored minorities in medical schools and the medical profession; (2) countering the effects of societal discrimination; (3) increasing the number of physicians who will practice in communities currently underserved; and (4) obtaining the educational benefits that flow from an ethnically diverse student body.

Powell rejected the first goal as "facially invalid." "Preferring members of any one group for no reason other than race or ethnic origin is discrimination for its own sake." To the argument that the program was necessary for improving health care in underserved communities, he echoed Justice Mosk's argument that there was "no evidence in the record indicating that petitioner's special admissions program is either needed or geared to promote that goal." Even at this stage the skimpy trial court record had come back to haunt the university lawyers.

Powell's approach to the remaining goals of the university was less direct. Here he would exercise his skills as a statesman and respond to political pressures by attempting to give something to both sides. "The state certainly has a legitimate and substantial interest in ameliorating or eliminating, where feasible, the disabling effects of identified discrimination," he said, addressing the university's argument that it wanted to counter the effects of societal discrimination. Earlier Powell had made clear that he thought the use of racial classifications appropriate in school desegregation cases. But in these cases, he noted, the classifications involved were "designed as remedies for the vindication of constitutional entitlement" and "the scope of the remedies was not permitted to exceed the extent of the violation." In other words, the school cases used race to remedy the effects of discrimination found by a court. In employment cases, Powell went on, the courts had fashioned racial preferences as "remedies for constitutional or statutory violations resulting in identified, race-based injuries. . . . Such preferences have also been upheld where a legislative or administrative body charged with the responsibility made determinations of past discrimination by the industries affected and fashioned remedies deemed appropriate to rectify the discrimination."

Powell had referred to these cases to support his argument that the university's more amorphous goal of remedying "societal discrimination" was insufficient. But he had also made an important concession to the forces supporting affirmative action. If a state legislature or federal agency wanted to use race as a criterion, it had to show past discrimination that made a race-conscious remedy necessary. Powell the statesman was aware of the two-edged effect of his argument.

But the university's fourth goal would allow Powell to uphold the concept of affirmative action and still order Bakke admitted. Using a somewhat novel approach, he argued that the pursuit of a diverse student body was essential to the university's exercise of academic freedom: the right to select its own student body. Although academic freedom was not a specifically enumerated constitutional right, it had long been viewed as a special concern of the First Amendment. Because the university's purpose of achieving diversity involved the exercise of a constitutional right, it was sufficiently compelling to meet the first requirement of the strict scrutiny test.

But the second part of the test had not been met, according

to Powell. "Petitioner's argument that this is the only effective means of serving the interest of diversity is seriously flawed. The diversity that furthers a compelling state interest encompasses a far broader array of qualifications and characteristics of which racial or ethnic origin is but a single though important element," Powell went on. "The experience of other university admissions programs, which take race into account in achieving the educational diversity valued by the First Amendment, demonstrates that the assignment of a fixed number of places to a minority group is not a necessary means toward that end."

Powell then referred to the Harvard College admissions procedure as an example of an acceptable program. "In such an admissions program, race or ethnic background may be deemed a 'plus' in a particular applicant's file, yet it does not insulate the individual from comparison with all other candidates for available seats."

The special admissions program at Davis had failed the strict scrutiny test because a set number of places had been set aside, and Powell found this not "necessary." Justice Brennan would find the necessity to which Powell referred more political than constitutional. The chief advantage of the Harvard program seemed to be that it did not make its system public. In dissent Brennan wrote, "It may be that the Harvard Plan is more acceptable to the public than is the Davis 'quota.' If it is, any state, including California, is free to adopt it in preference to a less acceptable alternative. . . . But there is no [constitutional] basis for preferring a particular preference program simply because in achieving the same goals that the Davis medical school is pursuing, it proceeds in a manner that is not immediately apparent to the public."

The gentleman from Virginia had written the ultimate political opinion. He had neutralized the anti-affirmative-action forces by admitting Bakke and holding that quotas were illegal.

And he had given his friends in the academic establishment what Mr. Cox had asked for: the freedom to continue to run their business the way they pleased. It was not clear that he had given minorities anything, but he had not shut the door on them entirely. It would be possible for them to claim victory and difficult for them to say they had been ignored.

Justice John Paul Stevens had authored the opinion for the bloc of four justices who had voted to order Bakke admitted because the Davis Medical School had violated Title VI of the 1964 Civil Rights Act. Stevens, the Court's most junior member, had been appointed by Gerald Ford in 1975 to replace an ailing Justice Douglas. A moderate Republican, Stevens had a reputation as a scholar at the University of Chicago and an able circuit court judge. He had not yet established a reputation on the highest court, but in his first years he had evidenced a strong, hard-eyed independence that led him to write more than his share of separate concurrences and dissents. There was some surprise that Stevens should align himself with the conservative wing of the Court, but the *Bakke* case had made for strange bedfellows. Stevens's eagerness to decide the case on the narrowest of grounds was not uncharacteristic, and it was certainly plausible that each of the justices who had joined his opinion had done so for very different reasons.

"It is always important at the outset to focus precisely on the controversy before the Court," began Justice Stevens. "This is not a class action. The controversy is between two specific litigants." Stevens was echoing the theme that Reynold Colvin had so often repeated to the Court. The critics in the eastern establishment had panned his performance at oral argument, but the "country lawyer" had made his point well. Colvin had focused on Bakke as an individual to stress the real human injury to his client. Justice Stevens's purpose was to frame the narrowest possible question for the Court's consideration. If it was possible for the Court to decide this case without saying anything about the broader constitutional and societal issues that had so sharply divided the nation, it should do so.

With this goal in mind Stevens pointed out that the trial court had ordered the university to consider only Bakke's application without regard to his race and that the order did not include any broad prohibition against the use of race in the admissions process. "There is no outstanding injunction forbidding any consideration of racial criteria in processing applications." Said Justice Stevens, "It is therefore perfectly clear that the question whether race can *ever* be used as a factor in admissions is not an issue in this case, and that discussion of that issue is inappropriate."

In his eagerness to avoid the more far-reaching and politically volatile constitutional issue, Stevens had ignored the language in the California Supreme Court's decision which stated in no uncertain terms that *"no applicant* may be rejected because of his race," an omission that Justice Powell was quick to call to his attention.

Stevens continued. "Both petitioner and respondent have asked us to determine the legality of the university's special admissions program by reference to the Constitution. Our settled practice, however, it to avoid the decision of a Constitutional issue if a case can be fairly decided on a statutory ground."

The statutory ground that provided Stevens with a way out of the constitutional issue was the Civil Rights Act of 1964. Colvin had made it part of his original complaint and then forgotten about it until Justice Brennan had brought it up during oral argument.

Section 601 of the 1964 act provides: "No person in the United States shall, on the ground of race, color, or national

origin, be excluded from participation in, be denied the benefits of, or subjected to discrimination under any program or
activity receiving federal financial assistance."

Stevens's position was that, as an admitted recipient of federal funds, the university was in clear violation of the statute.
The university had excluded Bakke from participation in the
Task Force program because of his race, an action expressly
prohibited by the plain language of the statute. There could
be no other result, argued Stevens, unless the statute's language misstated the central intent of Congress. Stevens was
convinced that it did not. "It seems clear that the proponents
of Title VI assumed that the Constitution itself required a
color-blind standard on the part of government," he argued,
quoting sections of the *Congressional Record* for support.
Stevens had adopted the "color-blind" argument advanced by
Bakke's supporters but he had carefully avoided giving it constitutional status by attributing this interpretation of the Constitution to the Congress rather than to the Court. "Congress'
expression of its policy to end racial discrimination may in-
dependently proscribe conduct that the Constitution does not.
However, we need not decide the congruence—or lack of congruence—of the controlling statute and the Constitution since
the meaning of Title VI's ban on exclusion is crystal clear:
Race cannot be the basis of excluding anyone from participation in a federally funded program."

By confining their decision to the statute, Stevens, Burger,
Stewart, and Rehnquist had managed to say nothing about
where they stood on the issue of whether race-conscious affirmative action violated the equal protection clause of the
Fourteenth Amendment. Their insistence that Title VI required
a color-blind administration of federally assisted programs may
have been one indication of how they would have stood on
the Fourteenth Amendment, but Stevens had gone to some

length to make clear the fact that they were not expressing their own views on whether the Constitution required the same thing as the statute, and this may well have been an indication that even this group of four had joined together only after mutual compromise—that perhaps the only thing that all four agreed on was the propriety of not divulging their views on the ultimate question.

Because Justice Powell chose to say what he thought about the meaning of the equal protection clause the four justices who signed the Stevens opinion would neither agree nor disagree with anything he had said except that Bakke should be admitted. "Accordingly, I concur in the Court's judgment insofar as it affirms the judgment of the Supreme Court of California," wrote Stevens at the close of his brief and rather cryptic opinion, "to the extent that it purports to do anything else, I respectfully dissent."

There was some speculation that the opinion authored by William J. Brennan had once been a draft of the majority opinion of the Court. In several places Brennan had used the active tense usually reserved for a justice who speaks for five or more justices rather than the subjunctive normally used in concurrence and dissent. Justice Stevens had openly chided him for presuming to explain the "central meaning of today's opinion." "It is hardly necessary to state that only a majority can speak for the Court or determine what is the 'central meaning' of any judgment of the Court," wrote Stevens in his opening footnote.

Had Brennan found himself speaking for more than four justices in this crucial case on race he is likely to have been at least as much surprised as pleased. The most senior justice on the Court, he had come to the high bench in 1956 and was one of only four justices remaining from the activist Warren Court. But two of those four, Stewart and White, were often found in the chief justice's camp, and increasingly Brennan found himself dissenting in important civil rights cases with only Marshall for company.

"Our Nation was founded on the principle that 'all men are created equal' yet candor requires acknowledgment that the framers of our Constitution, to forge the thirteen colonies into one Nation, openly compromised this principle of equality with its antithesis: slavery. The consequences of this compromise are well known and have aptly been called our 'American Dilemma.' " Brennan had begun the body of his opinion by calling to mind the initial hypocrisy in America's commitment to the equality of all men. It was an appropriate introduction. For the central theme of this opinion would be that law must be more than empty words. It must ensure the actuality of equal opportunity in a society where all were not yet equal. "We cannot . . . let color blindness become a myopia which masks the reality that many 'created equal' have been treated within our lifetimes as inferior both by the law and their fellow citizens," Brennan wrote at the close of a brief history of the Fourteenth Amendment.

Having established his theme in the clear rhetorical tones of an orator, Brennan would support it with an exhaustive marshaling of legislative history and case law that ran in excess of fifty pages. His first task was to give the lie to his brothers on the Court who had argued that Title VI standing by itself barred all race-conscious efforts to extend the benefits of federally funded programs to minorities. He agreed with Powell that Title VI prohibited only those uses of racial criteria that would violate the Fourteenth Amendment. "The history of Title VI," argued Brennan, "reveals one fixed purpose: to give the executive branch of government clear authority to terminate federal funding of private programs that use race as a means of disadvantaging minorities in a manner that would be prohibited by the Constitution if engaged in by government." He followed with seven pages of references to the legislative history to support his position that Title VI was intended to help eliminate privately initiated segregation and that race-conscious affirmative action had been anticipated as a means of carrying out that purpose.

Brennan further buttressed his position on the intent of Congress by referring to the regulations that had been devised to administer the statute. In several cases the Court had recognized that such regulations were a reliable indication of congressional intent, and the Court had found regulations construing a statute particularly deserving of attention when Congress had subsequently considered the regulations and left them unaltered. Brennan cited four different HEW regulations adopted to ensure the enforcement of Title VI. Where there was evidence of past discrimination these regulations not only were permitted but required race-conscious affirmative action. Even in the absence of prior discrimination, the regulation clearly allowed the consideration of race. In adopting subsequent legislation, Brennan noted, Congress had discussed these regulations and allowed them to stand.

Congress had also made clear that it did not intend Title VI to bar consideration of race in its passage of the recent Public Works Act. That legislation explicitly required that no grants be made for any local public works project unless the applicant gives satisfactory assurance that at least 10 percent of the amount of the grant will go to minority businesses. Congress was fully aware that Title VI would apply to these federal grants. "The enactment of the 10% 'set aside' for minority enterprises reflects a congressional judgment that remedial use of race is permissible under Title VI," concluded Brennan.

Finally, Brennan pointed to the Court's own prior decisions, noting that it had interpreted Title VI to require recipients of federal funds to depart from a policy of color blindness in a case in which the San Francisco schools were ordered to provide bilingual education for Chinese children. The Court had also, Brennan said, declined to adopt a "color-blind" interpretation of the voting rights and employment discrimination statutes by upholding Court-ordered racial preferences for minorities as a remedy for Title VII violations and by permitting states voluntarily to take race into account in establishing voting districts that would fairly represent the voting strength of minority groups.

Now Brennan turned to the equal protection argument. "The position summed up by the shorthand phrase 'our constitution is color-blind' has never been adopted by this Court as the proper meaning of the Equal Protection Clause," he began. "Indeed, we have expressly rejected this proposition on a number of occasions." With a brief flurry of case citations Brennan quickly disposed of Colvin's argument that racial classifications are per se invalid under the Fourteenth Amendment.

Then, adding a new twist to traditional equal protection analysis, he rejected both Bakke's claim that racial classifications always require strict scrutiny and the university's argument that the minimal scrutiny or rational basis test should apply when the purpose of such a classification is benign. Because the Court was faced with a problem it had never before confronted, the old definitions and tests were in many respects inapplicable.

The Court's prior cases made it clear that statutes that restricted "fundamental rights" or contained "suspect classifications" must be subjected to strict scrutiny; but no fundamental right was involved here, and whites as a class had none of the "traditional indicia of suspectness." As a group, whites had not been subjected to a history of purposeful unequal treatment, nor were they in a position of political powerlessness that required the Court to protect them from the majoritarian process. Finally, this was not a case in which racial considerations should be prohibited because they were irrelevant. But Brennan was equally uncomfortable with allowing a racial classification to be shielded against any real judicial scrutiny by the rational basis test.

The test that Brennan proposed lay somewhere in between the "we'll look with our eyes closed" approach of the rational basis test and the "hanging judge" approach of the strict scrutiny test. It was a test the Court had used in cases involving sex discrimination and statutes that discriminated against illegitimate children. In those cases the Court had held that the classification involved "must serve important governmental objectives and must be substantially related to the achievement of those objectives." Elaborating on this test in order to account for the "significant risk that racial classifications established for ostensibly benign purposes can be misused," Brennan proposed that to justify a benign racial classification, "an important articulated purpose for its use must be shown." Then he added that "any statute must be stricken that stigmatizes any group or that singles out those least well represented in the political process to bear the brunt of a benign program." This last requirement was designed to quell the fears that discrete white minority groups might be singled out for less favorable treatment.

Having stated his new test, Brennan spent the next ten pages of his opinion in another exhaustive chronicling of the law in support of his position that the Davis Medical School's stated purpose of remedying the effects of past societal discrimination was sufficiently important to justify the use of a race-conscious admissions program. One passage in this generally compelling analysis is worth special note because it places Bakke's claim in a perspective that has been lost amid the cries of "reverse discrimination." Brennan wrote, "If it was reasonable to conclude—as we hold it was—that the failure of minorities to qualify for admission at Davis under regular procedures was due principally to the effects of past discrimination, then there is a reasonable likelihood that, but for pervasive racial discrimination, respondent would have failed to qualify for admission even in the absence of Davis' special admissions program."

Brennan closed, first, by echoing Justice Tobriner's sentiments that the alternatives to considering race proposed by the majority of the California Supreme Court were fraudulent, and second, by exposing Justice Powell's baseless distinction between Davis's "quota" and what would surely become known as "the Harvard Plan":

"Davis' special admissions program cannot be said to violate the Constitution simply because it has set aside a predetermined number of places for minority applicants rather than using minority status as a positive factor to be considered in evaluating the applications of minority applicants. For purposes of constitutional adjudication, there is no difference between the two approaches. In any admissions program which accords special consideration to disadvantaged racial minorities, a determination of the degree of preference to be given is unavoidable, and any given preference that results in the exclusion of a white candidate is no more or less constitutionally acceptable than a program such as that at Davis."

That an opinion as strong as Brennan's should be joined by White and Blackmun as well as Marshall was perhaps the most encouraging note of the decision for minorities. Blackmun had been the biggest surprise for those who did not look past his rather consistent alliance with Burger on most issues. But for those who had followed the case closely, the Minnesota Republican's vote had come as less of a shock. While Blackmun was considered a "conservative" and a "strict constructionist," his record in the area of race and civil rights had been moderate. He had written for the majority in decisions that had given more protection to aliens and joined Brennan and Marshall in dissenting from the Court's decision in a California case which upheld a state constitutional amendment that had the effect of keeping blacks and poor people out of the suburbs.

It was Blackmun who had asked Cox whether racial preferences were not similar to athletic scholarships, and during oral argument in the *DeFunis* case he had asked a similar question, inquiring whether it would not be appropriate for a professional school to give preference to an applicant from an underserved geographic location. Blackmun's ten years as general counsel to the Mayo Clinic, located in his hometown of Rochester, Minnesota, had no doubt made him more aware of the peculiar problems connected with medical school admissions than were many of his brothers in the Court.

In a separate opinion Blackmun added some observations to the joint opinion written by Brennan. Repeating the theme he had pressed in oral argument, he said, "It is somewhat ironic to have us so deeply disturbed over a program where race is an element of consciousness, and yet to be aware of the fact, as we are, that institutions of higher learning . . . have given conceded preferences up to a point to those possessed of athletic skills, to children of alumni, to the affluent who may bestow their largesse on the institution, and to those having connections with celebrities, the famous, and the powerful."

And then, in an eloquent closing, he rephrased the words of Bork and McCree. "I suspect that it would be impossible to arrange an affirmative action program in a racially neutral way and have it successful. . . . In order to get beyond racism, we must first take account of race. There is no other way. And in order to treat some persons equally, we must treat them differently. We cannot—we dare not—let the Equal Protection Clause perpetrate racial supremacy."

There could be little doubt that Thurgood Marshall's presence at the secret deliberations of the Court had a profound effect on those deliberations and on the final decision. It is difficult to ignore the reality of race in America with a black man looking you in the eye. And Justice Marshall would not have been shy about verbally reminding his colleagues of that reality if for some his presence were not enough. His "to eat cake" exchange with Colvin at oral argument was evidence of the fact that age and position had not blinded Marshall to the plight of his people.

He had not been able to argue this case in Court, as he had in *Brown,* but as their peer his influence on the justices could be even greater. Behind the closed doors of the Supreme Court conference room and in private chats with his colleagues he was not limited by the same restrictions of time, form, and deference.

There were limits to what Marshall could do, for this was a different Court and a different issue from *Brown.* But his presence surely had far greater impact than his single vote. His hand was clearly evident in the joint opinion authored by Brennan. And no member of the Court dared offer the empty alternatives proffered by Mosk and the California Supreme Court. In his own separate opinion, Marshall articulated the thoughts of millions of black Americans. Unlike the other members of the Court, Marshall could not differentiate between the laws of the country and the treatment of blacks under those laws. "Three hundred and fifty years ago, the Negro was dragged to this country in chains to be sold into slavery," Marshall began. "Uprooted from his homeland and thrust into bondage for forced labor, the slave was deprived of all legal rights." Marshall was establishing the unique status of blacks in America, an experience that had been deliberately blurred by opponents of affirmative action and by members of the Court who argued that blacks were just one more ethnic group.

He reminded the Court of its own responsibility in relegating blacks to inferior status. "The position of the Negro slave as mere property was confirmed by this Court in *Dred Scott* v. *Sandford,* holding that the Missouri Compromise—which prohibited slavery in the portion of the Louisiana Purchase territory north of the Missouri—was unconstitutional because it deprived slaveowners of their property without due process." He noted that the Court had concluded that blacks were not intended to be regarded as citizens but were "regarded as beings of an inferior order . . . altogether unfit to associate with the white race, either in social or political relations: and so far inferior that they had no rights which the white man was bound to respect."

Marshall then traced the repeated failure of the Supreme Court to protect the rights of blacks after Emancipation, noting that even *Brown,* the case to which he had devoted most of his legal career, "did not automatically end segregation" or "move Negroes from a position of legal inferiority to one of equality."

"The position of the Negro today in America is the tragic but inevitable consequence of centuries of unequal treatment," he continued. "Measured by any benchmark of comfort or achievement, meaningful equality remains a distant dream for the Negro." Marshall's value to the Court once again was to touch on the reality of the black existence in America, a reality often lost in the efforts of the other justices to find a politically acceptable solution. "It is unnecessary in twentieth century America to have individual Negroes demonstrate that they have been victims of racial discrimination," wrote the Supreme Court justice whose color might still disqualify him from membership in some of Washington's most exclusive private clubs. "The racism of our society has been so pervasive that none, regardless of wealth or position, has managed to escape its impact.

"It is more than a little ironic," Marshall concluded, "that after several hundred years of class-based discrimination against Negroes, the Court is unwilling to hold that a class-based remedy for that discrimination is permissible."

Even as the justices attempted to explain the convolutions of their opinions, the major news organizations rushed to inform the world. In the early minutes the desire to score a "beat" outweighed the prudence required by such a complicated decision. The Associated Press scored a six-minute "beat" over UPI with a flat declaration that Allan Bakke had won his case. The wire service would spend the rest of the morning attempting to explain its initial bulletin.

It was just a few minutes after seven on the West Coast when the *CBS Morning News* was interrupted so correspondent Terry Drinkwater could inform early-morning viewers about the decision. Allan Bakke had won, Drinkwater told his audience, and the Supreme Court had outlawed racial quotas. "Some of these quotas are called affirmative action," he rambled with uncharacteristic partisanship. "But the important thing is—Allan Bakke won." On the other side of Los Angeles, the struggling *Herald-Examiner*'s morning edition would scream, "Bakke Wins." If the initial reports were something less than objective, it was a reflection of the perception in some quarters that the rights of white men were under siege. In the Washington bureau of the *New York Times*, an editor glanced at the wire stories about the decision and declared, "Well, that's one for our side."

As the news organizations scrambled to formulate more accurate assessments of the decision, various interests rushed to claim victory. A flock of reporters had been camped on the street outside the home of the most important figure in the case since the night before. But Allan Bakke remained true to his decision to avoid public comment about the case. He dashed out of his home with a newspaper over his face, slid behind the wheel of his Volkswagen Rabbit with only a mumbled acknowledgment that he had heard the Court's decision, and drove to work at NASA. He would leave it to his attorneys to declare that he was pleased with the outcome and that he intended to attend medical school in the fall.

Across the bay in Berkeley, University of California president David Saxon addressed a packed news conference. "I consider it a victory for the University of California," he declared. "The overall bulk of our admissions programs appear to be entirely lawful." Some days later university lawyers would issue guidelines to all branches of the institution about revisions in their affirmative action programs.

In Washington, Attorney General Griffin Bell said he and President Carter regarded the decision as a "great gain for affirmative action." Bell told White House reporters, "That is what we thought the law was."

In New York, Benjamin Hooks, the executive director of the NAACP, called the decision "a clear-cut victory for voluntary affirmative action." Hooks said he was disappointed that Bakke had won, but he added that he saw a strong ray of hope in the Court's decision. Urban League head Vernon Jordan also looked for the silver lining: "The most important thing is that a majority of the Supreme Court backed the use of race as a permissible factor in affirmative action programs."

But not all minority spokesmen viewed the decision with such immediate optimism. Operation PUSH president Jesse Jackson viewed the decision as part of a national move "to the right" and suggested that minorities might organize boycotts or sit-ins to emphasize their concerns. His reservations were echoed by Representative Parren Mitchell, chairman of the Congressional Black Caucus, who said the group's members were not pleased but did not view the outcome as "the death knell for affirmative action."

The greatest outrage at the decision was expressed by the groups that had organized to campaign against the case. The National Committee to Overturn the Bakke Decision and the Anti-Bakke Decision Coalition overcame their internal political differences to denounce jointly the Court's finding as "a bad decision with potentially devastating impact on race relations in this country." Within hours chapters of the organizations staged protests in a number of major cities.

Even the Jewish organizations, which had opposed any use of racial consideration, could find comfort in the decision. Arnold Forster, general counsel of the Anti-Defamation League of B'nai B'rith, said his organization was "comforted that, once and for all, the United States Supreme Court has held that racial quotas are flatly illegal."

The central message to the public seemed to be that everybody had won. Many commentators referred to the "Solomonic decision" of the Court and declared that the justices had given "half a loaf" to each side. The liberal position was that this decision was the best one possible because quotas were clearly indefensible and because the tenuous support for affirmative action was the most that could be hoped for. But many of the black spokesmen would begin to develop reservations as they analyzed the decision more carefully. They realized that the decision made affirmative action permissible and not mandatory. The white majority which Justice Powell suggested did not exist would be allowed to continue to provide minorities with access to the mainstream as long as it desired. But what the minorities recognized was that the *Bakke* case reflected a growing sense among the more fortunate that the poor had been given enough. In the words of pollster Mervin Field, "It has become much more acceptable to be less generous."

Because of the narrow scope of the decision, it was not immediately apparent what its effect would be in the important area of employment. But even if the Court upheld laws mandating affirmative action in employment, minorities had to worry about a possible translation of the national mood into congressional action. Already, conservative members of Congress had introduced legislation to undercut the government's ability to enforce affirmative action requirements.

None of America's traditional victims would be winners in the *Bakke* case. The Court had by the slimmest of margins held affirmative action programs permissible under certain circumstances, but there was no guarantee that white Americans would choose to continue these programs, which had only just begun to bring equal opportunity to racial minorities. Allan Bakke had been admitted to medical school, but while he had become a symbol for America's "forgotten" white men, Bakke, with his $28,000 NASA salary and engineer's degree, was hardly representative of the poor and working-class whites who the polls showed identified with him so strongly. And few of them would gain by his "victory."

The real winners had been the country's economically and educationally privileged. Mr. Cox had asked that the Court not interfere with the university's right to choose its students as it saw fit. Not only had his request been granted, but his own school, Harvard, the pinnacle of the academic elite, had been pointed to as the example of the way things should be done.

Shortly after the Court's decision, Derrick Bell, the Harvard Law School's first black professor and the author of a text on racism in American law, noted that once again the legitimate frustrations and angers of the majority of white Americans had been displaced onto blacks. At most schools minority admissions programs provided token access by minorities to an admissions process heavily weighted toward the upper classes. Poorer whites, Bell pointed out, considering their virtual exclusion from elite educational institutions, had every reason to complain, but the concern and hostility of whites focused not on the general admissions process and the most favored status it provided for well-to-do applicants but on the minuscule number of seats set aside for minorities.

"Opposition to racial quotas has been the slogan," said Bell, "but retention of superior societal status based on race has been the goal. Otherwise, why challenge a minority admissions procedure accounting for ten percent of the seats when class-based standards equally exclusionary for all but a few account for 90 percent of the seats?"

The Court had failed to address itself to the issues at the core of the national debate provoked by Bakke. By their silence, the justices who took the Stevens position alleging a violation of Title VI had sidestepped the serious questions raised about the meaning of race and the scope of racial problems still existing in the United States. And because of Justice Powell's concern about responding to the most immediate political pressures, he too had written an opinion that had avoided any clear position on the nature of the Constitution's commitment to resolving the American Dilemma of race and equality. Only the four justices who had joined the Brennan opinion had seen fit to confront the reality that a history of American racism had left the country divided by race and opportunity. The question of the meaning of the equal protection clause could not be answered without a decision on what equality meant. Did the Constitution require a maintenance of the existing inequities of opportunity, or did it require a fundamental readjustment of those opportunities?

Ultimately the greatest impact of the Court's decision would be outside the bounds of the laws it had handed down. Americans had looked to this respected and still-hallowed institution for guidance on a difficult and troubling issue. The justices had been aware of the most melodramatic aspects of the case and had done their best to sidestep the most obvious pitfalls by refusing to entangle themselves in semantic problems such as "goals," "quotas," and "qualifications." After all, one reason the Court had maintained its aura in a time of growing mistrust of government was its very cautious approach to jurisprudence. Even the favorite term of the meritocrats and journalists, *reverse discrimination,* was referred to only once in the massive opinions, and Justice Powell took care to wrap it in quotation marks.

It is not a little ironic that the script for this legal melodrama was little more than a reasonable facsimile of what had really transpired at Davis. Much of the Court's decision had turned on crucial "facts" that had become a part of the record through the stipulations and omissions of the university. Powell had held that the Task Force program constituted an unconstitutional quota because the record showed that whites were not allowed to compete for seats in the special admissions program while minorities were considered for every seat in the class. But a full examination of the admissions process as it actually operated raises considerable doubt whether either of these "facts" was true.

The final decision to order Bakke's admission was compelled because the university had conceded its inability to prove that Bakke would not have been admitted if the special admissions program did not exist. This concession had clearly been influenced as much by the university's anxiety to get to the Supreme Court and avoid a close examination of its admissions practices as by its belief that it could not meet the burden of proof.

Despite the fact that Justice Powell's opinion represented the views of only one member of the Court, schools throughout the country looked to his words for guidance in revamping their minority admissions programs. They argued that it was all they had to go on and that since Powell had taken such pains to chart a "middle course," it made perfect sense for them to follow his lead. But the lack of a clear majority position also provided a perfect excuse for institutions that wanted to rid themselves of minority admissions. They could argue that because of the murky nature of the Supreme Court's decision, they had to choose a conservative interpretation to avoid further legal challenges.

At some schools special committees for minority applicants were eliminated. On other campuses the definition of *disadvantaged* was broadened to include whites. Others tried to balance traditional admissions criteria with new ones that took race and economic background into consideration.

The new admissions procedure at Davis, introduced in the fall of 1978, sought that elusive "middle course." Under a computer-graded point system, applicants had to score at least 15 out of a possible 30 points to make the first cut. Points were awarded primarily on the basis of grades and test scores. Minority applicants automatically received an additional 5 points. Students who claimed to be disadvantaged also received 5 points and were asked to submit a brief written description of the nature of their disadvantage.

The 2,000 applicants to survive the first cut then were considered by a series of subcommittees. The first committee examined the credentials of applicants. A second group interviewed applicants, and a third subcommittee made the final decision on admission or rejection. Interestingly, the new plan took away the medical school dean's power to admit students at his own discretion.

But the decision ordering Bakke admitted legitimized the concept of a majority discriminating against itself, and there was a danger that zealots opposed to this practice would harm genuine efforts toward equality. If there was a serious omission by the Court, it was the failure to address the national mood which lurked around the edges of the stage on which the Bakke affair was played. The justices, no matter what their political or legal positions on the issues, surely could have addressed this important element in the melodrama and declared the continuing commitment of America to a real and tangible equality for all its citizens. By their failure to chastise the hecklers in the audience, they had given opponents of affirmative action the courage to continue their campaign.

Minority groups had sought some guarantee from the Court that the process of amelioration begun in the last decade would continue. But this was not a Supreme Court that wanted the role of protector which the Warren Court had accepted courageously. The frail majorities in this decision said simply that efforts to bring minorities closer to equality were allowable under the laws of the land. This caution, too, was in keeping with the traditions of this Court in avoiding a leadership role in the formulation of a national consensus. The broader issues of class and privilege sidestepped this time would undoubtedly come back to the Court in future cases.

For the time being, medical schools would continue to favor the children of the wealthy and exclude thousands of well-qualified applicants of all races. Just a few months before the decision, the *New York Times* had reported on a growing pattern of abuses of the admissions process by wealthy parents attempting to avoid the stiff competition for places. A study by Grace Ziem at Harvard University of the composition of medical students at U.S. universities shows that the percentage of students below the national median income has remained at 12 since 1920. It would probably have been unreasonable to assume that the Court would address the most serious problems of the medical profession which are rooted at least as much in class issues as in the racial history of this country. The exorbitant costs of medical care would not at all be affected, nor the basic nature of that care. The decision would have little impact on the infant mortality rate in the black and Hispanic ghettos of the country and would not visibly alter the racial makeup of the medical profession. While the chances for whites of being admitted into their desired professions had not been changed much by the *Bakke* decision, the ruling would clearly have a negative impact on the opportunities for minorities. The Supreme Court had attempted to find a neutral ground for a political decision, but because there could be no "benign" solution, the justices had not strayed from the traditions of America in their choice of victims.

Eleven

AFTER BAKKE: QUOTAS
AND A WHITE CLUB
BY THE BAY

Reporters have grown fond of referring to the *Bakke* case as "perhaps the most important Supreme Court decision since *Brown* v. *Board of Education*." In the 1954 *Brown* decision, the Court declared segregated school systems unconstitutional because they deprived black schoolchildren of the opportunity for an equal education. The decision itself was a narrow one; it did not outlaw all segregation but applied only to segregated schools. Only school systems where segregation was sanctioned by law were compelled to desegregate, and that was to be accomplished with "all deliberate speed." The narrow score and cautious tenor of the decision were dictated by the Court's sensitivity to the southern temperament and by Chief Justice Earl Warren's desire to achieve a unanimous ruling on the controversial case. The decision to treat the South gently meant that segregated school systems remained virtually intact for ten years following the decision.

But the importance of the *Brown* decision cannot be measured simply by its scope or the success of its implementation. Despite the Court's effort to limit the language of *Brown,* it became clear that the decision had, in effect, declared illegal all forms of state-sanctioned segregation. The Court went on to rely on *Brown* to declare unconstitutional segregated municipal buses, public parks and beaches, public golf courses, and other government-owned services and facilities.

Even more important was the fact that *Brown* spawned the mass movement for racial equality by declaring that the Constitution was squarely on the side of the struggle for equality and human rights. Equality was not just a gift to be bestowed by whites, but a birthright. Less than a year after the decision, Rosa Parks, a forty-three-year-old seamstress in Montgomery, Alabama, refused to give up her seat to a white man and sparked a yearlong boycott of public transportation led by Martin Luther King, Jr. The success of Montgomery led to other boycotts throughout the South. In 1960 college students launched the second stage of the movement with sit-ins at segregated lunch counters in North Carolina. The all-out campaign for civil rights had begun.

But while the Supreme Court had outlawed segregation in publicly owned facilities, lunch counters, hotels, barbershops, movies, and restaurants were privately owned and protected from court action by a constitutional rule called the state action doctrine. In 1883, in the Civil Rights Cases, the Supreme Court had struck down a provision of the federal Civil Rights Law of 1875 which had outlawed racial discrimination in inns, public conveyances, theaters, and other places of public amusement. The Court had said the Fourteenth Amendment applied only when the *state* deprived an individual of equal protection and said the law did not apply to wrongs that blacks might suffer at the hands of private individuals.

This decision was an invitation to discrimination by making it clear that government would do nothing to interfere with the discriminatory practices of individuals. The courts were also inactive in protecting the right of blacks to vote. The civil remedies for discriminatory administration of election laws depended on private litigation and even when a complainant could be found, the problems of collecting evidence or securing a favorable verdict in southern communities were insurmountable. But in 1963 the campaign of nonviolent confrontation with southern segregation reached its peak. National television audiences saw "Bull" Connor's troops use dogs, hoses, and cattle prods against children. When three little black girls were killed by a bomb in a Birmingham church, President Kennedy could no longer remain silent. His televised speech to the country challenged America to make freedom a reality for blacks as well as whites. "We are confronted primarily with a moral issue," he declared. "It is as old as the Scriptures and is as clear as the Constitution. If an American, because his skin is dark, cannot eat lunch in a restaurant open to the public; if he cannot send his children to the best public schools available; if he cannot vote for the public officials who represent him; if, in short, he cannot enjoy the full and free life which all of us want, then who among us would be content to have the color of his skin changed and stand in his place?"

A week after this extraordinary speech, Kennedy sent to Congress a comprehensive Civil Rights Bill. But it would take his assassination in Dallas, the killing of a white woman, Viola Liuzzo, in Alabama, massive marches in Washington and Selma, and the arm-twisting tactics of a southern president to enact the Civil Rights Act of 1964. The act outlawed discrimination in public accommodations, federally assisted programs, education, and employment. The relatively weak voting rights provisions were substantially strengthened by the Voting Rights Act in 1965. The mood of the country—despite some strong resistance—was one that supported equality for blacks, and Congress reflected that mood with a willingness to support Johnson's Great Society legislation.

Southerners quickly challenged the new legislation in the courts. The Supreme Court, however, supported the national mood in two public accommodations cases, avoiding the state action doctrine and declaring that racial discrimination in public places affected interstate commerce. In the two cases, *Heart of Atlanta Motel* v. *United States* and *Katzenbach* v. *McClung*, the Supreme Court made it clear that it was reversing its long-standing acquiescence in discrimination.

The High Court went on to affirm the Voting Rights Act in *South Carolina* v. *Katzenbach* and declared that "the time for deliberate speed has run out on school desegregation. The Court struck down freedom-of-choice plans and placed the burden on school boards "to come forward with a plan that promises realistically to work now."

Because the initial confrontations following the *Brown* decision had centered on desegregation and the vote, the employment provisions of the 1964 Civil Rights Act, Title VII, had received little attention. But it soon became clear that Title VII was the most radical provision of the 1964 law, for it contained the only hope of eradicating the economic caste system which placed blacks on the lowest rung of the employment ladder.

Title VII prohibited an employer from hiring, firing, promoting, or in any other way discriminating against an employee on the basis of race, color, religion, sex, or national origin. It also prohibited any segregation or classification of employees or applicants that would deprive the individual of employment opportunities or in any other way affect his or her status adversely. The act, originally applied to private employers, was amended to cover government employers in 1972 and also affected labor unions, employment agencies, and job-training programs.

It was not until 1971 that the Supreme Court addressed the legality of Title VII. *Griggs* v. *Duke Power Company* involved a class action suit brought by blacks working at the Dean River power-generating facilities operated by Duke in

Draper, North Carolina. Before Title VII became effective, the company had openly discriminated in hiring and assigned all blacks to the labor department, where the highest-paying jobs paid less than the lowest salaries in the other four departments.

In 1965 the power company had discontinued the overt policy of restricting blacks but, for the first time, made graduation from high school and satisfactory performance on two professionally prepared aptitude tests a condition for employment in the more desirable departments. White employees who had been hired prior to the adoption of the new requirements were allowed to continue working in the higher-paying departments and were promoted whether or not they had been graduated from high school and without having to take the new tests.

According to the 1960 census, only 12 percent of black males in North Carolina had graduated from high school, compared to 34 percent of white males. It was not surprising that 58 percent of the whites and only 6 percent of blacks who took the test passed. A crucial factor in the case was that neither of the aptitude tests measured the ability to learn or perform the jobs the company had to offer.

The federal district court that considered the case found that Title VII had not been violated and said that the law was not intended to be retroactive or to apply to discrimination in the past or to the impact of past discrimination on the racial composition of the company's work force, and the court of appeals agreed.

But the U.S. Supreme Court reversed the lower court's decision. The Court said the intent of Congress in enacting Title VII was clear: "It was to achieve equality of employment opportunity and remove barriers that have operated in the past to favor an identifiable group of white employees over other employees." Under the act, said Chief Justice

Warren Burger, writing for a unanimous Court, "practices, procedures or tests neutral on their face, and even neutral in terms of intent, cannot be maintained if they operate to 'freeze' the status quo of prior discriminatory employment practices.

"Congress has now provided that tests or other criteria for employment or promotion may not provide equality of opportunity only in the sense of the fabled offer of milk to the stork and the fox. On the contrary, Congress has now required that the posture and condition of the job seeker be taken into account. It has—to resort again to the fable—provided that the vessel in which the milk is proffered be one all seekers can use. The act proscribed not only overt discrimination but also practices that are fair in form but discriminatory in operation. The touchstone is business necessity. If an employment practice which operates to exclude Negroes cannot be shown to be related to job performance, the practice is prohibited," the Court asserted. "Good intent or absence of discriminatory intent does not redeem employment procedures or testing mechanisms that operate as headwinds for minority groups and are unrelated to measuring job capability."

Although the Court was technically just interpreting the provisions of the statute, its reasoning recognized a reality that had never before been articulated in its decisions. After 200 years of oppression, the Court said, equality could not be achieved by simply removing the mechanisms of political domination. It was fraudulent to speak of "neutral requirements" or a "fair contest" when a contestant had suffered the consequences of this oppression. The *Griggs* opinion also recognized that any requirement of intent would destroy any chances of achieving equal opportunity. Intent would be almost impossible to prove, especially since employers knew that racial discrimination was illegal. The new business necessity test assumed that any requirement that excluded blacks for reasons not related to the job had a discriminatory intent. In addition, intent was really irrelevant since the purpose of the law was not to punish evil employers but to ensure the removal of the barriers to equal employment.

The decision of the Supreme Court to look at results makes the *Griggs* case its most radical and far-reaching decision on the issue of race. The Court recognized that a conversion to a nonracist society required the removal of barriers much more complex and subtle than laws. Once it was demonstrated that the employer was using a test or requirement that had the effect of excluding minorities or maintaining the status quo, the burden was on the employer to prove there was a business reason for this practice. If *Brown* established racial equality in principle, *Griggs* required it in fact.

San Francisco is an unlikely setting for racial conflict. There is little evidence here, even in the poorest neighborhoods, of the bombed-out blocks of the South Bronx or the rows of deserted houses in Philadelphia or Detroit. The neighborhoods are culturally distinct: the Mission, with its Latin flavor and "English spoken here" signs; the Fillmore, still predominantly black but turning over to gay and white; North Beach, where the Chinese are replacing the Italians. But racial tensions are remarkably low. Whites, blacks, browns, and yellows move easily within integrated neighborhoods and interracial couples rarely attract attention. There is little evidence now of the attitude of twenty-five years ago when Nob Hill's famous Mark Hopkins Hotel had to clear its dining room of all white patrons before seating the family of one of the city's most prominent black doctors. San Franciscans today would find it difficult to believe that Willie Mays had so much trouble finding a house when the Giants abandoned New York in 1958.

Poverty is also well disguised in San Francisco. Tourists gape out of bubble-topped charter buses and never see a slum. The only obvious poverty is the self-imposed version among the remnants of the Haight-Ashbury counterculture.

But there is one section of San Francisco that has neither the look nor the feel of the rest of the city. Bayview-Hunters Point is on the southeastern tip of the city, isolated from more affluent and picturesque areas by the barrier of Highway 101. Chinatown may be the only ghetto that is a tourist attraction, but few casual visitors ever see the city's only nonintegrated black enclave. The best parts of Hunters Point look like neighborhoods in a slightly seedy southern town, but the barracks-like projects, built for the influx of blacks who worked in the shipyards during World War II, make it clear that this is what the social planners call the inner city. And it was here that another kind of racial conflict would bring up the question of "quotas," in a different context from the *Bakke* case.

For years the San Francisco Fire Department had operated as an exclusive white club. In 1967 the department had just one black member. Most of the fire fighters were Irish Catholic, and they ran the department like a family business, passing the jobs from father to son and from uncle to nephew. At one time in the city's history this might have been a reflection of the ethnic makeup of San Francisco. But according to the 1970 census, 43 percent of the city's population consisted of minority groups (15 percent black, 23 percent Asians, and 5 percent others). The city's high schools were more than 60 percent nonwhite. In the summer of 1969 a newspaper article had disclosed that there were only four black firemen in San Francisco. City fire fighters were well paid, and the twenty-four-hour shift system meant they worked only a three-day week, which gave them time to moonlight in second jobs. To the residents of Hunters Point, these jobs seemed very desirable, and they wanted to get more blacks in.

Another community concern was safety. After the riots of 1966, white firemen had declared that they were afraid to venture into Hunters Point and other black areas of the city. The residents were angered and naturally concerned that a result of the segregated fire department would be unanswered alarms and a loss of lives and property in their communities.

It took some time to collect the data, to find complainants, and to prepare the case, but in August 1970 the NAACP Legal Defense Fund and the California Rural Legal Assistance program joined the Neighborhood Legal Assistance in a suit against the San Francisco Civil Service Commission on behalf of the Western Addition Community Organization, the NAACP, and the Mexican-American Political Association. The complaint said the organizations represented "all Negro and Mexican-American San Francisco area adults fully qualified to be firemen" and "all Negro and Mexican-American San Francisco adults desirous of having their homes protected by an integrated department." The suit charged that the written examination used to select firemen violated the plaintiffs' rights to due process and equal protection of the laws.

WACO v. *Alioto* was an example of the kind of lawsuit that would become commonplace in the 1970s, attacking patterns and practices that had long been taken for granted and demanding a redistribution of opportunity and a more equal share of the nation's jobs. The cases aroused opposition among whites, like Bakke, for whom affirmative action programs amounted to reverse discrimination.

Although the U.S. Supreme Court's decision in *Regents* v. *Bakke* related to race-conscious admissions programs in the country's graduate schools and colleges, several of the justices had drawn analogies to employment cases. The Court had already agreed to hear several important job discrimination cases in the 1978–79 term, and the *Bakke* decision would ultimately have its greatest impact on the nation's working men and women.

Any measure of black opinion reports that employment is the primary concern. For the past twenty-five years, black unemployment has stayed nearly double the white rate, no matter what the economic situation. In 1966 the median non-white income was equal to the median white income in 1947. A 1967 study of poverty among nonwhites found that even when one discounted such variables as differences in education, "the sheer fact of being black explained 38 percent of the difference between the incidence of poverty for whites and Negroes." But while the pattern of economic exclusion was clear, the first stages of the struggle for equality did little to address these issues.

The Supreme Court's reasoning in *Griggs* was the basis of WACO's suit against San Francisco's all-white fire department. At the crux of the case was the city civil service examination results, used to fill vacancies in the department. Although applicants were also required to take an athletic ability test and a medical examination, the results merely determined minimal requirements. The sole factor in determining an applicant's position on the hiring list was his score on the written test.

The minority applicants complained that the written test was discriminatory because it was unrelated to the job of fire fighting and served as a barrier to minorities in competing for positions in the fire department. The exam's emphasis was on math, verbal ability, and reading comprehension. While 47 percent of the 150 questions tested these skills, 16 percent related to the general knowledge of mechanics and the physical properties of various materials, 11 percent to basic chemistry and physics, and 13 percent to responses in situations with which a fireman might be confronted. An item on one exam depicted a famous painting and asked the applicant to identify the artist. Perhaps a fire fighter might have to choose one day between saving a Van Gogh or a Cézanne, but the question seemed somewhat removed from "business necessity."

The job required physical ability and the capacity to perform under stress, the suit argued, but not mathematical, verbal, and reading skills. The emphasis of the examination and its weight in the selection process seemed misplaced. In fact, a report from the National Board of Underwriters had recommended that a written examination should constitute no more than 30 percent of the factors in selecting firemen. But San Francisco's fire department had chosen to ignore this recommendation.

The negative impact of the test on minority applicants was illustrated by the result of examinations given in December 1968. Just 101 of the 1,883 applicants allowed to take the test after meeting the physical, medical, and character investigations were black. Of the 662 who passed the test, 12 were black. Of the 350 who qualified for the hiring list, just 3 were black, and they ranked 239th, 304th, and 308th. Since 160 men would be hired from the list, none of the blacks would qualify for the fire department. On the basis of the *Griggs* decision, the department had to show that the test was related to the actual task of fire fighters, or it was illegal under Title VII.

On July 23, 1970, the lawyers at Public Advocates, the public interest firm now representing the minority organizations, filed a motion in the federal district court in San Francisco to stop the city's Civil Service Commission from using the results of the 1968 test and from using its format in future examinations.

The judge hearing the case was William Sweigert, a seventy-year-old Republican who had been appointed to the federal bench by President Eisenhower in 1959. A product of San Francisco's parochial school system, he had many old friends in the largely Irish-Catholic fire department hierarchy, and he was reluctant to find them directly at fault. Throughout the litigation, Sweigert would give the city every benefit of doubt, ruling against the defense only when the evidence was uncontradicted and when the law clearly allowed no other result.

Sweigert's initial response to the suit was to delay the administration of the written examination and request the city to devise a new, fairer test. But in the three years and numerous court hearings that followed, the Civil Service Commission seemed content to do little more than procrastinate and make excuses. Two new tests were proposed, but each test proved almost as discriminatory as, and no more job-related than, its predecessor. Sweigert considered the imposition of a quota an "extensive type of relief" and felt it "should be avoided, even if legal, unless necessary as a last resort."

By November of 1973 Sweigert's patience was at an end. There was still no valid written exam, and the more than 200 vacancies in the fire department were endangering the safety of the city's inhabitants. He went back to the most recently administered test and found a pool of 314 white and 118 minority applicants who had passed all segments of the test. He ordered the Civil Service Commission to create a dual list and to fill the vacancies by picking alternately from the list of white applicants and the list of minority applicants until the pool of minorities was exhausted. The quota order was temporary and could be altered or ended at Sweigert's discretion.

The ruling was received with a mixture of shock and resentment in the firehouses of San Francisco. The firemen's union had intervened in the suit and opposed any change of the old system. Although the case had been based on the *Griggs* theory of unlawful impact, it soon became clear that racial bias in San Francisco's fire department was not at all theoretical.

On January 21, 1974, the first class of recruits entered the Fire College. Forty-eight men had been selected—twenty-four whites and twenty-four minorities. Nine of the minority recruits were black, two were Asian, one was an East Indian, and twelve had Spanish surnames. Before 1957 new recruits had been immediately assigned to fire stations, where they received their training on an individual basis. The Fire College made that training more formal and socialized the recruit for his professional family. Because men's lives depended on skills and cooperative efforts, the Fire College placed great emphasis on building camaraderie and commitment to the team. The best and most respected veterans were assigned to teach at the college. The training was vigorous, but there was little formal testing. Instructors stayed after class to give recruits who needed help additional pointers, and the recruits were allowed to work with the equipment until they had mastered the necessary skills. In the entire history of the Fire College no man had ever been terminated because of substandard performance. One man had been dismissed for being drunk on the job.

But in the forty-eighth Fire College class the emphasis was not on training but on testing. Recruits were graded on attitude as well as on written and practical skills. Tests were given each Friday, and during the first six weeks of the eight-week course more than twenty-five different tests were administered. Tests were scored in an apparently arbitrary manner, and the passing score fluctuated from week to week. There were no provisions for retesting or makeups. Instructors refused to stay after class to give the recruits additional help.

Little of the family spirit remained, and the minority recruits felt they were being made to pay for the court order. Black candidates who were told by instructors immediately after a practical test that their performance was outstanding discovered later that they had been given failing grades. Others who took tests as part of a team that included white recruits were the only members of their team to receive low scores. Despite these pressures, after three weeks nearly all the recruits had passing grades.

On February 18, the fifth week of classes, a new grading system was introduced. The new deficiency point system meant that failure in one practical test could mean failure for the entire week. Within a few days eleven recruits were called to individual conferences and warned that their performance was substandard. They were told that they were in danger of termination and that they had two weeks to improve their records. Nine of the eleven were minorities, and none had received any prior indication that their performances had any serious deficiencies.

On March 1 three black recruits, Carl English, George Drake, and Jimmy Oates, received letters warning them that termination was imminent. Four days later they were called in and given letters of dismissal.

Ironically, two of the three blacks who had become scapegoats would have made it into the Fire College without the help of Judge Sweigert. Drake, a twenty-year-old Vietnam veteran and the winner of eight combat decorations, had scored 998.50 of the possible 1,000 on the 1971 test, which ranked him twenty-second on the master civil service list. English, an outstanding high school athlete who had completed a year at the University of California at Berkeley, was twenty-third on the original list.

A fourth recruit also dismissed had not been warned as the others had been. Dennis O'Leary had all the traditional San Francisco Fire Department credentials. His father and his uncle were firemen. After being graduated from high school, he had completed two years of junior college and received a degree in fire sciences. He told the court later, "I believe my termination was part of an active cover-up by the Department designed to obscure its efforts to remove black candidates from the Fire College." The fact that he had not received a warning letter seemed to support his suspicion that integration of the dismissals was an afterthought. He believed that he had been chosen because he had been friendly with some of the black recruits.

The recruits contacted Public Advocates, the public interest law firm that had taken over the original suit. The firm immediately filed a motion to reinstate the four recruits. The affidavits of the dismissed recruits were accompanied by a petition signed by 250 firemen who believed the terminations had been "arbitrary and unfair." Seventy-seven firemen agreed to assist in any additional instruction the four might need. The story of the dismissals had spread through the grapevine, and a large number of the club members were unwilling to go along. A similar petition signed by the forty-three remaining recruits was also attached to the motion. Two respected battalion chiefs were leading the campaign for decency. Robert and John Sherratt had witnessed the arbitrary and abusive treatment of the new recruits and refused to go along at great personal risk. But the leaders of the department stood firm and denied any wrongdoing. It would take four weeks of trial before the city agreed to a settlement, which reinstated the four plaintiffs in the next available Fire College class.

What this incident illustrates is both the power and the limitation of the law. In a city with the liberal reputation of San Francisco, the resistance to racial change was as real in the 1970s as it had been in the South a decade earlier. The law had bypassed the barriers to opportunity for minority groups, but it could not protect them from a will to resist. Critics of quotas might point to this resistance as an unavoidable result of groups pitted against each other by court decisions. But would there have been justice in allowing the selection process to continue unchanged because of fears that racial antagonisms would be exacerbated? The *Griggs* decision was an admission that racial attitudes were often subtle and extremely difficult to assess. Examining the impact of an apparently neutral selection process on minority groups revealed discrimination. Opponents of numerical goals avoid the reality of white resistance to the invasion of their exclusive little club. Sometimes the very real concern about social discomfort obscures the equally real right of economic opportunity, and in the more sophisticated language of our time, we tend to forget that resistance to change is not limited to one specific ethnic or economic group.

Judge Sweigert was not the only one to order employers to hire a specific percentage of minorities to correct the effects of discriminatory tests or former job requirements. Between 1971 and 1975 federal courts in virtually every circuit issued and sustained similar quota orders. Police and fire departments were ordered to hire according to numerical ratios in Minneapolis, Boston, Bridgeport, Los Angeles, Baltimore, Philadelphia, Montgomery, and San Francisco. When past discriminatory practices could be proved, unions were also subjected to numerical quotas. In the private sector, racial quotas were imposed on United States Steel, Goodyear Tire and Rubber, Detroit Edison, and other large corporations.

When it became clear that federal judges were willing to require that employers do something about desegregating their work force, many employers entered into consent decrees or voluntary affirmative action programs, either out of a new sense of social responsibility or concern about the costs of defending their actions in court. The battleground for equality was clearly economic, and state and federal agencies had become active advocates for minorities.

Executive Order 11246 gave the Labor Department the

power to require every federal contractor to have an affirmative action program. The Supreme Court upheld this order issued by President Johnson in a case attacking the Philadelphia Plan, which required goals for hiring minorities by contractors involved in federally assisted construction projects. In 1977 Congress would pass the Public Works Employment Act in an attempt to stimulate the economy and fight unemployment. The act required that all contractors receiving funds under the law set aside at least 10 percent of all construction funds for "minority business enterprises" when such businesses were available to do the work. This little-noticed provision would provoke a series of court battles over the concept of the economic quota.

But the enthusiasm for economic redistribution which had evolved out of the civil rights era began to wane in 1971, when the worldwide economic recession began to have an impact on the American economy. The continued expansion of the middle-class sector was no longer assured, and inevitably white males who were competing with women and minorities would soon be rushing into court with their own complaints. Like Bakke, they argued that employment programs which reserved a certain number of slots for minorities and women discriminated against them. Jobs and promotions should go to the best qualified and the most senior, they argued. They favored civil service examinations, like the one used to select firemen for San Francisco, which had been introduced by reformers to remove political favoritism and make sure jobs were awarded on merit alone.

Reynold Colvin's suit on behalf of the San Francisco school administrators had been one of the first of these "reverse discrimination" attacks on affirmative action in employment. The famous baby boom of the post–World War II period had made education a growth industry in the 1950s and 1960s, but the demographic changes in the 1970s forced a rapid contraction. School districts closed schools and laid off teachers. There was no longer a job in education for anyone who wanted one. The competition between blacks and whites was soon translated into a growing flood of challenges to affirmative action.

Brian Weber, a white laboratory technician at a Kaiser Aluminum plant in Gramercy, Louisiana, succeeded Bakke as the central character in the continuing racial melodrama plaguing the Supreme Court. His case, *Weber* v. *Kaiser Aluminum and Chemical Corporation,* was considered by the Court during its 1978–79 session. While he had not captured the public's attention as easily as Allan Bakke, his legal efforts promised to have a much broader impact on affirmative action.

Weber had applied for an on-the-job training program that would qualify him for a position with higher pay and better job security. But Kaiser had signed an agreement with the United Steel Workers Union to set up a program that would bring more minority workers into skilled positions. The minority population in the area around the Louisiana plant was about 43 percent, but until the affirmative action plan was implemented, only 5 of the approximately 290 skilled craftsmen at the plant were black. Under the agreement, one minority worker was to be picked for every white chosen until the percentage of minorities in skilled jobs was roughly equal to their representation in the population. Candidates for the program were picked from separate seniority lists for whites and minorities. When Weber applied for the general repairman program, three blacks and two whites were selected. He was not one of them.

Weber sued, charging that the labor agreement violated Title VII's prohibition of discrimination based on race. The federal district court and the Fifth Circuit Court of Appeals ruled in Weber's favor. The appeals court said there was insufficient evidence to show that Kaiser had engaged in past discrimination and that in the absence of such discrimination the quota system imposed by the company and the union violated Title VII.

American Telephone and Telegraph's affirmative action program was not exactly voluntary, but the company soon found itself a defendant in a reverse discrimination suit. In what had been described as the largest civil rights settlement ever, AT&T agreed in 1973 to a consent decree designed to end job bias against women, blacks, and other racial minorities. After months of negotiation, the Justice Department, the Equal Employment Opportunity Commission, and the Department of Labor filed a suit charging AT&T with discrimination against women and minorities in its 700,000-member work force. The same day a federal judge approved a consent decree the government had negotiated before filing the suit.

The agreement required AT&T to establish goals and timetables for preferential hiring and for promoting and transferring minority and women employees. Three unions representing company employees refused to accept the agreement and sued both AT&T and the government. In *Communications Workers of America* v. *EEOC* they argued that the program undercut seniority rights won in collective bargaining and violated the due process and equal protection clauses of the Fourteenth Amendment. In May 1977 the Third Circuit Court of Appeals upheld federal district judge Leon Higginbotham's ruling in favor of the consent decree. The circuit court ruled that "the use of employment goals and quotas admittedly involves tensions" with the Fourteenth Amendment but that the plan was "permissible because it seems reasonably calculated to counteract the detrimental effects of a particular identifiable pattern of discrimination." The U.S. Supreme Court would let the decision stand by refusing to review the lower court's ruling.

In *Kreps* v. *Associated Contractors of California* a group of contractors challenged the 10 percent "set-aside" provision of the 1977 Public Works Employment Act on the grounds that it violated Title VI of the Civil Rights Act of 1964, which bars discrimination in federally funded programs and the due process clause of the Fourteenth Amendment. A federal judge agreed, but the Supreme Court ducked the issue by sending the case back to determine whether it was moot because the money allocated to the act had already been spent.

In a case similar to the San Francisco suit against the fire department, a federal judge in Los Angeles found that city's fire department screening tests did not meet the *Griggs* standard of business necessity and set a quota of 20 percent for blacks and 20 percent for Mexican-Americans for new employees. The case, *County of Los Angeles* v. *Davis*, was taken to the U.S. Supreme Court.

Cramer v. *Virginia Commonwealth University* brought the issues raised by Bakke back to the academic setting and raised the additional issue of reverse discrimination by sex. James Cramer, a thirty-two-year-old sociologist who had taught at Virginia Commonwealth for a year, claimed he was denied tenure because the university chose to hire a "less qualified" woman under a voluntary affirmative action plan.

The common thread in all these cases is the argument by white males that they are being treated unfairly and that through no fault of their own they are being moved from the front to the back of the line. Their argument is that affirmative action changes the rules of the game and replaces mechanisms designed to assure fair competition. They are being made victims simply because they are white and male.

What these statements ignore is precisely what the Supreme Court recognized in *Griggs*—that the old rules of the game were not fair and that the merit system was limited to white males. Before 1954 the right of white men to superior and preferential treatment in the job market was never seriously questioned. When Congress and the courts made white male supremacy illegal in employment, both the formal and the informal systems of selection remained intact. There were the "old boy" systems of filling vacancies by word of mouth, the preferences for sons and nephews of employees, the stereotypes held by personnel directors about the kinds of people best suited for certain positions, the assumptions that certain ethnic groups had a natural monopoly in other positions, and the seniority systems that perpetuated the effects of past discrimination. During a period when federal agencies and the courts were willing to confront these much more complex obstacles to equality, they imposed goals and quotas with the objective of achieving results.

The "reverse discrimination" argument argues against any large-scale societal readjustments. It assumes that the pre-affirmative-action procedures were fairer than ones that take into account the dynamics and legacies of a racially conscious society. Both *Griggs* and Title VII address systemic and institutional policies that serve to exclude by race or sex. If an employer has used such devices or has discriminated against minorities in the past, the courts have allowed numerical readjustments.

Those who advocate a return to a nominally neutral system disclaim any societal responsibility for the position of minority groups, but they also want to reap the benefits of the acts in which they claim to have played no role. "Why should I be laid off when I've put in fifteen years at the plant when this black guy has only been here four?" says the white worker in defense of his seniority rights. But if the plant would not hire blacks ten or fifteen years ago, the black worker will never reap the equality of security granted his white counterpart. He will be laid off in recessions and be barred from promotion because of discriminatory acts ten or twenty years old. He continues to pay for the sins of those who would not hire him because of color.

When the U.S. Supreme Court agreed to hear the *Bakke* case, it had already made two substantial retreats from the spirit and principle of the *Griggs* case. *Washington* v. *Davis,* a 1976 decision, was almost identical to the San Francisco Fire Department case. Black applicants to the District of Columbia police force claimed that the written test used to help select recruits denied them equal protection by excluding a disproportionate number of blacks. The test failed blacks at four times the rate of whites and had no relationship to job performance, the plaintiffs argued. They made no claim of discriminatory intent or purpose. Then the police force in the nation's capital had been active and rather successful in attracting blacks. Using *Griggs* as a standard, a federal court of appeals agreed with the black applicants, saying that intent was irrelevant and that the discriminatory impact of the test was sufficient proof of a constitutional violation.

But the U.S. Supreme Court disagreed. When the applicants filed their suit, they were not yet protected by the amendments that extended Title VII to public employees. Their case was based on the Fifth and Fourteenth Amendments, and the question was whether the Court would extend the *Griggs* standard to the Constitution. Justice White, writing for a five-man majority, said the court of appeals was in error in applying *Griggs:* "We have never held that the constitutional standard for adjudicating claims of invidious racial discrimination is identical to standards applicable under Title VII and we decline to do so today. . . .

"The central purpose of the Equal Protection Clause of the

14th Amendment is the prevention of official conduct on the basis of race. . . . But our cases have not embraced the proposition that a law or other official act, without regard to whether it reflects a racially discriminatory purpose, is unconstitutional *solely* because it has a racially disproportionate impact."

In other words, the Court was requiring individuals or groups seeking constitutional protection from racial discrimination to prove intent or purpose. Where the Constitution was involved, the Court would ignore what it seemed to see so clearly in *Griggs*. Where tests and zoning ordinances had replaced "whites only" signs, the intention of institutions and individuals would be nearly impossible to prove. This apparent backward step was important because Title VII covered a limited area of conduct.

A year later the Court decided the case of *International Brotherhood of Teamsters* v. *United States*. This case involved a suit brought by the Civil Rights Division of the Justice Department against a large national trucking company and the union that represented most of its employees. The suit said the company had discriminated against minorities by hiring them only as servicemen or local drivers while reserving higher-paying long-distance jobs for whites. The suit charged that the seniority system in the collective bargaining agreements between the company and the union perpetuated or "locked in" the effects of past discrimination, because if a city driver wanted to transfer to the higher-paying positions, he had to forfeit all his seniority rights and start at the bottom. The government proved at the trial that the company had engaged in a pattern of discrimination against minorities in violation of Title VII. The vital question before the Court was whether, given proof of past discrimination, a seniority system that perpetuated past discrimination was unlawful.

The Supreme Court upheld the seniority system by making a distinction between seniority lost as a result of "post-Act discrimination" and seniority lost because of discrimination before the law was passed. The courts could make up for discrimination since 1964, but there would be no relief for "pre-Act discrimination." What happened was that the labor establishment, a powerful element in the civil rights struggle during the 1960s, had managed to insert a clause in the law immunizing seniority systems despite their discriminatory impact.

The Court rejected the government's argument that the clause was illegal by saying that such a finding "would place an affirmative obligation on the parties to the seniority agreement to subordinate [their] rights in favor of the claims of pre-Act discriminatees without seniority." After reviewing the legislative history, the justices concluded that "Congress did not intend to make it illegal for employees with vested seniority rights to continue to exercise those rights, even at the expense of pre-Act discriminatees." In the *Teamsters* case, the Court had attributed the choice of victims to Congress, and that choice was clear.

The Supreme Court had not been required to confront the issue of employment discrimination in the *Bakke* case, which centered on graduate school admissions. But the implications of *Bakke* for working men and women was clear enough. If affirmative action programs were outlawed, what was to prevent a return to the ancient practices that had always denied minorities access to the marketplace? The consensus for affirmative action was clearly a thing of the past in the face of tremendous economic problems and the intense competition for desirable positions.

Because the Court did not have the power to create full employment, it would have to decide whether the competition would be governed by the old rules that placed whites at the front of the lines or by the new laws that attempted to break the well-entrenched patterns of discrimination. Because, just like the men at the bottom of the San Francisco Fire Department hiring list, not all the people at the end of the line would get jobs, there could not be a neutral position that would harm no one. Someone had to be at the end of the line, and the Supreme Court was being asked to choose.

The Court would not make this choice in one crucial landmark decision. The *Bakke* case had proved that the Court was of many minds and that it would move cautiously on this very sensitive issue. In the cases challenging affirmative action in employment that were scheduled to come before the court in the 1978–79 term the Court was likely to base its decisions on the narrowest of grounds. It was also likely to attempt to avoid responsibility for the choice by throwing the issue back into the political arena as it had done in *Bakke*. But even if the Court upheld laws mandating affirmative action in employment, minorities had to worry about a possible translation of the national mood into congressional action. Already conservative members of Congress had introduced legislation to undercut the government's ability to enforce affirmative action requirements.

In California, the trend-setting state where it had all begun, the voters had overwhelmingly passed Proposition 13, a measure designed to limit property taxes and government spending, which would have a devastating effect on local governments' social welfare and affirmative action programs. Allan Bakke had left NASA and his suburban San Francisco home to enroll in his first year of medical studies amid the broad stretches of farmland at Davis. There were now 65 minority firemen among the 1,501 in San Francisco's previously all-white club. In the best tradition of the department several of them had found outside jobs to occupy their off days and supplement their income. Like all firemen, they tried to repress the constant fear that the next time they entered a burning building might be their last. They also tried not to think about Proposition 13 and the *Bakke* case. They had been given a piece of the American pie, but their position was a precarious one. Any combination of job layoffs or "reverse discrimination" suits might put their jobs in jeopardy.

Twelve

A CHOICE OF
VICTIMS

On Monday, September 25, 1978, Allan Paul Bakke joined 100 other first-year students to form the medical school Class of 1982 of the University of California at Davis. If Bakke's efforts over a five-year period had simply been one man's struggle to bring his dreams to reality, then the first day of classes would have provided a fit and anticlimactic end to the story. But the presence of reporters, cameras, and chanting pickets on the Davis campus thwarted any ideas Bakke might have had of ending his role as a symbol.

The story could not really end because some very serious issues remained. The U.S. Supreme Court had set down some rules that applied to only a very small segment of a very broad problem. The broader conflicts exposed by Bakke's determination to attend medical school had not yet been resolved. He had achieved a personal victory and given comfort to many who had serious questions about some of the methods used in the quest for equality in America. But there were also some who believed that Allan Bakke had helped curtail the aspirations of many others.

If there was a lesson in this case, it was that all the dreams of young Americans could not be fulfilled. The medical school process was a microcosm of a competitive process that was spreading to many areas of American life. According to the

U.S. Census Bureau, there would be more than 60 million Americans between the ages of twenty-five and forty-four by 1990. The competitive crush for places in professional schools would soon be extended into an intense and emotional struggle for scarce opportunities in other fields. The old myths about individual ambition and individual choice would now clash with the needs of society and the political realities of a very crowded future.

The *Bakke* case should have forced a sober examination of some very complex issues. How were we to choose the best doctors? How were we to choose from many well-qualified applicants for a few openings in many fields? What did tests really tell us, and what were their limits and values? What did "merit" really mean? Had we really achieved the equality that was so valued in America? But for the most part, the debate had not been enlightening. Too often it had got sidetracked into semantic cul-de-sacs such as "better qualified" and "less qualified." The issue of race dominated the debate around *Bakke,* and as often happened in American history, it helped obscure some fundamental economic problems.

At least the case had shown how artificial was the racial peace of the 1970s. There was plenty of evidence that the most cruel aspects of legal racism had been eliminated. Fundamental changes had taken place in the relationship between white and nonwhite Americans, and considerable progress had been made in employment, income, and social interaction. Because of such visible gains, many Americans found it difficult to accept the fact that so much more remained to be done.

The emotional rhetoric generated by the case pointed to a fundamental change in the country's perception of race relations. The problem posed was no longer a matter of granting rights to everyone but of allocating a limited number of opportunities. If there were no racial minorities, coming to grips with this fundamental challenge to our American myths would have been difficult enough. Now racial minorities were adding to the difficulties by demanding their fair share of these opportunities. If everyone who wanted to—and who had the ability—could not become a doctor or a lawyer or president, who would be chosen, and who would make that choice? It was easier to fall back on the ancient assumptions that those demanding their share who were not white were making unreasonable demands.

The country had clearly shifted away from the economic and political generosity that made the civil rights movement so successful in the 1960s. The Tax Revolt, highlighted by passage of California's Proposition 13, was an obvious sign of rebellion in the middle classes against the cost of government. Because this movement lacked ideology, minority groups feared it could be turned against them. Blacks and Hispanics had come to depend on government for employment and legal protection, and they worried that programs designed to help them particularly might be made scapegoats for fiscal problems for which they were not responsible.

A fundamental difference between blacks and whites lay in their different concepts of the role that government should play in their lives. The expression of middle-class sentiment in Proposition 13 had its applications in *Bakke* as well. At its core was a racial difference in perceptions of America. Most whites believed that our major racial problems had been solved, but most blacks did not. Justice Marshall, in arguing that the melting pot had not worked for blacks, reflected that minority perception. Without a national consensus to provide energy and momentum, the movement toward equality was stalled. Opponents of race-sensitive measures saw the country as a collection of competing ethnic groups whose only rights were individual and whose achievements were simply the result of merit. Such a vision of America was comforting to those in the best position to reap the benefits of privilege.

Racial minorities would find it difficult, in light of their own experiences, to accept such a picture of America. As long as opportunities were color-coded, there was a contradiction between the comfortable mythology of the meritocracy and the realities of American life. The sharp racial differences in life expectancy, medical care, income, job categories, education, and political power all were a part of that reality. Those who argued for improved educational opportunities rather than more drastic adjustments were ignoring disparities that went beyond differences in schooling. How would they explain that white high school dropouts had lower unemployment rates than black youths with some college education or that the economic gap between blacks and whites was widening despite growing numbers of blacks in higher education? The experience of professional schools and corporations had shown that *qualifications* was not such an easy term to define. A very real resistance to affirmative action came from a justifiable fear of competition. Just as whites wanted to narrow the competitive field as much as possible, minorities saw they needed government intervention to get a fair share.

"Victory for a White" said the subhead on the *New York Times* story about the Supreme Court's decision in the *Bakke* case. The year before, *Newsweek* had portrayed a black and a white in a tug-of-war over a diploma in its cover story on reverse discrimination. The presentation of whites as victims of affirmative action was the key to the controversy around the *Bakke* case, and considering the relative positions of whites and nonwhites in America in the 1970s, it was a gross distortion of reality. But the struggle for power had always been at the root of racial conflict in the country, and white resistance to civil rights had always been fed by a fear of losing control. Lost in the debate over preferential admissions was the fact that medical schools were more than 90 percent white, that 95 percent of law students were white, and that in virtually

263

every desirable job category, minorities came nowhere near having representation approaching their numbers in the population. After two decades of civil rights activism and ten years of feminism, being born white and male continued to be the best guarantee of success in America.

Historical and economic circumstances at the turn of the last century had enabled white ethnic groups to gain control of a number of powerful institutions—labor unions, political patronage systems, the film and information industries. These institutions had served as a base of power for the Irish, Italians, and Jews in their negotiations with the majority. In many instances the same institutions had opposed minority efforts to enter the political and economic mainstream. Blacks had been able to use a fortuitous combination of political and economic developments to apply *moral* pressure in the 1960s to make some gains. Attempts to disclaim any responsibility for past events were an effort to distort history and deny moral obligation for the majority to do something about the present.

Political and psychological resistance to the claims of minorities is an old tradition in America. As each new wave of immigrants arrived—and blacks took on the status of immigrants in 1954, when the U.S. Supreme Court granted them the rights guaranteed to the newcomers from Europe over the centuries—there was always a great deal of concern among the entrenched groups about the impact of those "fresh off the boat." At the turn of the last century white Anglo-Saxons worried that the character of the country would be altered by the influx of Jews and Eastern Europeans. The arguments made seventy-five years ago about preserving standards and "quality" are quite similar to those made today.

The American melting pot had actually been a divided plate, with each distinct group claiming its share by wielding its particular political and economic weapon. What the black and Hispanic newcomers now feared was that the plate would no longer expand to accommodate them. Economists were talking about a dual economy, with most minorities concentrated in the dead-end, low-paying jobs on the lower rung. For them affirmative action was a gateway into the more desirable track, and ruling in *Bakke,* the Supreme Court was defining not only their legal rights but their economic future.

The case had exposed the fragility of political alliances that had supported the cause of minorities in the past. Jews and blacks, old allies in the romantic days of the civil rights movement, had parted company over affirmative action. The labor movement had been so divided on the issue that the AFL-CIO had failed to file a brief in the case. After the Supreme Court's decision there were efforts by both sides to patch up the old wounds. But *Bakke* had provoked a great deal of bitterness, and many of the fundamental issues had not been resolved. Jews saw themselves as a beleaguered minority, one step away from an anti-Semitic backlash. But to blacks, Jews had achieved an enviable amount of power and the ability to manipulate public opinion in their own interest. The fundamental economic problems remained and the differences would not be resolved easily.

There was some discussion of new alliances between blacks and Hispanics, between the poor of different races, and between urban residents of various classes. But the old mistrusts continued to outweigh the new political necessities. The greatest obstacle of all, the absence of a political movement or figure that could provide common ground for unifying these divergent racial and ethnic groups, remained a major factor. In *Bakke* no major political figure had stepped forward to attempt a reconciliation of the opposing sides. The Carter administration had sought a political solution that pleased no one—and that did little to enlighten Americans about the real issue at stake.

The Supreme Court had disappointed the public by its failure to take a definitive stand on the issues, but the multiplicity of opinions was just a reflection of the complexities of the problem. Vietnam had taught America about the infinite shades of right and wrong in foreign policy. *Bakke* might extend this hard-earned wisdom into domestic policies and race relations. Efforts to define minority progress strictly with statistics avoided less tangible but equally important aspects of equality. In fewer than twenty-five years, blacks and other minorities had made great strides in overcoming hundreds of years of psychological damage caused by political oppression and white cultural supremacy. True equality would come only when people not only felt equal but also believed they were playing a role in determining the destiny of the country.

Finding a solution for the problems posed by the *Bakke* case would require a great deal of wisdom and an even greater degree of trust by both sides. The unequal nature of power in America would make this task extremely difficult. How would minorities be persuaded that institutions would do what was right without the pressure of law and government? Could they believe that the white majority had become "color-blind" in just two decades? Could whites be made to understand the real nature of economic struggles taking place and that minorities did not want lowered standards?

As long as race remains an issue in America, we will be unable to address the country's major structural deficiencies. In *Bakke* the issue of color had enabled many Americans to avoid the issues of class and privilege that contradict our most enduring myths. But as the nation matures and the conflicts deepen, we will have no choice but to confront the injustices that contradict these democratic ideals. No society can make winners of all its people. There are those who will not succeed in a system because of the flaws of that society or their own shortcomings. There are still some elements of American society who are anxious to assume—unobtrusively—that color is a justification for failure. It is perilous for any society to become comfortable with injustice. As America enters its third century, we see disturbing signs of complacency and intolerance. It is at our own peril that we become comfortable with our choice of victims.

SELECTED BIBLIOGRAPHY

Bell, Derrick. *Race, Racism and American Law*. Boston: Little, Brown & Co., 1973.

Blum, Jeffrey M. *Pseudoscience and Mental Ability*. New York and London: Monthly Review Press, 1978.

Carnegie Council on Policy Studies in Higher Education. *Selective Admissions in Higher Education*. San Francisco, Washington, D.C., London: Jossey-Bass Publishers, 1977.

Chase, Allan. *The Legacy of Malthus: The Social Costs of the New Scientific Racism*. New York: Knopf, 1977.

Ginger, Ann Fagan, ed. *DeFunis v. Odegaard and the University of Washington*. Dobbs Ferry, N.Y.: Oceana Publications, 1974.

Glazer, Nathan. *Affirmative Discrimination: Ethnic Inequality and Public Policy*. New York: Basic Books, 1975.

Jones, F. C. *The Changing Mood in America: Eroding Commitment?* Washington, D.C.: Howard University Press, 1977.

Kluger, Richard. *Simple Justice*. New York: Knopf, 1976.

National Urban League. "The State of Black America 1978." New York, 1978.

Bowman Gray Medical School,
Wake Forest, 16
Bradley, Joseph B., 80–81
Brennan, William, 185, 188, 214
decision in *Bakke* case of, 206,
212, 215, 216–21, 223, 229
Brennan, Mrs. William, 205
Brooks, Tom, 152–53
Brown, Edmund, 57, 70, 72–73
Brown v. *Board of Education*, 49,
103–4, 175, 185, 191, 199,
203–5, 223, 224, 234–35,
240
Buchanan v. *Warley*, 108
Burger, Warren, 176, 178, 188–89,
192, 197, 200, 205, 207,
221
decision in *Bakke* case of, 206
Griggs v. *Duke Power Company*
and, 238–39
Burt, Dr. Cyril, 135–36

Califano, Joseph, 164–65, 169
California Commission on Judicial
Performance, 73
California Constitution, 38
California Law Journal, 77
California Rural Legal Assistance
program, 242
California Supreme Court, 177,
178, 192
appeal of *Bakke* case to, 68–94
decision of in *Bakke* appeal, 181,
197, 200
final decision, 93–94
majority decision, 73–75, 76–
79, 80, 81–88, 89, 90, 110,
206, 209, 210, 221, 223
minority opinion, 75–76, 79–
80, 81, 87, 88–89, 209, 221
Supreme Court decision and,
206, 209, 210, 214, 216,
219, 220–21
justices. *See* Mosk, Stanley;
Tobriner, Mathew
petition for rehearing before,
91–92, 93
record of, 68–69, 82

Carmichael, Stokely, 149
Carter, Jimmy, 151, 162, 172, 226,
265,
solicitor's brief and, 166, 167,
190
CBS News, 145, 225
Chase, Allen, 132, 133–34
Chavis, Patrick, 117–18
Chen, Arthur, 122–23
City College of New York, 71
Civil Rights Act of 1964, 38
affirmed by Supreme Court, 236–
40
passage of, 236
Title VII of, 219, 237–40, 244,
251–52, 254, 255, 256–57
Title VI of, 189, 206, 208, 213,
214–15, 217–19, 229
Civil Rights Laws of 1875, 235
civil rights movement, 235, 236
Cobbs, Dr. Price, 159
Coblentz, William, 90
Coleman, William, 165, 177, 187
Colley, Nathaniel, 90, 177, 187
Colvin, Reynold H., 32–34, 35, 36,
64, 194–95
appeal of *Bakke* case to California Supreme Court and,
68, 69–70
appeal of *Bakke* case to U.S.
Supreme Court and, 175,
194–200, 201, 219, 223,
250
approach to *Bakke* case of, 36–
37, 44, 52, 53, 58, 190,
185–86, 213
deposition from Dr. Lowrey and,
45–48, 50
files complaint in Yolo County,
36, 37–38, 44, 57, 66
hearing to get Bakke admitted
and, 58–60, 62
Manker's decision and, 64–65
"Memo of Points and Authorities" of, 50–51
offer to drop case if Bakke admitted and, 48